Towards a just Europe

Manchester University Press

European Politics

Series Editors: Professor Dimitris Papadimitriou (University of Manchester), Dr Kathryn Simpson (Manchester Metropolitan University) and Dr Paul Tobin (University of Manchester)

The *European Politics* series seeks to tackle the biggest issues facing Europe in the twenty-first century.

Previously published under the *European Policy Research Unit (EPRU)* name, this long-established and highly respected series combines an important scholarly legacy with an ambitious outlook on European Studies at a time of rapid change for the discipline. Its geographical coverage encompasses the European Union, its existing and aspiring members, and 'wider Europe', including Russia and Turkey, and the series actively promotes disciplinary, theoretical and methodological diversity.

The editors particularly welcome critical scholarship on the politics and policy making of the European Union, on comparative European politics, and on contemporary issues and debates affecting the future of Europe's socio-political and security outlook. Key areas of interest include Brexit, the environment, migration, identity politics and the ever-changing face of European integration.

Previously published:

Regulating lobbying: A global comparison, 2nd edition
Raj Chari, John Hogan, Gary Murphy and Michele Crepaz

Towards a just Europe

A theory of distributive justice for
the European Union

João Labareda

Manchester University Press

Published by Manchester University Press
Oxford Road, Manchester M13 9PL
www.manchesteruniversitypress.co.uk

British Library Cataloguing-in-Publication Data
A catalogue record for this book is available from the British Library

ISBN   978 1 5261 5261 9   hardback
ISBN   978 1 5261 7450 5   paperback

First published 2021
Paperback published 2023

Typeset
by Deanta Global Publishing Services, Chennai, India

Contents

Acknowledgements   *page* vi

   Introduction: The problem of distributive justice in the EU   1
1 Two distributive duties   27
2 Democratic redistribution in the EU   60
3 Economic reciprocity in the EU   86
4 A moderate feasibility test for normative theory   119
5 Realizing distributive justice in the EU   144
   Conclusion: Towards a just Europe   163

   Bibliography   168
   Index   183

Acknowledgements

I have received a great deal of help and support, without which this book would never have been completed. I am very grateful to Rainer Bauböck, who supervised this research project with enormous dedication and enthusiasm. A very special thanks to Lea Ypi, Jennifer Welsh, and Andrea Sangiovanni, who provided constructive comments on a previous version of the manuscript. I am also grateful to Jean-Philippe Genet, Noel Malcolm, and Stefano Bartolini for encouraging me to think disruptively. A warm thanks, too, to Carlos Moedas, who gave me the opportunity to observe political processes from the inside and who inspired me to bridge theory and practice. I am thankful for a research grant awarded by the Portuguese Science and Technology Agency (Fundação para a Ciência e a Tecnologia (FCT)), without which this book would not have come to light. Last but not least, my biggest thanks to my parents and to Katharina. This book is dedicated to you.

Introduction: The problem of distributive justice in the EU

I. Robert Schuman revisited

Robert Schuman famously predicted that economic integration in the European Union (EU) would be followed by social integration.[1] Yet has this been the case? In recent years, distributive claims at the EU level have become more stringent than ever. In contrast with the so-called convergence thesis, the socioeconomic gap between centre and periphery in the EU shows no tendency to decrease substantially. Levels of material deprivation are, indeed, very high in a number of member states. More strikingly, the dramatic deterioration of the social outlook in certain member states is at least partially related to EU-led policies. This is most notably the case with the conditionality clauses of the Greek, Irish, and Portuguese adjustment programmes. The public debate on these matters has revealed strong divisions in Europe regarding the desirability and feasibility of social justice beyond national borders. Therefore, a number of questions need to be addressed. Do wealthier member states have the moral duty to assist distressed member states? What if socioeconomic inequalities result from poor policy choices? Is there any minimum level of assistance that should be regarded as necessary for EU citizens? What policy instruments would fairly distribute the benefits and burdens of European integration? Under what conditions would these be feasible? In short, what duties of justice are linked to EU membership, and how can they be realized?

This book will advance an account of distributive justice for the EU that aims to be both *plausible* and *feasible*. In this introductory chapter, I set the grounds for achieving these goals. The chapter is structured as follows. I begin by presenting three tensions that lead me to believe that the current distributions of wealth and income in the EU are unjust. Then, I list a number of familiar objections against distributive justice at the EU level, claiming that none of them is strong enough to prevent a more comprehensive debate on the matter. Subsequently, I introduce the research questions, and I show that the latter have not been satisfactorily addressed by the sub-fields of global justice and citizenship studies. I also identify a number of helpful insights advanced by the few existing publications on the topic. In a subsequent methodological section, I discuss the subject and scope of political theory, and I explain why it can help in addressing the research questions. Then I outline a step-by-step strategy to engage with the research questions. I conclude this Introduction by sketching the main arguments of the book.

II. The research puzzle

Three tensions in the European Union

This project stems from three tensions that, I shall argue, can be found in the EU today. These tensions are the following: (i) a discrepancy between the degrees of *political* integration and *social* integration in the Union; (ii) the existence of legal grounds for shared principles of justice, such as the EU Charter of Fundamental Rights, with a contrasting lack of mechanisms to provide and enforce them; and (iii) the fact that, under the principle of non-discrimination, EU citizens are entitled to the *same* set of social rights, but *only* when they live in the same member state. I shall discuss each of these tensions in turn.

The first tension lies in the gap between *political* and *social* integration in the EU. The key idea is that the extensive set of institutions, norms, and practices shared by all member states is at odds with the minimalistic social dimension of the Union. The Eurostat figures on poverty help to illustrate the point. In 2017, the governments of the Union – which altogether account for 24% of the world's wealth – were unable to meet the basic needs of 33 million EU citizens.[2] Yet deprivation levels vary dramatically across member states. In fact, in 2017 the percentage of individuals suffering from severe material deprivation in the EU ranged from 1.1% in Sweden to 31% in Bulgaria. Even if the three youngest member states (Bulgaria, Romania, and Croatia) are excluded from our analysis, differences in the incidence of poverty across the Union are astonishing. In fact, in the three best performing countries (Sweden, Luxembourg, and Finland), deprivation rates were lower than 2.5%; in turn, in the three countries showing the poorest performance (Lithuania, Hungary, and Greece), severe deprivation affects at least 12% of the population, with a figure of 21% in Greece. If the EU has integrated so many of the core competences of the nation-state, why should social policy be left behind?

I have implied that a divide between centres of political decision making and responsibilities for social provision is normatively problematic. Yet why is this the case? As Chapter 1 shall elaborate, individuals who are part of an institutionalized system of cooperation, which is simultaneously *coercive* and *democratic*, have duties of social justice towards each other. These obligations emerge from two interrelated concerns. First, having a real chance to participate in civic life presupposes a set of material conditions which generate social inclusiveness, time availability, and access to information. For example, in the absence of basic goods such as housing, healthcare, and education, the right to politically participate may become merely formal. Secondly, deprivation fosters the threat of arbitrary rule. In democracy, the ability to resist arbitrary power seems to be contingent on the availability of material means to either contest, or call for, the enforcement of the law, through the existing legal channels. Chapter 2 will show that coercion and democracy are key features of the present-day EU. EU institutions enact an extensive body of legislation, enforced by the Court of Justice of the European Union (CJEU) and by the domestic courts, with EU law having primacy over domestic law. In addition, the EU comprises a set of key democratic institutions, a citizenship status, and multiple *demoi*. Hence, if the link between coercion, democracy, and distributive justice is sound, the current "constitutional asymmetry" of the Union will have to be addressed.[3]

The second tension lies in the fact that, although EU treaties have established a number of social rights for EU citizens, they failed to assign corresponding duties to member states and EU institutions to bring them about. As a result, EU social rights lack any effective mechanism of enforcement. The foremost illustration of this ambivalence is the Charter of Fundamental Rights of the European Union. Article 33 of the charter establishes that the family shall enjoy not only legal but "economic and social protection".[4] In turn, Article 34 recognizes "the right to social and housing assistance so as to ensure a decent existence for all those who lack sufficient resources".[5] Article 35 adds that "[a] high level of human health protection shall be ensured" to every EU citizen.[6] However, Articles 51 and 52 state that the charter does not extend the competences assigned to the EU by the previous treaties, where social policy was defined as being a matter of member states' business. Hence, "for the EU institutions, the Charter creates an obligation to promote each of the enumerated rights, but denies them the capacity to extend their powers or tasks to secure its objectives".[7] In other words, the social rights prescribed by the charter do not generate any positive duty that may be invoked in court.[8] As a result, the binding effects of this document (as far as social rights are concerned) are mainly about deterrence: neither EU nor domestic institutions are allowed to promulgate laws and regulations that actively contravene the charter.

The current state of affairs is, therefore, problematic. On the one hand, member states seem to recognize that the Union should comprise a distributive dimension. This is patent not only in the charter, but in a considerable number of other political and legal documents produced throughout the history of the EU.[9] More stringently, the Treaty on the Functioning of the European Union (TFEU) specifically states that the EU "shall aim to eliminate inequalities", emphasising "the promotion of a high level of employment, the guarantee of adequate social protection, the fight against social exclusion, and a high level of education, training and protection of human health".[10] On the other hand, the reluctance of the EU to use the language of social rights when it comes to concrete policy actions "reflects precisely a fear of giving strong legal recognition and priority to particular social values in the face of competing economic interests".[11] In fact, most member states insist that social policy should remain within national borders, refusing to pay the costs of a just Europe. This mismatch between *goals* and *means* at the disposal of EU political institutions remains a source of contention. Crucially, any appeal to social rights will be effective "only if combined with arguments to show *who* should act, and *what* they should do".[12]

The third tension refers to the paradoxical implications of the EU principle of non-discrimination as far as social rights are concerned. Under this principle, a Spanish individual will benefit from similar social rights as a Dutch citizen if they move to work in the Netherlands – but *not* if they stay in Spain. This result is problematic for a number of reasons. First, by establishing a strong link between social rights and national job markets, this conception excludes people who are not in a physical condition to work or to cross the border – most notably, children, the elderly, and severely disabled people. This dramatically raises the moral risk of having first- and second-class EU citizens. Secondly, it is not necessarily true that a mobile Spanish worker enjoys the same social rights as local Dutch citizens. In fact, EU mobile workers are typically exposed to greater risks, particularly when it comes to contributory schemes, which are only activated after a given period of time. In addition, a few member states have recently increased the evidentiary requirements demanded from non-nationals to access social benefits, making the application process longer and harder. This suggests that, if non-discrimination is truly to apply, citizens of the EU polity should enjoy a level playing field of social rights.

The inadequacy of non-discrimination as a paradigm to achieve social cohesion in the Union is starkly revealed by the contrasting economic opportunities for citizens of different member states. For example, the GDP per capita and the level of unemployment vary greatly across member states.[13] It has often been argued that the disparities regarding the level of wealth can be explained by national policy choices. Yet, even if there is some truth in this argument, it fails to account for the *transnational* nature of the common market. Given the intensity of economic exchange and specialization within the EU, non-Dutch EU citizens make a major contribution to the prosperity of the Dutch market – even if they do not work in the Netherlands. Therefore, there is a moral problem of distribution of the benefits of integration. One cannot do away with this problem by simply referring to freedom of movement. Not every EU citizen can move to the Netherlands even if they wish to, given not only the physical constraints already mentioned, but also barriers such as language, family, and legal requirements for certain professions. Thus, the "poverty gap" seems to hide behind an "opportunity gap", which makes social convergence very hard. For all that has been said, the status quo "tends to create a category of European people excluded from the full benefits of European Union".[14] This suggests that non-discrimination must be complemented by additional distributive principles.

The three tensions presented in the previous paragraphs suggest the need to reassess the nature and scope of distributive duties in the EU. However, alternative views have challenged the claim that furthering social justice in the Union is both desirable and feasible. In the next section, I identify three types of concerns typically raised by the subscribers to these views.

Three objections against social justice in the EU

At least three types of objections may be raised against a comprehensive understanding of distributive justice in the EU. First, critics may claim that the EU is just an intergovernmental association; for this reason, distributive debates, as well as other dimensions of the so-called EU democratic deficit, are entirely misplaced.[15] The EU lacks a unified *demos*, as well as a widespread sense of social solidarity, which, so the argument goes, constitute prerequisites for any substantive scheme of redistribution.[16] According to this view, the EU should have a strong mandate to realize the single market, but leave aside issues not directly related to it, including social policy. It should be noted that a residual amount of social provision may yet be justified under this account, including access to urgent medical assistance and to public education. In fact, such services are currently provided to mobile EU citizens. However, the reasons for such concessions belong to the general goal of enhancing market efficiency – more specifically, correcting market failures and reducing transaction costs – and not to the realm of social justice.[17] Under this approach, redistribution is to remain exclusively attached to the nation-state. Therefore, the status quo presents itself as the most desirable alternative.

Secondly, critics may claim that the consequences of redistributing at the EU level are highly undesirable. To begin with, it has often been argued that EU institutions are excessively bureaucratic. Redistribution at the EU level would only add to this state of affairs by extending the number of tasks performed at the supranational level. Another concern is that redistribution at the EU level would create incentives for free-riding. On this view, relatively disadvantaged member states could then rely on others to afford their inefficiencies, instead of carrying out much-needed reforms. This could render the scheme economically unsustainable. In addition, critics may claim that a common redistributive scheme would imply levelling down a few of the already existing welfare systems – namely, the Nordic member states – and levelling up some others, especially Ireland. This standardization of social policy in disregard of national histories and political cultures may be an unacceptable price to pay for furthering social justice in the EU.[18] Thus the most desirable scenario is not one of redistribution at EU level, but one in which the coordination of national welfare policies is enhanced.[19]

Finally, critics have expressed concerns about how any redistributive scheme could be implemented. A preliminary observation is that any substantial scheme might be too costly. Since the EU does not have its own power of taxation, it is "limited both by its dependence upon member states for the implementation of whatever social policies would be decided, and by the reluctance of these polities to provide it with the funds necessary for any major effort at 'positive integration' via a common system of social redistribution or compensation".[20] In fact, the governments of those member states that would likely become net contributors to the scheme would find it very hard to justify any EU scheme to their electorates. Accordingly, the unanimity rule required for such reform would make its approval highly unlikely. Furthermore, after the Eurozone crisis, the refugee crisis, and Brexit have threatened the very existence of the EU, moving forward with social integration might be more than a step into the dark – it could constitute a final strike against the European project. Therefore, the already existing instruments, which include structural funds and certain "hidden" redistributive mechanisms, such as the bond-buying program of the European Central Bank, might be the best one could hope for.[21]

The need for answers

Although powerful, the objections I have listed do not defeat the project; on the contrary, they reinforce the need for an informed discussion. In fact, the current political debate has typically been framed as if one needed to choose between full-scale EU redistribution, regardless of current domestic preferences and past policy choices, on the one hand, and the status quo, where little redistribution exists, on the other. In addition, it is often suggested that social justice in the EU implies a federalist agenda for the Union. However, this is clearly not the case. Between these two extreme positions stand a number of possible arrangements with the potential to promote justice in the EU at an acceptable economic cost. These intermediate alternatives should be brought to light to be tested against the criteria of desirability and feasibility.

Furthermore, in this context feasibility should refer to a relatively broad timeline. If a political project is not immediately feasible, this does not mean that it should be discarded. As we shall see, for political theorists what matters is whether such a project is feasible under conditions that can be achieved in the future. Therefore, conceding the points raised by critics does not imply a move away from distributive claims. Even if it comes with some risks, distributive justice – I believe – is not a recipe for the end of Europe. Quite the contrary, it may bring about the prosperity, stability, and the sense of justice that are needed to hold the EU together. My task will rather be to develop an account of distributive justice that is robust enough to accommodate reasonable concerns such as levelling down, free-riding, and democratic legitimacy.

The research questions

I am now ready to systematize the research questions that I have been gradually approaching. The questions read as follows:

> *Does the political and economic configuration of the EU generate distributive duties amongst EU citizens, and/or between member states? If so, what are these duties and under what conditions do they apply?*

Some conceptual clarification is in order. By "political and economic configuration", I mean the institutional norms and practices governing the distribution of power and resources in a given territory. In the case of the EU, this includes, for instance, the EU treaties and legal principles, the coercive acts of the CJEU, the EU citizenship status, the procedures to appoint EU officials, the rules of the single market, and the monetary policy of the Eurozone. For strategic reasons, I avoid the more familiar terms "regime type" and "form of government" that are widely employed in the field of political science. The reasons are twofold. First, a lengthy and ongoing debate in EU studies has cast doubt on whether the EU fits the traditional terminology of statehood: is the EU a "federation", a "confederation", a "super-state", or an "international organization"? Since my main task is to investigate whether certain normatively relevant features – including coercion, democracy, and economic integration – are part of a sound account of the present-day EU, I do not need to make an ultimate judgement on which label should be used. It is enough for me to show that the EU is *sufficiently* coercive, democratic, and economically integrated to generate distributive duties. Secondly, the traditional terminology tends to leave economic institutions at a secondary level. For example, the concept of "regime type" focuses on political dimensions such as source of legitimacy, distribution of power, and constitutional structure. Yet economic institutions are a key defining component of the EU, and a candidate for generating distributive duties. Therefore, they should be granted greater prominence in my analysis.

In turn, the notion of "distributive duties" refers to the distributions of *wealth* and *income*, as well as primary goods that are directly linked to these distributions, such as housing, healthcare, and education. I exclude other sorts of morally relevant distributions, such as the distribution of political rights and social roles. Although social rights need political rights to be realized, the latter are already granted to a considerable extent by the criteria for EU membership.[22] The use of the plural "duties" is intentional. Indeed, it is assumed that distributive duties may present many forms and degrees, requiring differentiated treatment. This is based on the observation that a variety of issues – ranging from democratic redistribution to economic fairness to national responsibility – seem to be at stake. Similarly, it is assumed that distributive duties may refer to one or both types of relations: amongst EU citizens and between member states. In a polity as complex as the EU, there is no reason to assume that these are mutually exclusive. The conditionality element introduced in the second part of the question – the conditions under which distributive duties apply – raises the issue of feasibility, which, as I have been suggesting, is a key element of this project. Finally, it is assumed that there should be some sort of consistency between the political and economic configuration and the distributive duties. A comprehensive argument for that hypothesis will be presented in Chapter 1. For simplicity, I shall treat "distributive" and "social" justice interchangeably.

III. Literature

Global justice and citizenship studies

The project positions itself within two branches of literature: the debate on global distributive justice and the debate on multilevel citizenship in the EU. I argue that (i) in the way in which it is presently framed, the debate on global justice does not provide satisfactory answers to the research questions, and that (ii) the multilevel citizenship approach raises a problem of allocation of social rights which has not yet been properly addressed by the proponents of this view.

Literature on global distributive justice is usually divided into two main types of positions: statism and cosmopolitanism. Statist authors establish a strong link between redistribution and the nation-state system. Their arguments seem to rely on a critical distinction between *duties of justice* – morally obligatory requirements that hold on a permanent basis – and *humanitarian duties* – often supererogatory and always limited in their scope and duration.[23] Statists, on the one hand, claim that although humanitarian duties may apply beyond national borders, redistribution as a potentially large-scale duty of justice applies only at the domestic level. In this account, social rights are said to presuppose the existence of a set of civic bonds, social interdependencies, and a common institutional framework which can only be found within the borders of the state. The strategies to justify this link are diverse, ranging from social contract theory (famously, in the case of John Rawls), to the notion of membership of a national political community (influentially presented by David Miller), to the idea of subjection to a coercive system (notably advanced by Thomas Nagel).[24] In a variety of fashions, all statist authors assign international redistribution a secondary, typically minimalistic, role.

On the other hand, cosmopolitan authors claim that borders are morally irrelevant as far as distributive justice is concerned. Although a variety of cosmopolitan arguments can also be found, their structure is identical at least in two regards. First, cosmopolitans take individuals – not states – as the critical unit of concern for global justice.[25] Accordingly, they think in terms of direct obligations of each individual towards the rest of the world, even when they regard the nation-state as a significant political entity.[26] This significantly differs from statists, who tend to think of duties beyond borders in terms of an inter-state framework. Secondly, cosmopolitan approaches are ultimately grounded on the idea of the moral arbitrariness of birth. Underlying this idea is the claim that the distribution of wealth should not be shaped by features for which individuals cannot be held responsible – what Ronald Dworkin has dubbed "brute bad luck".[27] Cosmopolitans argue that, since no one chooses their place of birth, no one should, at least in principle, face harsher life prospects because of their nationality. Although it is to different degrees, all (moral) cosmopolitan authors call for substantial redistribution at the global level.[28]

In the way in which it is presently framed, the debate does not provide satisfactory answers to the research questions. The EU does not seem to fit in any of these two paradigms: it is neither a state nor a world without borders. This complicates the task of addressing the problem of distributive justice in the EU. On the one hand, if the degree of political and economic integration of EU member states is taken into account, a statist view will seem unsuitable. Given the supranational character of EU institutions and the transnational nature of the common market, it seems unsound to treat borders as set in stone. On the other hand, applying a cosmopolitan argument to the Union would mean that the duties of a French citizen with respect to a Polish citizen would be the same as their duties with respect to an Australian. This result would contravene the intuition that the extent of redistribution should be somewhat proportional to the level of moral proximity. How would statists and cosmopolitans react to these charges?

Statists would argue that, since the EU is a voluntary agreement amongst sovereign nation-states, their case – particularly, the coercion-based formulation – accommodates the reality of the Union. Given that member states have all agreed to join the EU and retain the right to leave, so the argument would go, any coercive power that the EU may hold against them is "on lease" from member states. EU member states are bound to each other only within the domains specified by their agreement. Thus distributive justice claims would only apply if member states choose to bring this issue to the treaties. However, this argument is unsatisfactory at least for two reasons.

First, as Chapter 2 will demonstrate, the fact that EU membership is voluntary does not exclude that EU institutions and practices might be (highly) coercive. Even if the EU's right to coerce is "on lease", distributive justice may be in order during the term of that lease. Secondly, it should be noted that consent is not the only relevant input of a compelling theory of justice. Having agreed with a certain state of affairs does not necessarily make it just, as the "happy slave" case illustrates. Therefore, if redistribution is to remain within the national borders in the context of EU membership, further justification should be advanced.

Cosmopolitans, in turn, would argue that the EU demonstrates the plausibility of their case. This is not only because the level of interdependence amongst member states is very high, but also because the EU has a supranational citizenship status, which recognizes the equality of all EU citizens. Therefore, once egalitarian redistributive policies are put into force, the EU will become a case study of how equality is to be realized beyond borders, without necessarily abolishing the nation-state. However, the claim that *equality* should be the leading distributive value of an account of distributive justice for the EU polity has to be challenged. As I will argue in Chapter 2, at the heart of the Union lies a tension between *equality of status* and *self-government*, which renders the cosmopolitan case for the EU unconvincing. One instance of such a dilemma is that, if the autonomy of member states is to be taken seriously, their different welfare regimes will have to be (at least partially) accommodated by any account of EU social justice. This, in turn, will compromise the goal of achieving equality. In addition, it is plausible to think that, since the strength of social solidarity tends to be much higher amongst national citizens than amongst EU citizens, egalitarian redistribution would most likely be grossly unfeasible. Is there a theoretical framework, other than statism and cosmopolitanism, which would be more suitable to the EU?

The issue of distributive justice in the EU has received little attention from political theorists. As the subsequent chapters will show, the few existing contributions suffer from one of two shortcomings: they are either too short, raising some key questions and offering general guidelines, or too loose, focusing on one particular form of injustice – say, tax competition or the crisis of sovereign debt – without offering a broader picture of the many problems at stake. Hence, a systematic articulation of principles of distributive justice for the European Union seems to be largely missing. Two recent developments in the fields of EU studies and political theory have created a momentum for an informed debate. The first is the so-called normative turn in EU studies, which has brought different aspects of the EU polity under normative scrutiny.[29] The second is the emergence of what Laura Valentini dubs the "third wave" of global justice studies, which attempts to go beyond the statist-cosmopolitan framing of the debate.[30] Despite their increasing attention to the EU, political theorists have only marginally addressed the problem of distributive justice in the Union, while the "third wave", however promising, "is still in its infancy".[31] Therefore, these significant developments still have to be substantiated in comprehensive answers to the research questions.

This study also draws on a branch of scholarship within citizenship studies, which has been advancing the notion of multilevel citizenship in the EU. Since its establishment by the Maastricht Treaty of 1992, the nature of EU citizenship has been a matter of intense dispute. A few legal scholars have stressed the limitations of EU citizenship, namely the lack of an EU people and a common identity.[32] Alternatively, other authors have welcomed this new status, treating "the overlap of citizenship and nationality as a matter of historical contingency".[33] In a search for a middle ground, a number of studies have linked the notion of EU citizenship not to a single EU *demos*, but to multiple *demoi*.[34] Similarly, a few scholars have investigated the perspectives for EU citizenship as a function of different political models of the EU.[35] Despite the diversity of approaches, the "dominant conception of citizenship" still regards the latter as "a unitary and homogeneous legal status granted to an individual by a sovereign state".[36]

In a recent essay, William Maas made a convincing case against the "dominant conception of citizenship".[37] Maas discusses different *levels* of citizenship, which include "citizenship not only of the state but also of the sub-state, suprastate, or non-state political communities".[38] In the specific context of the EU, Rainer Bauböck has similarly argued for the existence of three levels of citizenship – local, national, and supranational – where EU citizenship is "one layer in a multi-level model of democratic membership".[39] One of the advantages of the multilevel approach is balancing the special character of nation-state membership with the derivative, yet significant, nature of EU citizenship. Indeed, "[t]he reality of European citizenship is not 'either/or', it is 'both/and'".[40] In addition, this approach allows us to situate the rights and duties of EU citizenship within a multilevel scheme of rights and duties, which may vary in scope and degree, translating a complex hierarchy of civic affiliations.

If the model of multilevel citizenship is to be accepted, a key question will have to be addressed. At least since the aftermath of the Second World War, social rights have gradually become a constitutive dimension of democratic citizenship. In fact, most modern democratic polities are committed not only to political equality, but also to a (variable) degree of socioeconomic equality. How does this social dimension of citizenship fit within the model of multilevel citizenship? In other words, at what level should redistribution take place? Are social rights to be fulfilled at one specific level of citizenship, or should they be allocated across the different levels? In the context of EU membership, are there any distributive requirements linked to EU citizenship, or is social justice within the exclusive domain of the nation-state?

Although a number of studies on the notion of "EU social citizenship" have been produced, the issue of how different levels of citizenship are to interact in terms of distributive justice has been for the most part neglected.[41] The way in which responsibilities are to be assigned remains unclear. Most literature on European social welfare still operates under the assumption of territorial nation-states. Yet, in an EU where individuals have multiple affiliations and are highly mobile, this premise must be challenged. The existing literature seems to put the reader in a difficult position: they either have to endorse a full-scale conception of EU social citizenship, or to accept a residual model where distributive justice is almost exclusively the business of the nation-state. Since each of these options is problematic, a more nuanced approach seems to be needed. Hence, the question: in a multilevel polity such as the EU, who owes what, to whom?

Therefore, this project aims to fill two gaps in the literature: the place for the EU in the global justice debate and the assignment of social responsibilities in the context of multilevel citizenship in the EU.

A few clues about a sound answer

Although the number of works on distributive justice in the EU is very limited, the few existing contributions offer important insights regarding the tensions which are at stake. A preliminary issue has to do with the way of framing the problem of distributive justice in the Union. This point is neatly captured by Philippe Van Parijs in his correspondence with John Rawls. According to Van Parijs, the relevant factual question about the EU is "not whether there is one or more ethnoi involved (a matter of cultural distance), nor whether there currently happens to be a common demos (a matter of political institutions and of sufficiently common public space), but whether the circumstances (mobility, contact, interdependencies, etc.) are such that there *should* be a common demos – if only to enforce the requirements of justice".[42] Thus the issue is not whether one can find an EU people with a widespread sense of social solidarity, on the grounds of which social rights can be justified and endorsed. This mere replication of the domestic experience of the member states would be unsuitable for a supranational polity which is politically and sociologically at odds with the nation-state. Rather, my investigation should focus on whether the circumstances of justice of the present-day EU, *in their own terms*, are strong enough to generate distributive duties amongst member states and/or EU citizens.

Another important insight has been captured by John Rawls in his answer to Van Parijs. Rawls asks, "Isn't there a conflict between a large free and open market comprising all of Europe and the individual nation-states, each with its separate political and social institutions, historical memories, and forms and traditions of social policy?".[43] Indeed, Rawls's highly influential theory of justice presupposes a background of shared political and social institutions, which he claims to be found only at the nation-state level. It has been rightly argued that this assumption is unsuitable for a world which is no longer grounded on the absolute sovereignty of nation-states and where interdependence is very high.[44] Yet Rawls raises a very important point regarding the EU: how could a common conception of justice fit a variety of member states with contrasting political cultures? For instance, is it right to think of harmonizing social policy in a context where social preferences and needs are potentially very different? In turn, this raises the question of which distributive value should be at the heart of a conception of justice for the EU – for example, equality, sufficiency, merit, and so on. Thus, a satisfactory account must (i) substantiate what a common conception of justice would look like, and (ii) persuade that such a conception of justice would be feasible, despite the diversity of political cultures across the Union.

Andrea Sangiovanni, in turn, has drawn our attention to the undertheorized notion of solidarity in the EU. Despite its recurrent appearances in the legal and political discourse of both EU institutions and member states, the substantive content of solidarity remains vague and ambiguous.[45] Thus Sangiovanni opportunely asks, "what kinds of principles, policies, and ideals should an affirmation of solidarity commit us to?"[46] In one of his articles, Sangiovanni rejects three models currently available – statist solidarity, post-national solidarity, and solidarity as fraternity – suggesting that a model based on reciprocity is more suitable for the EU. He claims that "the most plausible view will begin with the special character and nature of European social, political, legal, and economic *cooperation*".[47] He thus rejects the argument that "our relations as subjects of coercion, bearers of an identity, or democratic citizens" may trigger such norms.[48] However, solidarity may be a composite value, expressed in more than one currency. In other words, coercion, democracy, and reciprocity may *all* – at least in principle – trigger distributive claims in the EU. For this reason, unpacking the ideal of solidarity and applying it to the EU entails a background theory of distributive justice, which specifies the conditions under which each particular duty of justice is activated. Thus, a systematic treatment to the research questions will imply a preliminary discussion of the more general question: why should we redistribute?

An additional challenge has been raised by the works of Jürgen Habermas and Claus Offe, who have highlighted issues of institutional legitimacy and capacity at EU level which are strongly linked to the goal of EU redistribution. Thus, in an EU polity which lacks a centralized government, as well as legal competences on social policy, how should distributive justice be realized? In short, Habermas suggests that this problem could be solved by bringing the EU one step forward towards a federation of states, which would create and enforce civic solidarity amongst all Europeans.[49] Yet if feasibility is to be taken seriously, his key concern for political agency

should be reformulated to allow for more modest, non-federalist alternatives. Hence, what minimum level of political reform would be required
for distributive justice to be realized in the EU? In Offe's view, this issue
has become particularly tricky since the onset of the economic crisis,
"which has deactivated potential crisis managers and agents of change".[50]
According to Offe, "the question of who is sufficiently legitimated and otherwise resourceful to formulate and implement a strategy that might move
Europe to any desirable and sustainable post-crisis future, and according to
what kinds of rules and procedures, is without a widely accepted answer".[51]
Thus, a compelling answer to the research questions has to specify the institutions which could realize distributive justice in the Union.

IV. Method

The discipline of political theory

At this point, it is worth clarifying the field of studies in which this study
is situated. What is a "political theory"? Is political theory about "theory"
in a proper sense? What exactly do political theorists mean by the term
"political"? What is the place of this discipline *vis-à-vis* the broader fields
of social science and philosophy? I shall address these questions in turn. To
begin with, the common denominator of competing political theories is the
moral evaluation of politics, which prescribes standards of behaviour for
political actors. Political theorists ask what societies *should* look like – a
goal which contrasts with the empirically driven tasks of describing and
explaining what a given society *is* or *was* at a particular moment of time.[52]
With this purpose in mind, political theorists engage with moral reasoning,
which may be defined as the abstract examination of the notions of "good"
and "evil", usually followed by the adjudication of "right" and "wrong"
courses of action.[53] This task is not one of pure intellectualism, irrelevant
for "practical" life. First, moral reasoning is a defining trait of human
beings from early childhood.[54] Second, enfranchised citizens are regularly
asked to choose amongst competing sets of public policies with morally relevant implications. Yet notice that the goal of political theory is not just to
advance a list of morally loaded claims about politics, as any other political
party. The main distinguishing feature of the discipline is to advance *justifications* for such claims, which fulfil certain *criteria of validity*. This points
to the reason why political theory is, indeed, about "theory".

There are at least two ways of conceiving of "theory". In a strict sense,
theory is a set of systematically articulated propositions, which describe
and/or explain a given phenomenon, verifiable (at least in principle) by
means of a replicable test.[55] Thus a key feature of a "theory" in this sense
is being *falsifiable*.[56] This definition applies largely to the theories of natural sciences and to the theories of social sciences which follow a positivist

approach. However, a *normative* theory is neither true nor false, it is more or less *plausible*.[57] This apparently lower threshold of what counts as a moral theory is nonetheless quite demanding. A normative theory is plausible at least if (1) it offers a reasonable answer to a given question; (2) it is internally consistent, that is, it does not show any logical flaw; (3) it is consistent with basic facts about reality; (4) it is consistent with other widely shared theories which are beyond its subject of study; and (5) it gives reasonable answers to the main objections against it.[58] This point can be illustrated by referring to two influential normative theories with contrasting implications: John Rawls's and Robert Nozick's accounts of distributive justice.[59] Surely, one can argue that one is more *plausible* than the other, but any categorical demonstration of what justice requires seems impossible. Accordingly, this book shall elaborate an account of distributive justice for the EU which is a "theory" only insofar as it attempts to meet the five plausibility requirements here listed.[60]

Yet what exactly is "political" about political theory? In the field of political theory, delimiting the domain of the "political" has proven difficult for at least for two reasons. First, the boundaries of the so-called *public* and *private* spheres are highly disputed. For instance, for liberal political theorists, the firm and the family belong to the private domain, provided that certain golden rules are followed, such as paying taxes and abstaining from violent behaviour.[61] Instead, for republican and feminist political theorists, the public realm comprises all fields of social life where arbitrary power may be brought about, which notably includes the firm and the family.[62] Secondly, the key unit of analysis of the "political" varies across different paradigms. Competing accounts focus on individual agency, social and economic structure, institutional design, and power relations.[63] However, this fluidity of the concept of the "political" may be more of an advantage than a problem. One reason is that, if political theory is to provide practical guidance in a diverse and changing world, it must be somewhat responsive to contextual challenges. For example, the normative assumption of secularism, largely accepted in the West, would not have fitted medieval Europe, nor does it suit a number of present-day Islamic states. This suggests that a helpful understanding of the "political" will be more modular than universalist.[64] The study of politics should, then, incorporate, rather than exclude, different angles and perspectives.[65] This fully applies to the current debates on distributive justice, where a variety of paradigms are engaged in constant dialogue.

Political theory is a promising field to address the research questions presented already. As we have seen, this discipline goes beyond what there *is*, asking about what there *should* be. In this sense, it may be useful for an EU which seems too attached to the status quo, at least as far as social policy is concerned. Yet, if political theory is not an empirical social science, it is not a synonym of political philosophy either. In fact, political theorists draw heavily on the insights of empirical sciences such as sociology, political science, psychology, and economics to a much greater extent than their philosopher counterparts. In addition, most of them seem to believe that the feasibility prospects of a given theory should be taken into account. For instance, they tend to exclude proposals which seem wholly unfeasible, as well as to specify institutional arrangements through which their theories could be realized. This peculiar position between social science and philosophy is promising for this investigation, which aims to address a normative question with many empirical inputs and implications, and which intends to reach multidisciplinary readers. I can only hope to provide an account which is sufficiently comprehensive and clear to bridge multiple concerns from different fields.

The method of reflective equilibrium

I have briefly sketched the subject of political theory. Now, my question will be, *how* can one come up with a sound political theory? In order to develop a theory of distributive justice for the European Union, this study will rely on the method of "reflective equilibrium", a process of inductive moral reasoning which builds on our *intuitions* about morality, taking into account certain *empirical facts* about human beings and the societies in which they live.[66] The main goal of this method is to achieve a stable moral account – an "equilibrium" or, in other words, a reasonable articulation of values in tension. This can be done by thoroughly engaging with conflicting intuitions about "right" and "wrong", in light of certain empirical elements, which help in translating abstract values into applied moral norms. This procedure is in notorious contrast to comprehensive moral doctrines such as utilitarianism and deontology, according to which a particular understanding of "right" and "wrong" is absolute and exclusive. In addition, the method of reflective equilibrium sustains that normative judgements are subjected to constant revision, particularly in the face of relevant empirical developments. Thus defined, reflective equilibrium raises a number of questions. First, what exactly is an *intuition*? Is it the equivalent to an opinion? Second, why do intuitions matter? Third, how should we proceed from a loose set of intuitions towards a systematic political theory? And how exactly can we adjudicate conflicting intuitions? Fourth, at what stage of the process should empirical facts come into play? Are they the starting point of the theory, a constitutive part of the theory, or an *ex post* feasibility test of the theory? In what follows, I shall sketch an answer to these questions.

One may define ethical intuition as "an initial, *intellectual* appearance", "whose content is an evaluative proposition".[67] Intuitions draw on a vast repertoire of mental and psychological resources, including ideas, experiences, feelings, and dispositions, to offer a preliminary assessment of the moral status of a given action or state of affairs. They are not "natural", in the sense of being prior to socialization. In fact, they are influenced by internalized norms of behaviour. Intuitions are a good starting point for moral reasoning for at least two reasons. First, they reflect the moral knowledge learnt through life in society. Although the existing moral conventions may be morally wrong, they are useful, either as an input, or as an object for critique.[68] Secondly, intuitions are a widely available resource for moral judgement amongst human beings. Of course, not all of us share exactly the same intuitions about the same event. This indicates that intuitions do not necessarily reveal what is right – recall that I defined them as "appearances". In addition, intuitions may be ambiguous, or even contradictory. This is why the content of intuitions is "raw material" which needs to be critically examined.[69]

A key challenge for political theorists is to coherently articulate plausible intuitions with opposite implications. Consider the ongoing debate on collective security and individual liberty, where two competing concerns are at stake. On the one hand, it seems necessary to give the authorities appropriate means to protect civilians from serious threats against their security. On the other hand, doing so seems to imply an undesirable reduction of individual freedom, placing too much power in the hands of unaccountable agencies. How can we adjudicate? This can be done in a number of ways. One is to search for the most salient moral concern amongst a set of competing concerns. In my example, this would mean claiming that one value – liberty or security – has moral priority over the other. Another strategy is to investigate the conditions under which each of the conflicting claims may apply. For instance, one may claim that, in principle, liberty has priority over security, but this changes when one is faced with certain types of threat. An alternative approach is to deconstruct the trade-off, arguing that it does not apply from a given instructive point of view. Thus, it may be argued that one is not free if one is not safe, which suggests that the two concerns are closely linked. These and other strategies illustrate how reflective equilibrium may be reached.[70]

Finally, in this book, I propose the view that empirics can rightly play three types of roles in normative theorizing. First, they may be the *starting point* of a given normative claim, originating the so-called practice–dependence approach. For instance, one may plausibly argue that the current refugee crisis in Europe gives rise to certain moral claims against EU member states. This function of empirical facts explains why normative theories which are grounded on contrasting descriptive claims about the world may come to very different conclusions.[71] Secondly, empirics may be a *constitutive part* of the theory. This means that a political theorist may refer to key social and psychological facts throughout their search for reflective equilibrium. For example, they may reject a Platonic abolishment of families based on the psychological needs of children and the emotional attachment of their parents. In this case, empirical facts substantively reveal whether a certain course of action is right or wrong. Thirdly, empirical facts may be employed as a *feasibility check* on the theory. For instance, once the theory has been outlined, one may test its economic viability. Given that reflective equilibrium is always revisable, the purpose of this test is mainly pedagogical – that is, if a theory is deemed unfeasible, a compromise between desirability and feasibility may then be sought. As will become apparent, my research relies on empirical facts at each of these three levels.[72]

Strategy to tackle the research questions

In the first part of this book, I will develop a normative argument for distributive justice in the EU. The argument will be built in three logical steps. First, I will address the general question: why should we redistribute? This exercise will allow me to identify a number of duties of justice and the conditions under which they apply. Second, I will investigate whether the current political and economic configuration of the EU fulfils the conditions identified in the first step. To do so, I will need to provide a descriptive account of certain key features of the present-day EU. Third, I will discuss the way in which responsibilities to fulfil the duties identified in the second step should be allocated amongst EU institutions and member states. At this point, I will be ready to advance concrete policy proposals. These three steps will, I hope, lead me to a coherent normative approach to the problem of distributive justice in the EU.

The second part of the book shall discuss the feasibility prospects of my normative account. The argument will unfold in two logical steps. First, I will investigate which criteria should be used to test the feasibility of a given normative proposal. Second, I will apply these criteria to my account of distributive justice. In doing so, I will discuss a variety of scenarios which may increase or decrease the feasibility prospects of my proposals. If successful, this strategy will allow me to formulate an account of distributive justice for the EU which is both plausible and feasible.

V. An overview of the argument

To conclude this Introduction, it will be useful to sketch the arguments which are put forward in this book. In Chapter 1, I introduce two distributive duties: the democratic duty to redistribute and the duty of economic reciprocity. The democratic duty to redistribute consists of providing the means for political participation and resistance to power to all the members of a polity. In turn, the duty of economic reciprocity requires a fair distribution of the gains of economic exchange amongst all market participants. I argue that each of these duties implies its own policy instruments. The democratic duty to redistribute is to be translated into a basket of basic goods, which includes (i) means of subsistence, (ii) healthcare, (iii) education, and (iv) resources for due process in court. In turn, the duty of economic reciprocity is to be realized mainly through labour regulation and economic and monetary policy. The geographical scope of application of these duties depends on whether the conditions which trigger them are met. These conditions are, in the former case, comprehensively institutionalized democratic and coercive institutions and, in the latter case, varying degrees of economic integration – national markets, free trade areas, and the global market.

In Chapter 2, I argue that, at the EU level, coercion and democracy are sufficiently institutionalized to activate the democratic duty to redistribute. First, I argue that the EU has the capacity to generate the generalized compliance of its members with its laws. This is achieved through a complex combination of domestic and supranational norms and institutions, from the stage of law enactment to that of law enforcement. I claim that the fact that the EU does not possess a unified monopoly of force in the Weberian sense is not an ultimate obstacle, since its supranational institutions can rely on national courts and police forces to enforce EU law. Secondly, I argue that the EU is a "demoicracy", with key democratic institutions, a citizenship status, and a plurality of *demoi*. I argue that the institutional architecture of the EU fulfils the basic requirements of democratic legitimacy, that the profuse practices linked to EU citizenship make it much more than an empty box, and that the absence of a single European people does not defeat redistributive claims at EU level. I argue that responsibilities to realize democratic redistribution in the Union should be shared by the three levels of government – local, national, and supranational. I claim that the trade-off between equality of status and self-government can be successfully addressed by relying on the familiar principles of proportionality and subsidiarity. In my account, this means that the EU should act as a safety net for domestic social citizenship, supplementing national welfare systems whenever they fail to meet the requirements of the democratic duty to redistribute.

In Chapter 3, I claim that the duty of economic reciprocity applies to a Union where the common market, the single currency, and freedom of movement decisively shape the distribution of wealth. I claim that the patterns of economic specialization resulting from the combined effect of EU integration and globalization created a "distributive vicious circle", which hinders worse-performing member states from improving their condition. I argue that the current design of the common market and the Eurozone are partially responsible for the practices of "social dumping" in the Union, as well as for the levels of indebtedness faced by a number of member states – despite the fact that poor policy choices also played a role. Accordingly, I claim that the costs of the present crisis should be fairly shared by all member states. In addition, I argue that free movement creates a number of social risks for mobile EU workers. I suggest that realizing the principle of non-discrimination implies making the opportunities of the common market accessible to all, which, in turn, requires a degree of redistribution. I present a number of policy proposals, including a coordinated EU minimum wage, a minimum EU corporate tax rate, and an EU Fund for Global Competitiveness (FGC). Thus, a combination of pre-distributive instruments (e.g. rules of cooperation) and redistributive instruments (e.g. inter-state transfers) is desirable to realize social justice in the EU.

In Chapter 4, I distinguish "temporary" from "pervasive" unfeasibility. Temporary unfeasibility results from circumstances that can arguably be overcome, such as the preferences of voters at a specific moment in time. In opposition, pervasive unfeasibility is linked to barriers that human agency cannot reasonably be expected to overcome, such as the efficiency costs associated with certain policy proposals. I argue that the debate amongst political theorists should focus on pervasive unfeasibility, leaving temporary feasibility for political strategists. Furthermore, I claim that, in order to be manageable, a test on pervasive unfeasibility has to refer to a particular paradigm of social order, such as liberal democracy – what I dub "constrained" feasibility tests. I thus present four criteria for assessing the feasibility status of a liberal democratic theory of distributive justice: (1) fitting the political culture of a given community, at least to a certain degree; (2) being economically sustainable; (3) being translatable into functioning policies and institutions; and (4) being consistent with the degree of social solidarity amongst the individuals who are to be bound by the proposed policies. I claim that to be feasible, an account of distributive justice has to meet each of these four criteria.

Finally, in Chapter 5, I claim that the policy proposals presented in the previous chapters are feasible in the long run if a number of requirements are met. First, any scheme of distributive justice at the EU level has to be compatible with a plurality of welfare regimes in the Union. I argue that the EU threshold of basic goods is consistent with this requirement insofar as it draws on an existing "overlapping consensus" regarding primary goods. In addition, since my proposal allows member states to diverge above the sufficiency level, it does not imply the harmonization of social policies. Secondly, I claim that any feasible EU scheme has to imply a relatively small amount of inter-state transfers. This is achieved by my proposal through a focus on pre-distribution, which is expected to considerably reduce the level of deprivation in the EU. Thirdly, I argue that an economically sustainable scheme needs to be financed through public policies which anticipate increasing social needs in times of crisis. My proposals do so by prescribing the accumulation of public savings in times of prosperity. Fourthly, I claim that a new institutional framework is needed at the EU level to realize distributive justice. In addition to a change in the treaties conferring social policy competences to the EU, I propose the creation of an EU agency for social justice, with the task of dealing with the main budgetary and operational challenges of distributive justice.

Notes

1 Robert Schuman, *The Schuman Declaration* (9 May 1950).

2 Calculations based on Eurostat, "Severely Materially Deprived People" (2018). This category is composed of individuals who experience at least four out of nine of the following deprivation indicators: cannot afford (i) to pay rent or utility bills, (ii) to keep home adequately warm, (iii) to face unexpected expenses, (iv) to eat meat, fish, or a protein equivalent every second day, (v) a week's holiday away from home, (vi) a car, (vii) a washing machine, (viii) a colour TV, or (ix) a telephone.

3 Fritz W. Scharpf, "The European Social Model: Coping with the Challenge of Diversity", *Journal of Common Market Studies* 40 (2002), pp. 645–670.

4 Charter of Fundamental Rights of the European Union, Article 33.

5 Charter of Fundamental Rights of the European Union, Article 34.

6 Charter of Fundamental Rights of the European Union, Article 35.

7 Jeff Kenner, "Economic and Social Rights in the EU Legal Order: The Mirage of Indivisibility", in Tamara K. Harvey and Jeff Kenner, *Economic and Social Rights under the EU Charter of Fundamental Rights: A Legal Perspective* (Oxford, 2003), p. 24.

8 This has been demonstrated by a number of recent decisions by the CJEU. Consider, for instance, the decision on *Elisabeta Dano and Florin Dano* v. *Jobcenter Leipzig*. The court ruled that "[e]conomically inactive EU citizens who go to another Member State solely in order to obtain social assistance may be excluded from certain social benefits". See Press Release 146/14 by the Court of Justice of the European Union, 11 November 2014.

9 These documents include the European Social Charter (1961, revised in 1996); the Community Charter of the Fundamental Social Rights of Workers (1989); the Treaty on European Union (TEU), establishing EU citizenship and the principle of solidarity (1993); and the European Commission's White Paper on Social Policy (1994).

10 TFEU, Articles 8 and 9.

11 Gráinne De Búrca, "The Future of Social Rights Protection in Europe", in Gráinne De Búrca, Bruno de Witte, and Larissa Ogertschnig (eds), *Social Rights in Europe* (Oxford, 2005), pp. 14–15.

12 Onora O'Neill, *Justice Across Boundaries: Whose Obligations?* (Cambridge, 2016), p. 5 (emphasis in original).

13 See Eurostat, "GDP per Capita in PPS" (2018) and "Unemployment Rate" (2018).

14 Miguel Poiares Maduro, "Europe's Social Self: The Sickness Unto Death", in Jon Shaw (ed.), *Social Law and Policy in an Evolving European Union* (Oxford, 2000), p. 334.

15 See, for instance, Andrew Moravcsik, "In Defence of the 'Democratic Deficit': Reassessing Legitimacy in the European Union", *Journal of Common Market Studies* 40 (2002), pp. 603–624.

16 See, amongst others, Dieter Grimm, "Does Europe Need a Constitution?", *European Law Journal* 1 (1995), pp. 282–302.

17 As an illustrative example, consider the European Health Insurance Card. This insurance allows every EU citizen to receive medical treatment in another member state on the same terms and at the same cost as nationals of another member state. Yet this insurance has two important caveats. First, it only applies to temporary stays. Second, member states have the right to charge the country of origin for the services provided to its citizens. Therefore, access to healthcare should be interpreted as a facilitator of freedom of movement, rather than as a redistributive policy.

18 Giandomenico Majone, "The European Community Between Social Policy and Social Regulation", *Journal of Common Market Studies* 31 (1993), pp. 160–161.

19 Fritz W. Scharpf, *Governing in Europe: Effective and Democratic?* (Oxford, 1999), Chapter 5.

20 Philippe C. Schmitter and Michael W. Bower, "A (Modest) Proposal for Expanding Social Citizenship in the European Union", *Journal of European Social Policy* 11 (2001), p. 55.

21 Klaus Tuori, "Has Euro Area Monetary Policy Become Redistribution By Monetary Means? 'Unconventional' Monetary Policy as a Hidden Redistributive Mechanism", *European Law Journal* 22 (2016), pp. 838–868.

22 For instance, EU citizens can freely express their views on social justice, they can organize a petition to the European Parliament calling for social reform, and they can run for an EU office on a social justice platform.

23 As noted in Laura Valentini, "Justice, Charity, and Disaster Relief: What, if Anything, is Owed to Haiti, Japan, and New Zealand?", *American Journal of Political Science* 57 (2013), 491–503.

24 See John Rawls, *The Law of Peoples* (Cambridge MA, 2001); David Miller, *On Nationality* (Oxford, 1997) and *National Responsibility and Global Justice* (Oxford, 2007); and Thomas Nagel, "The Problem of Global Justice", *Philosophy and Public Affairs* 33 (2005), pp. 113–147.

25 See, for instance, Peter Singer, "Famine, Affluence and Morality", *Philosophy and Public Affairs* 1 (1972), pp. 229–243; Thomas W. Pogge, *World Poverty and Human Rights* (Cambridge, 2008); Charles R. Beitz, *Political Theory and International Relations* (Princeton, 1999); and Simon Caney, *Justice Beyond Borders: A Global Political Theory* (New York, 2005).

26 Cosmopolitans do not necessarily reject the idea of the nation-state as such; they may argue, for instance, that the nation-state system is the best means to implement a cosmopolitan conception of global justice. On this view, see Lea Ypi, "Statist Cosmopolitanism", *Journal of Political Philosophy* 16 (2008), pp. 48–71.

27 See Ronald Dworkin, *Sovereign Virtue: The Theory and Practice of Equality* (Cambridge, MA, 2002).

28 A number of authors have distinguished moral cosmopolitanism from other types of cosmopolitanism, such as its political and cultural counterparts. See, amongst others, Charles R. Beitz, "Cosmopolitanism and Global Justice", *The Journal of Ethics* 9 (2005), pp. 11–27; and Fred Dallmayr, "Cosmopolitanism: Moral and Political", *Political Theory* 31 (2003), pp. 421–442.

29 For an overview of this normative turn, see Heidrun Friese and Peter Wagner, "Survey Article: The Nascent Political Philosophy of the European Polity", *Journal of Political Philosophy* 10 (2002), pp. 342–364.

30 See Laura Valentini, *Justice in a Globalized World: A Normative Framework* (Oxford, 2011), p. 4.

31 Ibid.

32 See, for instance, Carlos Closa, "Citizenship of the Union and Nationality of Member States", *Common Market Law Review* 32 (1995), pp. 487–518; and Dieter Grimm, "Does Europe Need a Constitution?", pp. 282–302.

33 Elizabeth Meehan, *Citizenship and the European Union* (Bonn, 2000), 4. See also Antje Wiener, "Assessing the Constructive Potential of Union Citizenship – A Socio-Historical Perspective", *European Integration Online Papers* 1 (1997).

34 See Kalypso Nicolaidis, "The Idea of European Demoicracy", in Julie Dickson and Pavlos Eleftheriadis, *Philosophical Foundations of European Law* (Oxford, 2012); and J. H. H. Weiler, "To be a European Citizen – Eros and Civilization", *Journal of European Public Policy* 4 (1997), pp. 495–519.

35 See Richard Bellamy and Dario Castiglione, "Between Cosmopolis and Community: Three Models of Rights and Democracy within the European Union", in Daniele Archibugi, David Held, and Martin Köhler (eds), *Re-imagining Political Community* (Stanford, 1998); and Rainer Bauböck, "Why European Citizenship? Normative Approaches to Supranational Union", *Theoretical Inquiries in Law* 8 (2007), pp. 453–488.

36 Willem Maas, "Varieties of Multilevel Citizenship", in William Maas (ed.), *Multilevel Citizenship* (Philadelphia, 2013), p. viii.

37 Ibid.

38 Ibid., p. 1.

39 Rainer Bauböck, "The Three Levels of Citizenship within the European Union", *German Law Journal* 15 (2014), p. 751.

40 Espen D. H. Olsen, "European Citizenship: Mixing Nation State and Federal Features with a Cosmopolitan Twist", *Perspectives on European Politics and Society* 14 (2013), p. 508.

41 The exceptions are Michael Keating, "Social Citizenship, Solidarity and Welfare in Regionalized and Plurinational States", *Citizenship Studies* 13 (2009), pp. 501–513; and Andreas Føllesdal, "Federal Inequality Amongst Equals: A Contractualist Defence", *Metaphilosophy* 32 (2001), pp. 236–255. However, Keating addresses the general problem of social citizenship in the context of multiple affiliations, without focusing on the EU. In turn, Føllesdal's is an account of distributive justice for federations, and thus is not necessarily suitable for the EU.

42 Philippe Van Parijs, "Première Lettre", in John Rawls and Philippe Van Parijs, *Three Letters on* The Law of Peoples *and the European Union* (2003) (emphasis in original).

43 John Rawls, "Deuxième Lettre", in John Rawls and Philippe Van Parijs, *Three Letters on* The Law of Peoples *and the European Union.*

44 See, for instance, Thomas W. Pogge, *Realizing Rawls* (Ithaca, 1989); and Allen Buchanan, "Rawls's Law of Peoples: Rules for a Vanished Westphalian World", *Ethics* 110 (2000), pp. 697–721.

45 Note, for instance, that the word "solidarity" features 15 times in the consolidated version of the Treaty on European Union.

46 Andrea Sangiovanni, "Solidarity in the European Union: Problems and Prospects", in Julie Dickson and Pavlos Eleftheriadis (eds), *Philosophical Foundations of European Union Law* (Oxford, 2012), pp. 385–386.

47 Ibid., p. 410 (emphasis in original).

48 Ibid.

49 Jürgen Habermas, "The Postnational Constellation and the Future of Democracy", *The Postnational Constellation: Political Essays* (Cambridge, 2001).

50 Claus Offe, *Europe Entrapped* (Cambridge, 2015), p. 4.

51 Ibid., pp. 4–5.

52 There are also a number of works in "conceptual" political theory, which claim to combine both types of questions. One of the main goals of this approach is to give substantive content to key concepts such as "institution", "state", and "political party". According to this approach, sound *theoretical* definitions are grounded on certain normative commitments. An illustrative example presented to me by Stefano Bartolini is that a compelling definition of social institution *should* exclude corruption, even if the latter is embedded in the social norms and practices of a given country. In turn, "conceptual" political theory becomes an empirically driven enterprise when it translates a given theoretical definition into an *operational* definition – that is, a set of criteria that can be quantified for the purpose of hypotheses testing. For instance, corruption may be operationally defined as "having received at least one bribe in 10 years' time". For an influential discussion by one of the main representatives of this tradition see Giovanni Sartori, "Concept Misformation in Comparative Politics", *American Political Science Review* 64 (1970), pp. 1033–1053.

53 This definition thus includes the two existing types of moral reasoning – theoretical and practical. See Henry S. Richardson, "Moral Reasoning", in Edward N. Zalta (ed.), *Stanford Encyclopedia of Philosophy* (Fall 2018), https://plato.stanford.edu/archives/fall2018/entries/reasoning-moral/ (Accessed 3 October 2019).

54 See, for instance, Sophia F. Ongley, Marta Nola, and Tina Malti, "Children's Giving: Moral Reasoning and Moral Emotions in the Development of Donation Behaviors", *Frontiers in Psychology* 23 (2014), pp. 1–8.

55 The caveat "at least in principle" refers to cases where, although it is possible to conceive a test in which a given theory could be proven wrong, the technology required to perform such test is not (yet) available. This applies to many theories regarding the origin and expansion of the universe.

56 See Karl Popper, "Science: Conjectures and Refutations", in *Conjectures and Refutations: The Growth of Scientific Knowledge* (London, 1963). Popper's approach has been influentially challenged by Thomas Kuhn, for whom falsification does not necessarily lead to the rejection of a given theory, since it may still be the best available paradigm to explain the majority of the events. See Thomas S. Kuhn, *The Structure of Scientific Revolutions* (Chicago, 2012).

57 Certain moral theories appear to be imminently false. For instance, consider the case of doctrines which advocate the supremacy of a certain race. Yet, in my

view, the falsehood rather lies on the empirical premise on which this theory is predicated. As a *normative* theory, race supremacy is, thus, utterly *implausible*.

58 These criteria are inspired by the discussion by Mark Timmons, *Moral Theory: An Introduction* (Lanham, 2001). I leave aside the question of whether standards of plausibility may be contingent on cultural or religious beliefs, which determine what is accepted as a sound premise. For instance, Divine Command theory and most versions of Natural Law theory are entirely built upon the assumption of the existence of God. More generally, as Thomas Kuhn has argued, standards of proof are to a great extent determined by membership of epistemic communities with given sets of beliefs.

59 See John Rawls, *A Theory of Justice: Revised Edition* (Cambridge MA, 1999); and Robert Nozick, *Anarchy, State and Utopia* (Malden, 1974).

60 Against my view, the so-called moral realists have claimed that moral knowledge, if at all possible, must be grounded on "moral facts". A justification for the rejection of moral realism cannot be presented here. For an influential statement of the realist position by one of its main proponents, see Thomas M. Scanlon, *What We Owe to Each Other* (Cambridge MA, 1998).

61 See Paul Kelly, "How Political is Political Liberalism?", *Liberalism* (Cambridge, 2005).

62 See, for instance, Philip Pettit, "Freedom in the Market", *Politics, Philosophy and Economics* 5 (2006), pp. 131–149; and Catherine A. MacKinnon, *Toward a Feminist Theory of the State* (Cambridge MA, 1998).

63 See, respectively, F. A. Hayek, *The Constitution of Liberty* (Abingdon, 2006); John Rawls, *A Theory of Justice: Revised Edition*; Robert Dahl, *Democracy and its Critics* (New Haven, 1989); Elizabeth Anderson, "What is the Point of Equality?", *Ethics* 109 (1999), pp. 287–337.

64 On this point, see Dipesh Chakrabarty, *Provincializing Europe: Postcolonial Thought and Historical Difference* (Princeton, 2000).

65 A number of calls for eclecticism can be found in the different fields of the social sciences. For instance, in the field of international relations, see Rudra Sil and Peter J. Katzenstein, "Analytical Eclecticism in the Study of World Politics: Reconfiguring Problems and Mechanisms across Research Traditions", *Perspectives on Politics* 8 (2010), pp. 411–431.

66 Norman Daniels, "Reflective Equilibrium", in Edward N. Zalta (ed.), *The Stanford Encyclopedia of Philosophy* (2013), http://plato.stanford.edu/arch ives/win2013/entries/reflective-equilibrium/ (Accessed 1 June 2016).

67 Michael Huemer, *Ethical Intuitionism* (New York, 2005), p. 102 (emphasis in original).

68 In fact, there are many moral conventions which are not disputed by any major moral theory, except under exceptional and delimited circumstances. Consider the moral norms against murder, theft, and lying.

69 There has been much discussion on the epistemic status of intuitions. Most notably, a number of important experiments have challenged the validity of intuitions as a basis for moral reasoning. For an overview of the existing empirical research on intuitions, and the claim that the available results do not compromise their epistemic status, see John Bengson, "Experimental Attacks on Intuitions and Answers", *Philosophy and Phenomenological Research* 86 (2013), pp. 495–532.

70 This may lead one to ask whether political theory is epistemologically equivalent to *opinion*. However, this view appears to be unsound. In fact, the demanding plausibility criteria outlined in this section are not required by opinions in a proper sense, which do not have to be logically coherent or comprehensively engage with alternative points of view. Surely, subjective beliefs and experiences may play a role when choosing between equally plausible views. Yet this proposition also applies to empirical social sciences and even to some natural sciences, whenever competing paradigms of explanation are available. In fact, the quality of a method of reasoning does not seem to be determined by its ability to produce a single answer to a given question, but by its degree of success in excluding answers which are implausible.

71 For instance, consider the empirical assumptions of John Rawls and Charles Beitz on interdependence at the global level. See John Rawls, *The Law of Peoples* and Charles R. Beitz, *Political Theory and International Relations*.

72 In Chapter 4, I shall discuss the existing literature on the concept of feasibility.

1

Two distributive duties

I. Introduction

This chapter addresses the question: why should we redistribute? I suggest that at least two different types of distributive duties may coexist. The first duty derives from membership of a polity – a democratic duty to redistribute. The second duty is related to participation in the market, understood as a system of cooperation – a duty of economic reciprocity. I claim that each of these duties implies different distributive mechanisms. While the democratic duty to redistribute relies heavily on income redistribution, the duty of economic reciprocity focuses on regulation. They also vary in their territorial scope of application. The democratic duty to redistribute applies to contexts in which democracy and coercion are comprehensively institutionalized. This typically refers to the nation-state, but it can also go beyond its borders, in the presence of a sufficiently institutionalized apparatuses at the international level. In turn, the duty of economic reciprocity applies to contexts of regular economic exchange, varying according to the degree of economic integration: namely, national markets, free trade areas, and the global market.

I begin with a criticism of Thomas Nagel's article, "The Problem of Global Justice". I argue that insofar as Nagel formulates the problem of global justice in "either/or" terms (i.e. either duties of distributive justice apply exclusively within the boundaries of the nation-state or they apply beyond them), his argument is problematic. Then, I propose an alternative approach to global justice, which addresses different claims of justice separately. I also introduce three conceptual distinctions that are instrumental to the rest of the chapter: pre-distribution versus redistribution, redistribution versus rectification, and moral versus political duty. In the subsequent sections, I discuss in turn the democratic duty to redistribute and the duty of economic reciprocity. These sections follow the same structure. Each begins with a justification of the duty on the grounds of a particular form of injustice followed by an explanation of what specific distributive instrument should be used to deal with it. Subsequently, each discusses major objections to the argument, and each concludes with an investigation of the geographical scope of application of the duty. The last section of the chapter concludes the discussion.

II. A multi-layered approach to distributive justice

Justice beyond borders: not "either/or"

In his influential article "The Problem of Global Justice", Thomas Nagel discusses the scope of distributive responsibilities amongst human beings.[1] Nagel frames the problem in "either/or" terms: *either* duties of justice apply within the boundaries of the nation-state, *or* they apply beyond its borders. The "either/or" setting seems to be grounded on two main assumptions, each of them challenging the hypothesis that distributive justice should apply to the EU. First, Nagel assumes that the problem of global justice can be soundly formulated in terms of the relation between *justice* and *sovereignty*. This becomes clear in his treatment of Thomas Hobbes, for whom "actual justice cannot be achieved except within a sovereign state", which offers the apparatus to realize justice.[2] According to Nagel, "if Hobbes is right, the idea of global justice without a world government is a chimera".[3] Second, Nagel assumes that duties of distributive justice may be soundly treated as a unified category. This is apparent in his continuous reference to the duties of "socioeconomic justice", which contains a variety of things. According to him, socioeconomic justice includes "a right to democracy, equal citizenship, nondiscrimination, equality of opportunity, and the amelioration through public policy of unfairness in the distribution of social and economic goods".[4] As we shall see, each of these assumptions is problematic.

First, the direct correspondence between *justice* and *sovereignty* seems hard to sustain in a globalized world. Even if, as Nagel suggests, claims of justice were strictly linked to coercion, one could think of several examples of coercive practices in the international arena, including colonialism, the exploitation of labour by multinational firms, and unfair patterns of international trade. This suggests that, in the global arena, "there are not just concrete relations of unequal power, but also more or less fixed patterns of domination".[5] Furthermore, the alleged lack of a coercive institutional network which would render justice beyond borders possible should be challenged. Although there is nothing like a world state, a number of international institutions, such as the United Nations (UN), the World Trade Organization (WTO), and the International Criminal Court (ICC), hold considerable coercive power in relation to their members. As Chapter 2 will demonstrate, this applies stringently to the European Union. Thus, at least in principle, a sound political morality will be "sensitive to the circumstances and associative conditions", yet "without being statist".[6] If a case for a special duty amongst compatriots is to be made, one needs to specify *how* exactly domestic coercion generates distributive duties. As it stands, Nagel's first assumption seems to dismiss too quickly candidates for duties of justice which are not strictly linked to sovereignty.

Secondly, Nagel's treatment of duties of socioeconomic justice as a single category is misleading. The fact that *certain* distributive duties may result from subjection to the monopoly of force does not imply that *all* such obligations must be linked to the nation-state. The setting whereby one faces a choice between full-scale redistribution beyond borders and no redistribution at all discards, by definition, the plausible hypothesis that different levels of redistribution may apply to different territorial boundaries. There may be "[s]everal ways of living out this interregnum".[7] In fact, at least theoretically, there could be as many types of distributive duties as the different forms of injustice one can list, with each of the duties presenting its own scope of application. This insight has been captured by a number of authors who link particular forms of injustice, such as gender inequality, colonialism, and climate change, to independently standing distributive claims.[8] None of these claims has to be incompatible with domestic redistribution at a more ambitious scale. Hence, "if we could make practical the idea of a gradual redistribution of weights between standards, this might be the least bad approach".[9] For this reason, it seems worthwhile to unpack Nagel's all-encompassing notion of socioeconomic justice.

The adoption of an alternative framework is critical for our discussion on the EU. Notice that, were Nagel's assumptions to be adopted, distributive justice in the EU would indeed be a chimera. For one thing, making a case for EU redistribution would imply demonstrating that the EU is a conventional state, which is highly implausible. For another, the failure to distinguish different categories of duties would mean that duties of justice at the EU level would be similar to the ones at the nation-state level. This seems not only philosophically undesirable but also grossly unfeasible, if we consider the contrasting degrees of social solidarity at each level of government in the Union. A framework intended to analyse distributive claims in the EU should, in principle, allow for different scales of redistribution and for a set of alternative instruments. A "one-size-fits-all" approach to distributive justice would lead to an implausible setting whereby *either* EU citizens do not have any duty of justice towards each other, *or* they have exactly the same duties as they have towards their compatriots. This setting fails to accommodate the intuition that justice should be somewhat proportional to the degree of political and economic integration that is at stake. In what follows, I shall present an alternative approach, which will help us in addressing claims of justice in the EU.

A multi-layered approach to distributive justice

In this chapter, I propose an alternative approach to the problem of global justice. As we have seen, one possible strategy is to search for a moral argument on the grounds of which duties of socioeconomic justice beyond borders are, altogether, *either* excluded *or* justified.[10] Alternatively, one may start the other way around. This means considering unjust states of affairs that ought to be prevented, or minimized, through distributive justice. Each of the duties of justice may have its own territorial scope of application, depending on the scale of injustice which is being addressed. To illustrate the point, consider the three following examples of injustice: (i) young workers of country X are asked to pay disproportionate taxes to finance the excessively high pensions of retired citizens; (ii) an explosion in a nuclear facility in country Y, which was built unilaterally next to the border with country Z, causes severe human and material damage in both countries; (iii) a group of private rating agencies sets the terms of access to capital for small countries in accordance with the financial interests of the former. It is clear that the territorial scope of the injustice varies across cases. In the first case, the scope is national, in the second it is transnational, and in the third it is global. It is thus reasonable to think that the scope of corresponding duties of justice should vary accordingly. The question of whether a specific duty applies beyond borders should then be addressed in light of the particular form of injustice that is at stake.

The claim that different forms of socioeconomic injustice in the EU should be addressed separately has a moral and an empirical foundation. At the moral level, each form of injustice seems to require an appropriate instrument that can effectively remedy it.[11] In fact, a widely employed redistributive device such as tax policy may leave certain types of injustices untouched, or address them only marginally. Consider the case of exploitation, understood as taking unfair advantage of a worker. If it is wrong to exploit workers, then exploitation should be prevented in the first place through appropriate labour regulation. This indicates that distributive *goals* and distributive *instruments* should be aligned and presupposes a separate treatment of different types of injustices. At the empirical level, it seems helpful to think of realizing justice in the EU in incremental terms – that is, by identifying ways of eliminating or minimizing specific forms of injustice.[12] In this sense, the multi-layered approach is practice dependent, which will allow me to integrate abstract principles of justice with the concrete reality of the EU.[13] In a context of political cultures and standards of ethical reasoning as diverse as the Union, this strategy seems more promising than searching for an idealistic blueprint of a well-ordered EU.

A conclusion that logically follows from this approach is that different duties of justice may refer to different types of moral agents. Thus, in this account, certain duties refer to the relations amongst fellow *citizens*; others refer to the relations between *states*; and others refer to the *international community* as a whole.[14] Once again, it would be misleading to assume that these units of moral concern are mutually exclusive – in other words, that there is a single "subject of justice".[15] The reason is that socioeconomic injustice can be produced by actors at multiple levels. Thus, in the previous examples, (i) illustrates injustice amongst fellow citizens; (ii) is a case of inter-state injustice; and (iii) is an instance of injustice in the international order. A subsequent concern is whether a single account of distributive justice can integrate claims predicated on different units of moral concern. This seems particularly relevant for our discussion on the EU, where justice between EU citizens seems often in tension with justice between member states. Can the two approaches coexist? The answer is affirmative, since the duties of a state are not detachable from the duties of its citizens. To say that state X has a duty towards state Y is to say that the citizens of state X have a duty towards the citizens of state Y, mediated through political institutions. Hence, different units of concern are interrelated sources of duties of citizenship.

Under the multi-layered approach, the "problem of global justice" will, in fact, comprise a constellation of problems, with the moral status of borders *not* being decided once and for all. The multi-layered approach begins with a diagnosis of specific forms of injustice; it then selects the appropriate mechanisms to prevent or correct an unjust state of affairs; and it finally assigns responsibilities. Why should we prefer this approach to alternative strategies? The multi-layered approach is desirable for four reasons. First, it captures the diverse nature of distributive duties, instead of treating them, as well as the instruments to realize them, interchangeably. Secondly, it seems easier to create a broad consensus around concrete forms of injustice, and to justify distributive policies in terms which are instrumental to deal with such forms of injustice, than to agree upon an abstract ideal of justice.[16] Thirdly, the multi-layered approach conciliates the seemingly conflicting intuitions that (i) more comprehensive assistance should be provided for those who are closer to us, but (ii) something serious should be done to alleviate economic injustice towards the rest of the world. Finally, the multi-layered approach is not over demanding, since, as we shall see, a great deal of assistance to non-nationals is to be delivered through regulation, not actual redistribution. This increases the prospects for moral motivation and political feasibility of the theory.

In addition, this approach is particularly suitable to the EU. In the following sections, I shall suggest that at least two fundamentally different types of distributive duties may coexist: the democratic duty to redistribute and the duty of economic reciprocity. Each of these duties comprises different territorial scopes and distributive mechanisms. While the democratic duty to redistribute applies only to democratic polities and relies heavily on income redistribution, the duty of economic reciprocity applies to contexts of regular economic exchange and focuses on regulation. These two distributive duties are not intended to be exhaustive, in the sense of capturing *all* legitimate claims of justice. This selection has the specific purpose of addressing the problem of distributive justice in the EU as defined by the research questions that were presented in the Introduction. Therefore, my argument does not exclude the existence of additional duties of justice, grounded on other morally relevant features and with broader scopes of application – notably, duties towards third-party states.

Three conceptual distinctions

Before beginning our discussion on distributive duties, three key conceptual distinctions are in order. First, I should distinguish *pre-distribution* from *redistribution*. Both are forms of distributive justice, but their aims are quite different. The goal of pre-distribution is levelling the playing field.[17] This means assuring that all individuals face framework conditions that are considered to be fair. To realize this goal, pre-distribution may establish a set of rules governing relations and exchanges. As an illustrative example, consider the case of minimum wage regulation. In turn, redistribution aims to attain and maintain a particular distributional pattern. The main concern of redistribution is to replace non-conforming distributions with the ideal pattern. Thus, redistribution requires continuous rearrangements of the market outcomes. The typical instruments to perform this task are tax policy and social benefits. Hence, one can say that, while pre-distribution focuses on the *prevention* of unjust states of affairs, redistribution focuses on the *minimization* of injustice.[18] This study will address both types of distributive justice.

Theoretically, there should be a presumption in favour of pre-distribution. The reason is that it is better to prevent an evil than try to correct it. Why is this the case? First, avoiding injustice and human suffering is a desirable thing. Secondly, if wrongdoing takes place, one will never be sure that it can and will be corrected. Even the most generous compensation devices often fail to reach the intended recipients. Thirdly, the need for compensation puts the victim in a position of vulnerability, since the offending agent may fail to fulfil its obligations. However, this does not mean that distributive justice should only rely on pre-distribution, since some unjust states of affairs cannot be prevented by any pre-distributional device. For example, in a market economy, a minimum wage will not prevent the emergence of significant economic inequalities. Redistribution will be morally required if a small number of individuals hold nearly the totality of the wealth in the society, even if the rules of the game have been fair. Therefore, for justice to be realized, a combination of pre-distributive and redistributive devices seems to be required. This claim may be summarized in the following formula: *injustice should be prevented whenever possible and corrected whenever needed.*

A second distinction contrasts *pre-* and *redistribution* with *rectification*. Both pre- and redistribution aim at realizing a certain distributive pattern, which is defined by a given conception of justice. Examples of different distributive patterns are the ones proposed by egalitarian justice, sufficientarian justice, and left libertarian justice. Instead, the purpose of rectification is to correct any wrongdoing perpetrated in the past. Its aim is, whenever possible, to restore an original state of affairs or, alternatively, to offer compensation for past wrongdoing. This suggests that, unlike pre- and redistribution, rectification is exceptional and episodic: its ceases once the restitution or compensation has been fulfilled. For example, while economic interdependence may generate pre- and redistributive claims, colonialism may only originate rectification claims. Therefore, pursuing a certain distributive ideal and correcting past wrongdoing are different goals, which may require different distributive instruments. Given its focus on the current duties between EU member states, the present study will focus on pre- and redistribution.

A third distinction highlights the difference between *moral* and *political* duties. While moral duties refer to the moral agency of every human being, political duties are based on membership of a polity and are mediated by political institutions. These categories are not mutually exclusive. For instance, one may have a political duty (as a citizen) to ensure, through the payment of taxes, the provision of basic goods to those who cannot afford them, plus a moral duty (as a human being) to share part of one's net income with those who are still relatively disadvantaged after redistribution. The fundamental difference between the two is linked to the use of coercive power to enforce a particular distributive pattern. Thus, the question of why we should redistribute cannot be detached from that of why, and up to what point, we can legitimately coerce individuals to give up part of their income for redistribution. Since this study is interested in whether EU member states can legitimately be sanctioned to transfer shares of their wealth to other states, it shall focus on political duties.

III. The democratic duty to redistribute

Democracy and distributive justice

In what sense can coercion be said to generate distributive duties? The link between these two concepts is not straightforward. A tradition in the history of political thought, including authors such as Thomas Hobbes, David Hume, and Thomas Nagel, has defined justice as the solution to the dilemma of collective action. Since individuals are only willing to comply with norms if they are assured that others will also comply, stable patterns of conduct arise only in the presence of a coercive system. Justice is thus the set of norms rendering life in society possible, backed by a monopoly of violence. Yet this definition does not say much about *distributive* justice. In fact, it is hardly the case that redistribution is an enabling condition of life in society. Many regimes have endured without redistributing wealth, and this remains the case in some regions of the world. Nagel is not sufficiently clear regarding the way in which coercion and duties of socioeconomic justice are linked. His argument systematizes the claim that redistribution should not be global in scope, yet a positive justification for domestic redistribution seems to be mostly missing.

The claim that *not all* coercive systems generate distributive claims is somewhat trivial but is worth remembering. In fact, it would be odd to think that the sailors of a ship are entitled to redistribution by virtue of being under the orders of the same captain. Similarly, it seems implausible that duties of justice apply to the prisoners of a given detention facility due to their subjection to the same monopoly of violence. Hence, the link between coercion and distributive justice is not straightforward. Accordingly, one must specify the link between these two concepts. As suggested already, a promising method to address this issue is identifying risks and threats raised by coercive power, and then checking whether particular distributive devices would be effective in preventing these forms of injustice. Since the present investigation is ultimately interested in the European Union, I shall focus on the issue of coercive power in democratic regimes. To understand the dangers raised by coercion in a democratic polity, we first should have a closer look at the structure of democratic citizenship.

Whenever understood as "a status of equal and full membership in a polity", citizenship combines a *participatory* dimension with a *coercive* dimension.[19] While the coercive dimension means that citizens are required to comply with the laws of the polity under the threat of harmful consequences for failing to do so, the participatory dimension implies that citizens have a say in the making of the laws which bind them. That these two dimensions are interrelated has been a central claim of different traditions of political thought. For instance, Jean-Jacques Rousseau suggested that the use of coercion would be justified as long as the law translated the "general will" – which he regarded as the overlap of each informed individual will.[20] Alternatively, John Locke put great emphasis on the limitation of coercive power, which he treated as a necessary evil.[21] Each of these views incorporates an important insight: coercion is legitimized *both* by democratic self-rule and by a number of constraints imposed on it. This point will be central in our discussion on distributive justice. As I shall argue, distributive justice is linked to democracy and coercion insofar as it assures that each citizen has a real chance to be involved in the ruling of the polity, and that coercive practices remain within the delimited domains prescribed by the law. Let me, then, introduce the democratic duty to redistribute.[22]

The democratic duty to redistribute consists of providing *the means for political participation* and *resistance to power* to all the members of a polity. On what grounds is this duty justified? The answer combines two related types of concerns and may be summarized as follows. In order to have a *real chance to participate in civic life*, citizens must benefit from a set of material conditions. In the absence of a list of basic goods, their right to participate is merely formal. In turn, exclusion from participation due to the lack of material resources creates the *risk of arbitrary rule*. If citizens do not have the chance to have a say in the legislative procedure, nor the resources to contest executive and judicial decisions, they become mere subjects to power.[23] Distributive justice may thus be regarded as a prerequisite for democratic citizenship. Note that democracy is hereby understood as a particular institutional network, which includes elected officials, free and fair elections, inclusive suffrage, the right to run for office, freedom of expression, the right to seek for alternative sources of information, and associative rights.[24] Therefore, on this account, coercion justifies redistribution only when combined with democracy.

Distributive justice, translated into the provision of basic goods such as healthcare, education, and appropriate labour regulation, generates opportunities to participate in civic life at least in three ways. First, distributive justice promotes *inclusiveness*. Sick individuals unable to afford medical treatment, retired citizens without decent pensions, homeless people, unemployed citizens without any source of income – all lack the most basic material conditions to be politically engaged citizens. Secondly, distributive justice may increase the *time available for participation*. Under the conditions of modern capitalism, many individuals are forced to work several jobs to generate enough resources to assure their subsistence. This leaves little time for any type of political participation. By establishing a minimum wage, regulating working hours, and supplementing lower salaries, the state thus increases the prospects for participation. Finally, distributive justice provides *educational tools to engage with the debate*. Through a public system of education, the state promotes the functioning required for informed participation in civic life. In the absence of material inclusiveness, time to participate, and appropriate educational tools, the right to participate may become merely formal.[25]

In turn, distributive justice prevents arbitrary rule by empowering citizens to fight for their own rights. It does so by granting them the material means to act within judicial institutions whenever potential abuses are at stake. If one lacks such means, one becomes vulnerable to arbitrary acts by public authorities, as well as other powerful private agents. Having a chance to be part of the law-making process is not enough to realize democracy; it is also critical that these laws are duly enforced. Thus, equal and full membership of a polity presupposes the means to access judicial institutions which continuously interpret and reinforce rights. In the absence of these means, citizenship will become a status of subjection, justifiable only on Hobbesian grounds.[26] Implied in this argument is the claim that the state apparatus (including courts, police forces, state bureaucracy, and so on) ought to be ready to justify the use of coercion in particular cases on grounds of public reasons – that is, reasons that every citizen can be reasonably expected to endorse.[27] Thus distributive justice provides the basic material conditions which allow citizens to demand state responsiveness and to appeal against any abuse that they may suffered.

The threshold of basic goods

I should now specify which goods are implied by the democratic duty to redistribute. I have been claiming that a key purpose of distributive justice is to empower citizens for democratic life and to protect them from arbitrary power. Having these goals in mind, we may derive a list of basic goods, which includes the provision of (i) the means of subsistence, (ii) healthcare, (iii) education, and (iv) resources for due process in court. Notice that these basic goods can be provided in a number of different ways. Thus, the means of subsistence may be assured through a decent salary from a private firm, an unemployment subsidy, or a retirement pension. Likewise, resources for due process may be provided in the form of a public defendant or an allowance that enables the citizen to pay the fees of a private lawyer. Although there may be sound normative reasons to prefer some forms of social provision to others, these also must be equated with considerations regarding efficiency and political culture, as we shall discuss in Chapter 4. The main general guarantee that the state should offer is that nobody is left behind. Hence, the threshold is universal in the sense that all citizens are equally entitled to attain it.

Let me provide some further clarification. I am aware that the concept of means of subsistence becomes problematic when linked to an objective understanding of what is "good enough". In his classical formulation, Harry Frankfurt asserts that saying that a person has enough means "that he is content, or that it is reasonable for him to be content, with having no more money than he has".[28] In turn, Roger Crisp has suggested that a virtuous spectator who is particularly concerned for those who are badly off is capable of setting a "compassion threshold at some absolute level of welfare".[29] However, these claims seem to ignore the subjectivity and context-dependency of human needs. Consider the case of internet access. One may argue that internet access is not required for survival in a strict sense, or even that one can pursue a decent life without internet access. Yet one may also argue that internet access is key to inclusion in contemporary societies and thus should be listed as a basic need. In addition, what is regarded a basic need within a given culture may not be seen as such in a different cultural context; and what is today a basic need may not have been a basic need a few centuries ago. Do these remarks defeat the prospects for any meaningful notion of means of subsistence?

However relevant, these philosophical difficulties seem to be solvable in the empirical world. Institutions such as universities and firms provide their incoming members with estimations of living costs in a particular city or country. The state proceeds similarly when it calculates social indexes or when it adjusts the salaries of public servants to the living costs of a particular region. This rather intuitive understanding of means of subsistence as the ability to afford living costs is the one that most matters to us.[30] In addition, note that if the means of subsistence are provided through lump sum transfers, each citizen will be able to discretionally decide what is most basic for them. The fact that our threshold of basic goods is defined in instrumental terms (i.e. the means to realize democracy) as opposed to utilitarian terms (i.e. a given utility level which is deemed acceptable) saves it from the charges of arbitrariness faced by other threshold accounts.[31] Therefore, the subsistence component of the threshold is compatible with the subjectivity and context-dependency of human needs.

A more nuanced approach is needed when it comes to setting thresholds on healthcare, education, and due process in court. On the one hand, certain basic standards can hardly be controversial. For instance, it seems difficult to conceive of a decent educational system in which students fail to learn how to read and write, or to speak of a fair trial in the absence of the right to an attorney. In fact, institutions working in the field of international human rights have been defining basic components of these thresholds. Thus the World Health Organization (WHO), UNICEF, and the European Court of Human Rights have listed, respectively, essential health services to ensure universal coverage, basic skills that should be developed in every school, and the substantive and procedural requisites of a fair trial.[32] The fulfilment of these minimum requisites resonates well with the ideal of an inclusive and non-arbitrary democratic society. On the other hand, the diversity of health, educational, and legal systems across states seems to be an unavoidable consequence of democratic self-government. Accordingly, it would seem undesirable to define exhaustively the services that each threshold should cover, since this would hinder a great deal of meaningful democratic choices by local communities. Consider, for instance, the ability to select the specific contents to be taught in a history class and the exact length of mandatory schooling. Thus each political community should have a say in the concrete specification of each basic good. In Chapter 2, I will discuss how to balance these two concerns in the context of EU membership.[33]

The diversity of existing institutional settings shapes, in turn, the feasibility prospects for competing strategies to fulfil the thresholds in a given political culture. For instance, the debate on whether it is preferable for the state to subsidize private healthcare insurance or to run itself a public healthcare system should consider the historical experience of each community. As I shall suggest in Chapter 4, a plausible argument on distributive

justice should combine a degree of universality of the distributive values
(such as sufficiency, equal opportunity, and free choice) with the acceptance
of different local interpretations of the meaning of these values, as well
as what the best ways to realize them are. In fact, a democratic threshold
which tried to replicate the same exact standards of justice in every country would constitute an undemocratic attempt of social engineering, which
could fail to collect a minimum degree of public support. Normative theorists thus have the difficult task of calling for change, while understanding
that the possibilities for change are conditioned. I shall come back to this
point in Chapter 4.

In my account, the provision of means of subsistence – unlike access to
healthcare, education, and resources for due process – should be conditional upon willingness to work and need. Why are these conditions relevant? The first reason is that a model of social justice deeply grounded on
democratic ideals seems to imply not only responsibilities for democratic
institutions, but also a number of commitments on the citizen's side. These
include paying taxes and avoiding unnecessary waste of public resources,
but also being willing to work. In fact, only an efficient economy with
high employment levels makes democratic redistribution possible in the
first place.[34] This renders unjust the scenario where some citizens free-ride
on the work of others. A second reason is that a need-based approach is
more compatible with a widespread sense of justice – a key feature of well-
ordered societies.[35] In fact, it seems hard to accept that wealthy citizens
should be provided with (extra) means of subsistence, when they clearly
do not need them.[36] For these reasons, the democratic duty to redistribute
is consistent with the rejection of an unconditional basic income.[37] Note,
however, that this reasoning does not apply to healthcare, education, and
due process.[38]

Objections discussed

I have attempted to establish a strong link between redistribution and
democracy. It may be suggested that, by logical implication, undemocratic
states are not required to engage with distributive justice. This perverse
implication would be both philosophically implausible and historically
inaccurate, since a number of autocratic regimes have put in practice comprehensive redistributive plans. Yet the argument I have been pursuing
does not force me to endorse such a conclusion. I have, indeed, argued
that democracy offers a moral ground to link coercion and distributive
justice, but it need not be the only one available. For instance, in a coercive
socialist state, comprehensive duties of distributive justice may emerge from
the ultimate goal of enforcing equality amongst the citizens. In addition,
there may be duties of distributive justice which apply independently of the
regime type. This is the case of the duty of economic reciprocity, which will

be discussed later in this chapter. Thus, the absence of democracy does not exempt the state from distributive obligations.

Another important question is the place for immigrants, who are equally subjected to state coercion, in this theory. In fact, the threat of arbitrary discrimination seems particularly worrying for voiceless minority groups facing scarcity of resources, as immigrants often do. I have argued that, if the democratic duty to redistribute applies only when coercion is combined with a comprehensive right to participate, then only citizens can fully qualify for it. Yet this does not exclude the claim that some components of the threshold may be due to immigrants – particularly, the means for contestation, which must be independent of citizenship status. Thus a state cannot "exempt itself from the demands of justice simply by ensuring that the coercion to which it subjects persons is *pure* coercion, without any pretense of accountability".[39] Under the multi-layered approach to distributive justice, the fact that non-citizens do not fully qualify for the democratic duty to redistribute does not mean that they are not entitled to redistribution at all. As we shall see, immigrants are entitled to both economic reciprocity and humanitarian assistance. In addition, it should be noted that the democratic duty to redistribute does not apply necessarily to the citizens of a nation-state: they can be the citizens of a local or supranational democracy.

Another challenging objection is that the main goal of distributive justice should be promoting the ideal of equality, rather than just sufficiency. This point deserves careful consideration for two reasons. First, the egalitarian paradigm seems to be the dominant view within the literature on distributive justice. Secondly, in most historical cases, redistribution has been closely associated with a fight against inequality. Given that my purpose is not to discuss the merits of egalitarianism, it will be more useful to formulate the egalitarian claims in terms of a critique to the argument that was presented in the previous paragraphs. More specifically, a luck–egalitarian critique of the democratic duty to redistribute should translate the insight that "the fundamental distinction for an egalitarian is between choice and luck in the shaping of people's fates".[40] Therefore, luck–egalitarians may ask at least two questions. First, is it not the case that participation and resistance to arbitrary coercion requires not only a number of basic goods, but also a reduced degree of socioeconomic inequality? Second, to what extent does the democratic duty to redistribute neutralize luck and other morally arbitrary factors in life? How does this duty relate to other democracy-independent requirements of justice?

It is true that highly unequal shares of wealth and influence constitute a threat to democratic life. Those who hold office, those who see their interests better represented, and those who are defended by the most talented lawyers are often part of circles of affluence and power. These circles are not openly accessible and tend to reproduce themselves across generations.[41]

The multi-layered approach addresses this problem in two ways. First, the democratic duty to redistribute establishes a common ground that allows the citizen to fight for their rights. Although there is still a relative advantage for the wealthier, everyone may be said to have a reasonable chance to participate and to resist arbitrariness. In this sense, this duty works as an *equalisandum* of democratic opportunities, reducing the impact of an otherwise fully arbitrary distribution of wealth and influence.[42] Secondly, by calling for fair wages, the duty of economic reciprocity is expected to ensure that the degree of economic inequality is consistent with democratic life. As we shall see, although the duty does not exclude inequality in principle, it does reject the kind of extreme inequality that is so disruptive of democracy. In fact, the implications of my proposal may in some cases be more demanding than a number of egalitarian theories.[43]

Coercion and democracy beyond borders

An issue that remains to be discussed is whether democratic redistribution applies beyond borders. In the existing literature, one finds two main types of claims. On the one hand, it has been claimed that, at the international level, there is no coercive institution comparable to the state. By this account, "[n]o matter how substantive the links of trade, diplomacy, or international agreement, the institutions present at the international level do not engage in the same sort of coercive practices against individual moral agents".[44] This point is illustrated by the lack of key coercive institutions such as courts, police forces, and armies at the international level, apart from a few exceptions, such as the ICC, which are nonetheless grounded on voluntary membership. On the other hand, it has been argued that the international arena constitutes "a *context of force and domination*".[45] According to this view, even if global coercion is qualitatively different from state coercion, this does not mean that the former should be ignored.[46] Courts and armies are not the only institutions capable of exercising coercion. For example, exploitation of labour by multinational firms and unfair patterns of international trade are recognisable expressions of abusive coercive practices. Thus, the capitalist economic order has been described as one of "dominance and subordination".[47] If both accounts seem to have a point, what can be said about the scope of the democratic duty to redistribute?

In the formulation presented here, the democratic duty presupposes not only coercion but also democracy. Now, a democracy beyond borders can only be found in terms very different from the ones which were previously equated with democratic redistribution. In fact, most of the key democratic institutions listed by Robert Dahl are missing at the global level. As an illustrative example, none of the global coercive institutions – the UN, the WTO, the International Monetary Fund (IMF), and so on – organizes (free and fair) elections for the top positions in their bureaucratic apparatuses.

This by no means implies a denial of the ongoing process of globalization of politics. It is true that global politics "is not an occasional matter of sparse agreements; it seems, despite all the uncertainties of the situation, to be enduring and institutionally dense".[48] In addition, there are reasons to believe that a "global civil society" is emerging.[49] However, the requirement of providing the material means for political participation and resistance to power is only meaningful in the presence of an institutional network in which these two goals can actually be achieved by the citizens. Such an institutional network is largely absent at the global level. Surely, democracy at the global level may need to be conceived in different terms than at the national level.[50] A conception of global legitimacy may take states – not citizens – as key mediating actors, focusing, for instance, on mutual advantage, moral decency, and institutional integrity.[51] Yet again, an account of distributive justice which is based on individual citizens – such as the democratic duty to redistribute – cannot apply to a global democracy conceived in such terms.

However, the dismissal of a democratic duty to redistribute beyond borders comes with two caveats. First, the diagnosis presented in the previous paragraphs will have to be revised in case comprehensive institutional reforms take place at the global level. More specifically, this will apply if, at any point, a "process of consent enables all persons to have a kind of say in a process of fair voluntary association among societies".[52] As an illustrative example, consider a scenario in which Jürgen Habermas's proposal of a World Parliament comes into practice.[53] Secondly, the EU is a notorious exception to the state of affairs described here. As I shall argue in Chapter 2, the EU is, on the one hand, a *system of coercion*, capable of producing the generalized compliance of its citizens through a complex combination of domestic and supranational institutions, and, on the other hand, a *democratic regime*, with key democratic institutions, a citizenship status, and multiple *demoi*. As I shall claim, these features provide solid grounds for the duty of democratic redistribution to apply in the Union, which means that an EU threshold of basic goods is morally required. In turn, the unjust economic world order and the coercive nature of global capitalism will have to be tackled through an alternative distributive instrument. The next sections will sketch what that instrument might be.

IV. The duty of economic reciprocity

Why economic reciprocity matters

Reciprocity is a key term in the lexicon of political theory. Yet the current meaning of the word is entirely modern.[54] In medieval scholastic thought, the idea of reciprocity was so much embodied in the concept of justice that these two terms would not be addressed separately. Thus, the *just* price of a good would also be a *fair* price – a price that, according to most historians, "corresponded to a reasonable charge which would enable the producer to live and to support his family on a scale suitable to his station in life".[55] A few centuries later, liberalism radically challenged this way of understanding economic justice. Thus, the earlier "moral economy" was replaced by a market economy in which prices were no longer a matter of justice but of efficiency. Amongst other things, this implies that prices should be determined by the equilibrium between demand and supply, and that markets should be as competitive as possible. A problem with this view is that, unlike the prices of other goods, wages – that is, the price of labour – are not morally neutral.[56] Indeed, salaries shape decisively the life prospects of workers, and they constitute an indicator of the worth of individual efforts. Therefore, acknowledging the fact that a free market is the most efficient mechanism to allocate resources is different from saying that each of its outcomes is morally acceptable.[57] One way to attempt a reconciliation between justice and efficiency is to elaborate the concept of economic reciprocity.

The concept of economic reciprocity has two main elements. To begin with, it refers to an exchange which generates a *mutual advantage*.[58] An exchange in which one of the parties collects all the benefits is clearly not a reciprocal one. An illustrative example is forced labour.[59] Yet reciprocity is not only about mutual advantage. A full-time worker of a highly profitable company on a very low salary is, most likely, better off than if they were unemployed, but this is not enough to deem the relation reciprocal.[60] In fact, economic reciprocity also presupposes *mutual respect*.[61] In the context of economic exchange, mutual respect has at least two important implications. First, the goals and interests of *all* parties involved should be considered. Since the majority of individuals work primarily to obtain the means for their subsistence, this suggests that wages should at least be sufficiently high to fulfil such a purpose. Secondly, the distribution of the outcomes resulting from the exchange should be proportional to the inputs provided by each party, measured not only in crude terms of economic added value, but also in terms of effort and time. Given that work is a fundamental dimension of human life, a failure to receive a fair share may damage self-respect, as well as the social recognition for one's contribution. Thus, reciprocity comprises both *mutual advantage* and *mutual respect*.

Yet one may ask, why are economic agents morally required to reciprocate? In a society with division of labour, an economic activity can only be profitable if associated with many other activities. Adam Smith famously stated that this scheme of cooperation does not arise out of the generosity of the market players, but as a result of their individual interests.[62] Yet the arguably egoistic motivations to cooperate do not substitute for the need for cooperation. For example, the CEO of a big company can only successfully play their role if someone else answers the phone at the reception desk. Such interdependence applies not only to delimited schemes of cooperation, such as a particular industry or service, but to the economy as a whole. In fact, one could hardly get rich through one's own endeavours if there was no one else to provide food and water, to make the streets relatively safe, to educate children, and so on. Since the market is a system where each job is the pre-condition for other jobs, reciprocity is morally required. However, this claim raises issues of moral responsibility illustrated by Robert Nozick's influential Wilt Chamberlain thought experiment.[63] In fact, if a market outcome such as poverty is the *unintended* result of a number of *voluntary* exchanges, why should *I* bear the responsibility for it?

Iris Marion Young offers an enlightening conceptualization of the type of responsibility that should be equated with the market. As she notes, in moral and legal theory, the concept of responsibility usually involves considerations regarding (i) the *intent* to produce a certain outcome and (ii) the strength of the *causal link* between a specific course of action and such an outcome.[64] However, in the context of market exchange none of these dimensions is clearly present. When one buys a cheap t-shirt made in a country where child labour is permitted or tolerated, one does not intend to say that exploitation of children is acceptable. In addition, the purchase of one t-shirt can hardly be the cause of an exploitative system which produces millions of them. Yet, as Young suggests, this does not mean that responsibility is absent at all. In fact, "all those who contribute by their actions to structural processes with some unjust outcomes share responsibility for the injustice".[65] This implies that "one has an obligation to join with others who share that responsibility in order to transform the structural processes to make their outcomes less unjust".[66] Surely, certain agents are personally liable for economic wrongdoing, such as the owners of child-exploiting factories in our previous example. This, however, does not substitute for the moral relevance of being part of, and benefiting from, a system that produces injustice.

My adoption of Young's model, instead of the Rawlsian original position, has to do with the role played by "structure" in each theory. I have been suggesting that the duty of reciprocity applies to any context of *regular economic exchange* where there is *division of labour*.[67] Now, a claim of reciprocity in these terms does *not* presuppose the existence of a comprehensive set of social institutions according to the Rawlsian "basic structure". The latter includes features as varied as the political constitution, the legal system, and the conception of family of a given society.[68] Young's model of social connection cited already is consistent with the idea of a less comprehensive, and yet decisive, "economic structure". An economic structure comprises, for instance, patterns of division of labour, conditions of access to capital, endowments of natural resources, terms of trade for goods and services, and formal rules of cooperation beyond the state's control, such as foreign taxes and tariffs, exchange rates, and border control regimes. The notions of "basic" and "economic" structure are not mutually exclusive, but they have different distributive implications.[69] As we shall see in Chapter 3, the idea of "economic structure" is more suited to the EU, since there is no European basic structure in a proper sense.

Realizing reciprocity will imply state intervention regarding *both* labour relations and the economic structure. In fact, neither of the two dimensions is enough to assure that a given market substantiates reciprocity. For instance, in the presence of a fair economic world order, relations between workers and firms could still be unfair if local labour regulation failed to protect the interests of the former. Similarly, if local labour regulation is fair but the economic structure is not, certain workers will always find themselves in a relatively worse-off position, regardless of their efforts.[70] This is why reciprocity can only be realized if both *transactional* and *structural* arrangements are fair. As we shall see in the next section, realizing reciprocity requires different types of distributive instruments for each of these levels – labour law and economic/monetary policy, respectively. This suggests that, when discussing ways to realize reciprocity, it is better to think in terms of states and international/supranational organizations than in terms of individuals or firms. In fact, if the altruism of human beings is, indeed, limited, one should not expect reciprocity to emerge voluntarily; coercive policy instruments will need to be employed.[71] In addition, the state, the EU, the WTO, and so on are the best available proxies of economic structure due to their capacity to regulate the economy and to shape its possible outcomes.

Against this view, it has been argued that state intervention in the market is morally undesirable. Robert Nozick has famously claimed that implementing a given pattern of distributive justice undermines individual freedom, since it implies "continuous interference with people's lives".[72] As I have suggested, market outcomes result from the *aggregation* of an asymptotical number of actions, which means that they depend very little on each particular choice.[73] It can be very hard for individuals to make predictions regarding the consequences of crucial economic choices such as choice of a profession, particularly given the frequency of external shocks to the labour market in advanced capitalist economies.[74] This is not to say that the state should aim at neutralizing option luck, but that freedom in the context of the market has a qualified meaning. In fact, it should not be understood merely as a negative status, translated only into contractual freedom and property rights, but also as the opportunity to receive a fair share of the output resulting from labour.[75] Only the latter can bring about economic recognition for one's efforts, which as we have seen is a requirement of mutual respect. Therefore, since one's degree of control over market outcomes is very limited, state intervention aimed at achieving reciprocity is compatible with a concern for individual choice.[76]

A final point to be made is that economic reciprocity and democracy are interrelated. In fact, a lack of reciprocity may be said to undermine democratic life in at least three ways. First, individuals whose goals and interests are not considered by their employers are socialized in a framework of coercive relations. For instance, many workers do not have a reasonable chance to say "no" to unfair demands, nor to engage with meaningful discussion regarding their roles and remuneration. The internalization of this logic of powerlessness at work is hardly a promising background for participatory self-government. Secondly, a concentration of economic power in relatively few hands, followed by the emergence of extreme inequalities, is at odds with democracy. The reason is that individuals with disproportional shares of income are in a much better position to influence the outcomes of the political process.[77] Thirdly, a pervasive lack of reciprocity likely undermines trust in democratic institutions and demobilizes citizens.[78] This may ultimately create opportunities for undemocratic alternatives that claim to be more effective in achieving a distribution of wealth that benefits the poor. For all these reasons, a reciprocal economy is a better fit for a democratic regime.

Labour regulation and economic and monetary policy

The best means to address unfairness is preventing it from happening in the first place. Alternatively, one could think of letting the market work freely and then redistributing its outcomes. The difficulty with this approach is that it only addresses the problem of disrespect for people to a limited extent. For instance, it is implausible to argue that exploitation is acceptable as long as there is redistribution. Of course, it is better to have some kind of compensation if one is exploited, but this misses the point that exploitation ought to be avoided in the first place. One could also argue that, in the presence of an appropriate salary, exploitation would no longer deserve such a label. Yet it is clear that child labour and excessive working hours would not be acceptable even if they were generously paid. This suggests that a comprehensive body of labour regulation is required to assure economic reciprocity at the level of discrete transactions. This does not exclude that compensation may be due in some particular cases, namely a failure to fairly regulate in the past. However, these cases fall under the specific category of rectification, which, as we have seen, deserves separate treatment. For all of these reasons, *current* deficiencies in reciprocity have to be addressed not through redistribution but by solving the problems at their very source.

Therefore, the state should use labour law to establish fair terms of cooperation amongst the members of the polity. This includes a variety of rules, namely the establishment of a minimum wage, the limitation of the number of working hours, the promotion of decent working conditions, the specification of objective criteria for assessment and firing, the right to maternity leave and illness leave, the prohibition of child work, and so on.

The minimum wage is of special interest for distributive justice. By setting a decent lower cap for remuneration, exploitation can be contained to a considerable degree. A question that will arise is how high the minimum wage should be. Since salaries ought to translate into respect for people and their work, the minimum wage cannot be lower than the amount that allows for one's subsistence in a given place and time. Thus, a full-time worker must have a reasonable expectation of living from their minimum wage. As we shall see, transitional economies may be temporarily excluded from this requisite, but wealthy economies under cyclical crisis should not.

Another critical dimension of sound labour regulation concerns the proportionality of salaries. As we have seen, fairness requires not only the avoidance of exploitation but also the rejection of extreme inequality. Ideally, this would be translated into a legal formula of the sort, *the highest salary in a firm should not be higher than X times the lowest one*. However, this raises the question of how much inequality is acceptable – that is, which figure X should assume. This problem can only be addressed within the context of a particular political culture and the distributive preferences of its citizens. As we shall see in Chapter 4, normative theory can advance principles of justice with a claim of universality, but the application of such principles has to be sensitive to the context where they are applied. The task of conferring meaning to abstract principles should be mainly local. Thus, a political culture that puts great emphasis on individual choice may publicly justify a higher degree of inequality than a political culture that focuses mainly on structural phenomena. A compromise capable of fostering a widespread sense of justice will always have to be negotiated by social actors.

It may be added that there are alternative ways to promote proportional salaries that can be regarded as acceptable proxies to the ideal case. One example of an alternative mechanism is limiting the salaries and bonuses of top managers. The appeal of such an instrument is considerable. First, a maximum wage directly addresses the problem of extreme inequality. Although it may leave inequality in small and medium-size firms untouched, it corrects the most flagrant cases of inequality. Secondly, it is much easier to implement than a fully proportional scheme. Indeed, in labour markets displaying a high rotation rate, it would be very hard to constantly check whether a given proportionality rule is being applied in each particular firm. Thirdly, an economy with a minimum and a maximum wage constitutes a highly intelligible scheme of cooperation. The citizen may easily understand the degree of reciprocity implied in market relations and produce moral judgments about it. This is an important advantage because market relations are often so complex and diffuse that it gets very hard for the ordinary citizen to develop an informed opinion about them.

In addition, it should be noted that fair labour regulation contributes to our general goal of preventing arbitrary power. It is fair to acknowledge a qualitative difference between state power and economic power. Unlike public officials, business managers cannot arrest people nor send them to war. However, arbitrary economic power can still be very harmful for individuals. In the presence of objective rules for cooperation, employees have clear expectations regarding the outcomes of different ways of behaving. If these rules are fair, they allow for a sense of mutual respect. In addition, labour regulation provides the necessary conditions for workers to fight for their rights whenever these are violated. Amongst these are the right to associate with unions and the rules for firing, which should prohibit the dismissal of employees on the grounds of legitimate vindication of rights. Since individuals can be the best guardians of their rights, labour regulation rightly offers them the means to resist arbitrary power in the context of market exchange.

As I have argued, the duty of economic reciprocity applies not only to labour relations but also to the economic structure. Thus, public policies with a significant impact on the main features of this structure should not only serve efficiency goals – indeed, they ought to incorporate distributive concerns. Amongst the several policy domains which shape the economic structure of a given polity, economic and monetary policy deserve special attention. For instance, an apparently harmless decision such as targeting a certain exchange rate may have dramatic distributive consequences for the well-being of certain groups of citizens. The impact of monetary policy on the welfare of individual actors will vary according to the type of goods or services they produce, the factor which is the main source of their income (i.e. labour or capital), their dependence on external markets, and so on. Thus, a strong currency may harm the low-skilled workers, who become less competitive in the global market, but may be desirable for certain capital-intensive businesses. This reasoning can be extended to other policy choices that shape one's chances to succeed, independent of one's efforts.

I have claimed that economic and monetary policy should be interpreted as distributive instruments – but what exactly is a fair economic and monetary policy? Fair policies will take the interests of everyone into account and prioritize them according to criteria of equality of opportunity. Yet the exact implications of this statement will have to be grasped in the specific context of a particular market and its institutional setting. For example, in a capital-intensive economy which depends heavily on the banking sector, it may be preferable to target a high exchange rate and redistribute the capital gains. By contrast, a strong currency may have highly undesirable consequences for a labour-intensive economy, which cannot be reasonably tackled through redistribution. The distributive consequences of economic and monetary policy are amplified at the regional and global levels, where the conflict of interests amongst economies with very different profiles is apparent. The policies adopted by international institutions should not depend on the outcome of struggles that tend to reflect the relative power of different economies. Instead, the distributive implications of economic and monetary policy ought to be duly weighted, in a search for a compromise which treats each actor fairly. In Chapter 3, I will apply this exercise to the (combined) policies of EU member states.

Objections discussed

A number of objections may be advanced against the account of economic reciprocity presented here. To begin with, liberal economic theory will want to explain income inequality in terms of added value. What you get as a salary is a function of your contribution to the productive process. However, one should be sceptical about a model of remuneration whereby someone can contribute 183 times what the other person contributes.[79] Of course, salaries have to be linked to productivity. Some activities and tasks generate more wealth than others, and so they are capable of higher returns. Hence, the principle that salaries should vary according to the nature of individual inputs is not problematic; what is dramatic is the disproportionality in the application of this principle. Earning, say, 10 times what someone else earns is different from earning the 183 times just mentioned. Nowadays, we witness an increasingly unfair division of the benefits of cooperation.[80] Such a development is built upon a purely mathematical understanding of added value, which fails to capture the high degree of interdependence of social roles. If justice is to prevail, this narrow approach has to be abandoned.

In recent years, a number of international organizations, including the Organisation for Economic Cooperation and Development (OECD) and the IMF, have called for greater job flexibility. These institutions have suggested that by softening labour regulation, states create better conditions for economic growth and, consequently, for higher levels of employment. The duty of economic reciprocity is ready to accommodate the claim that firms need to adjust their resources to the business cycle to a certain degree, but it does not do so at any cost. Reciprocity does not ask firms or the state to artificially maintain jobs when they are no longer necessary or profitable. As François Quesnay famously illustrated with the case of servants in pre-revolutionary France, work has to be socially productive for a given economy to be sustainable.[81] Any feasible model of economic interdependency presupposes that the tasks performed by workers are indeed required for the functioning of the cooperative scheme. Therefore, respect for workers does not imply granting everyone a job, nor assuring that workers can engage with their favoured professional activity. It does mean, however, that socially productive workers have to be decently paid and adequately treated and that their rights should not be alienated for the sake of greater economic growth.

What can be said, then, regarding unemployment benefits? Although a case can be made on the grounds of reciprocity claims, unemployment is better addressed by the democratic duty to redistribute. One could argue that, insofar as "creative destruction" is a requisite of growth, the participants of the scheme should share its burdens and reciprocate to those who lose their jobs.[82] However, this claim is problematic. It implies, for instance, that the land owners of the Industrial Revolution should have compensated farmers for losing their jobs due to the increasing use of machines in the fields. An analogous contemporary example is the use of information systems, which increasingly substitute for human work. These examples indicate that the causes of unemployment are often exogenous to the scheme of cooperation. In other words, unemployment originates not only in the way in which we cooperate with each other in a market economy but also in significant changes in the production functions. This suggests that unemployment should be treated not as an issue of mutual advantage and economic responsiveness but rather as a matter of protecting the vulnerable citizen. Therefore, the unemployed should be entitled to state support on the grounds of the democratic duty to redistribute.

Another objection is that economic crisis may justify the levelling down of social protection due to a decrease in available resources. This trend has been observed in a number of EU member states in recent years. From the standpoint of distributive justice, this claim is unacceptable. It is precisely when economic performance worsens that individuals become more vulnerable. If labour regulation, as well as the democratic threshold of basic goods, do not apply to hard times, then they are of a limited practical use and lose much of their philosophical appeal. The point here is not challenging the Kantian maxim that *ought* implies *can*.[83] Alternatively, I would like to suggest that distributive justice presupposes a particular way of managing public finance. In prosperous times, states should save enough resources to allow for social provision during hard times. To use familiar economic terminology, states should adopt counter-cyclical macroeconomic policies. This means, on the one hand, that they should increase taxes when the economy is doing well and reduce them when growth slows down, while, on the other hand, they should expect an increase of social expenditure under adversity and its decrease in prosperous times. I shall discuss the prospects for this strategy in Chapter 5.

Reciprocity beyond borders

If reciprocity matters, it should matter beyond borders. Indeed, "[i]t is clear that interdependence in trade and investment produces substantial aggregate economic benefits in the form of a higher global rate of economic growth as well as greater productive efficiency".[84] The key question is precisely how much it should matter. There are at least three different answers to this problem. A first thesis is that the international system of cooperation is fundamentally different from the one that operates within the state, regarding the scope and intensity of exchange, the distribution of social roles, and the instruments available for economic arbitration. Accordingly, there can be no duty of global reciprocity in a proper sense.[85] An opposite view will be that, despite significant differences at the level of institutionalization, a globalized economy presupposes a global scheme of cooperation, without which state-level cooperation can no longer subsist. Therefore, with some necessary adjustments, the principles of economic justice applying to the state should also apply to the international scene.[86] Finally, an intermediate position will suggest that reciprocity should be somewhat proportional to the degree of political and economic integration.[87] Thus national markets, free trade areas, and the global market all raise claims of reciprocity, which vary in scope. Which of these views is the most consistent with the argument that we have pursued so far?

The idea that reciprocity should be proportional to the degree of economic integration is consistent with a rejection of the "either/or" formulation proposed by Thomas Nagel. To deny that global interdependence raises crucial issues of reciprocity is to forget the deplorable conditions under which many of the goods available in national markets are produced elsewhere in the world. In turn, to assert that principles of economic justice should apply beyond borders without making any further distinction is to miss the point that the economic interdependence between, say, Portugal and Spain is much higher than that between Portugal and Ecuador, in terms of international trade and foreign investment indicators.[88] Instead, the proportionality approach allows us to propose a global minimum of reciprocity, while maintaining that reciprocity should vary according to the intensity of economic exchange. Yet if this approach is to be adopted, we need to specify what proportionality means. How much reciprocity is due to each country and region? This question can only be addressed by referring to the institutionalized norms and practices of a given market, which constitute its framework of exchange. Thus, in Chapter 3 I shall discuss economic justice in the European Union in a context of free trade, free mobility of workers, and a single currency.[89] In what follows, I shall explain what I mean by a global minimum of reciprocity and provide justification for it.

The global minimum of reciprocity consists of a body of labour regulation that should be applied at a global scale. As I have argued before, the goal of reciprocity is not to compensate for exploitation but to prevent exploitation from happening in the first place. Thus, if child labour or forced labour are being used in a given country, redistributing the profits of international trade will not solve the problem. Although global redistribution could ameliorate the conditions of those who receive extremely low salaries, a decent minimum wage will likely do the job more effectively, since there will be no uncertainty about whether the assistance gets to the intended recipient.[90] The global minimum is justified by the fact that international trade is a multilevel network. Thus, although Portugal does not have a significant economic relationship with Ecuador, it is indirectly linked to that country through its relations with other countries that produce some of their goods in Ecuador. The idea of a global minimum suggests not only that every country should adopt minimum standards of labour regulation, but also that restrictions should be imposed on those countries that fail to meet the standards. The natural candidate to articulate a global minimum of this sort and to seek its enforcement would be the International Labour Organization (ILO).[91] Hence, while claims of reciprocity should vary according to the degree of economic integration, a global minimum should always be observed.

V. Conclusion

I have argued that the responsibilities to redistribute wealth are better captured by a multi-layered approach. I discussed two main duties: the democratic duty to redistribute and the duty of economic reciprocity. The democratic duty to redistribute consists of providing the means for political participation and resistance to power to all the members of a polity. In turn, the duty of economic reciprocity prescribes a fair distribution of the gains of economic exchange. As far as policy instruments are concerned, while the democratic duty to redistribute should be translated into a basket of basic goods, the duty of economic reciprocity should be realized mainly through labour regulation. Each of these duties may apply beyond borders, whenever the appropriate conditions which trigger them are met.

Notes

1 Thomas Nagel, "The Problem of Global Justice", *Philosophy & Public Affairs* 33 (2005), pp. 113–147.
2 Ibid., p. 114.
3 Ibid., p. 115.
4 Ibid., p. 127.
5 Rainer Forst, "Towards a Critical Theory of Transnational Justice", *Metaphilosophy* 32 (2001), p. 166.
6 Joshua Cohen and Charles Sabel, "Extra Rempublicam Nulla Justitia?", *Philosophy & Public Affairs* 34 (2006), p. 149.
7 A. J. Julius, "Nagel's Atlas", *Philosophy & Public Affairs* 34 (2006), p. 191.
8 See, respectively, Susan Moller Okin, *Justice, Gender, and the Family* (New York, 1989); Lea Ypi, Robert E. Goodin, and Christian Barry, "Associative Duties, Global Justice, and the Colonies", *Philosophy & Public Affairs* 37 (2009), pp. 103–135; Simon Caney, "Just Emissions", *Philosophy & Public Affairs* 40 (2012), pp. 255–300.
9 A. J. Julius, "Nagel's Atlas", p. 192.

10 In fact, a few influential works in both statist and cosmopolitan fields have adopted an "either/or" strategy similar to Nagel's. For instance, John Rawls assumes that if there is not such a thing as a global basic structure, significant distributive requirements will not apply beyond borders. In a similar fashion, but reaching an opposite conclusion, Peter Singer implies that, if individuals are equally worthy, borders must be morally irrelevant for distributive judgements. In each of these accounts, there seems to be little room for a middle ground. See John Rawls, *The Law of Peoples* (Cambridge MA, 2001); and Peter Singer, "Famine, Affluence and Morality", *Philosophy & Public Affairs* 1 (1979), pp. 229–243.

11 This point is implicit in those accounts of distributive justice that give distinct (but complementary) normative treatments to the issues of (i) elaborating an ideal of justice and (ii) assessing the means to realize it. Two outstanding examples are Elizabeth Anderson, "What is the Point of Equality?", *Ethics* 109 (1999), pp. 287–337; and Nancy Fraser, *Social Justice in the Age of Identity Politics: Redistribution, Recognition, Participation* (Berlin, 1998).

12 This strategy has noticeable affinities with the approach adopted by Amartya Sen. Sen's theory aims "to clarify how we can proceed to address questions of enhancing justice and removing injustice, rather than to offer resolutions of questions about the nature of perfect justice". See Amartya Sen, *The Idea of Justice* (London, 2010), p. ix.

13 Simon Caney has stressed that a theory of justice beyond borders may operate at three different levels: first, it may explain how domestic principles relate to global principles; second, it may specify the content of the principles (either domestic or global) and the institutions required to realize them; third, it may apply general principles to specific issues, such as the requirements of justice in the EU. As Caney notes, "the third level can be performed only by integrating principles (i.e. level-2 analysis) with an enormous amount of empirical detail". In starting its reflection from current forms of injustice in the EU, the multi-layered approach facilitates the task of putting flesh on the bones of abstract principles of justice. See Simon Caney, *Justice Beyond Borders: A Global Political Theory* (Oxford, 2005), p. 4.

14 This claim is consistent with a variety of accounts of global justice that propose a substantive distinction between injustice at the *state* level and injustice at the *global* level. See, for instance, Michael Walzer, "Achieving Global and Local Justice", *Dissent* 58 (2011), pp. 42–48; and Miriam Ronzoni, "The Global Order: A Case of Background Injustice? A Practice-Dependence Account", *Philosophy & Public Affairs* 37 (2009), pp. 229–256. In opposition, such a distinction is absent from most universalist accounts of morality, which are structured around the rights and duties of *individuals* (even if these are to be realized through political institutions). See, for example, Simon Caney, *Justice Beyond Borders: A Global Political Theory*; and Peter Singer, "Famine, Affluence and Morality".

15 John Rawls famously claimed that the basic structure is the primary subject of justice "because its effects are so profound and present from the start". Yet from this claim it does not follow that other stringent sources of injustice which are (arguably) unrelated to the basic structure should be ignored. See John Rawls, *A Theory of Justice: Revised Edition* (Cambridge MA, 1999), pp. 6–10.

16 A similar point has been made by Judith Shklar, for whom starting from a basic level of moral agreement about injustice seems promising. See Judith N. Shklar, "Putting Cruelty First", *Daedalus* 111 (1982), pp. 17–28.

17 The idea of levelling the playing field is key in the vast literature on equality of opportunity. For an influential statement of the level playing field ideal, see John E. Roemer, *Equality of Opportunity* (Cambridge MA, 1998). The term "pre-distribution" was coined by Jacob Hacker. See Jacob S. Hacker, "The Institutional Foundations of Middle Class Democracy", *Priorities for a New Political Economy: Memos to the Left* (London, 2011), pp. 33–38.

18 Note that the prefixes *pre-* and *re* are entirely conceptual and do not entail a temporal dimension. The key point is to distinguish two fundamentally different strategies to achieve distributive justice: (i) changing the rules of the game and (ii) changing the outcomes of that game.

19 For the definition of citizenship as a status of equal and full membership in a polity, see Rainer Bauböck, "Recombinant Citizenship", in Martin Kohli and Alison Woodward (eds), *Inclusions and Exclusions in European Societies* (London, 2001), p. 39.

20 Jean-Jacques Rousseau, *The Social Contract* (Oxford, 1998).

21 John Locke, *Two Treatises of Government*, ed. Peter Laslett (Cambridge, 1988).

22 As will become apparent, the argument draws on the republican tradition of political theory. However, as Cécile Laborde has pointed out, "[t]he republican tradition seems to have a blind spot about global justice". In fact, in a recent article, Philip Pettit addressed the problem of global republicanism without including a distributive dimension. My argument aims to help fill this gap. See Cécile Laborde, "Republicanism and Global Justice: A Sketch", *European Journal of Political Theory* 9 (2010), pp. 48–69; and Philip Pettit, "The Globalized Republican Ideal", *Global Justice: Theory, Practice, Rhetoric* (2016), pp. 47–68.

23 Notice that this idea is premised on a norm of democratic inclusion. If democracy could simply exclude those who are not sufficiently well off to participate, then there would not be a redistributive requirement on these grounds. This was one reason why ancient democracies were generally not redistributive and excluded slaves and working populations.

24 Robert Dahl, *Democracy and its Critics* (New Haven, 1989), p. 221. My adoption of this institutionalist definition of democracy is due to its plausibility and simplicity. Note that the discussion on whether participation should be more direct, or more comprehensive, than the one implied in Dahl's account is not critical to my argument. In fact, if distributive justice applies to a "minimalist" conception of representative democracy, on the grounds that citizens should be provided with the means to participate, it will necessarily apply to more ambitious approaches to democracy.

25 This argument has some affinities with the capability approach advanced by Amartya Sen and Martha Nussbaum in recent years. However, unlike the capability approach, the democratic threshold presupposes not only the development of a number of democratic functionings but also *actual attainment* of a level of sufficiency compatible with democratic life. See Amartya Sen, *Development as Freedom* (New York, 1999); and Martha C. Nussbaum, *Creating Capabilities* (Cambridge MA 2011).

26 Thomas Hobbes famously justified subjection to the sovereign on the grounds that it is preferable to the state of nature, which for him was necessarily a state of war. See Thomas Hobbes, *Leviathan*, ed. Noel Malcolm (Oxford, 2014), especially Chapter 14.

27 See John Rawls, "The Idea of Public Reason Revisited", *The University of Chicago Law Review* 64 (1997), pp. 765–807.

28 Harry Frankfurt, "Equality as a Moral Ideal", *Ethics* 98 (1987), p. 37.

29 Roger Crisp, "Equality, Priority, and Compassion", *Ethics* 113 (2003), p. 757.

30 Difficulties in determining what exactly a threshold of sufficiency should comprise have been faced since the preparatory works for William Beveridge's Report on Social Security in the United Kingdom, which eventually led to the first comprehensive social security scheme. As in many later schemes, these definitional difficulties did not prevent the scheme from being implemented and collecting broad support from civil society. For an overview of the debate amongst the members of the Beveridge committee regarding the conception of basic needs, see Jose Harris, *William Beveridge: A Biography* (Oxford, 1997), especially Chapter 16.

31 The utilitarian threshold account of Harry Frankfurt has been rightly accused of arbitrariness, notably by Paula Casal and Richard Arneson. A recent work by Liam Shields has re-examined the prospects for sufficientarianism, showing that this objection can be avoided. See Paula Casal, "Why Sufficiency is Not Enough", *Ethics* 117 (2007), pp. 296–326; Richard Arneson, "Distributive Justice and Basic Capability Equality: 'Good Enough' Is Not Good Enough", in A. Kaufman (ed.), *Capabilities Equality: Basic Issues and Problems* (London, 2005), pp. 17–43; and Liam Shields, *Just Enough: Sufficiency as a Demand of Justice* (Edinburgh, 2016).

32 The WHO mentions the essential healthcare services of "prevention, promotion, treatment, rehabilitation and palliation". In turn, UNICEF lists the following basic skills: foundational skills, digital skills, transferable skills, and job-specific skills. Finally, the European Court of Human Rights puts forward criteria such as independent and impartial tribunals, a fair administration of evidence, and a reasonable length of procedures. See, respectively, WHO, "Universal Health Coverage", https://www.who.int/health-topics/universal-health-coverage#tab=tab_1; UNICEF, "Skills Development", https://www.unicef.org/education/skills-development; and European Court of Human Rights, *Guide of Article 6 of the Convention on Human Rights: Right to a Fair Trial* (2019) (Accessed 27 February 2020).

33 It should be anticipated that allowing member states to define the exact specifications of the thresholds will not make the role of EU institutions redundant, nor merely equivalent to the status quo. As I shall claim, in addition to establishing a minimum common denominator, EU institutions should be responsible for ensuring the actual *attainment* of the threshold by EU citizens from distressed member states. In my account, the EU would work as a safety net for domestic welfare state systems. This differs fundamentally from the current state of affairs, where the EU is not responsible for enforcing most social rights.

34 The reasons are twofold. First, there would be little wealth to redistribute in an economy where only a few people engage in productive activities. Second, in face of pervasively low rates of participation in the job market, the costs

of universal social provision would reach unsustainable levels. This judgement will need to be revised if, as some authors have predicted, massive technological shocks substantially decrease the need for labour. Yet we seem to be somewhat far from this scenario, since some of the most technologically advanced economies in the world are precisely the ones operating close to full employment levels. Consider, for instance, the cases of Germany and Japan.

35 John Rawls, *A Theory of Justice: Revised Edition*, pp. 295–296. Elizabeth Anderson would object that, since conditionality implies means tests, it actually undermines the general sense of justice insofar as it requires citizens to justify themselves and their life story before state officials. See Elizabeth Anderson, "What is the Point of Equality?", pp. 287–337. However, if a choice has to be made between these conflicting claims, it seems much more harmful to a general sense of justice that some citizens may unfairly live at the expense of others.

36 Proposals for an unconditional basic income have been advanced in a number of countries. It is probably not a coincidence that the countries in which such proposals have received stronger support (namely, Switzerland and the Netherlands), the level of poverty is notably low. Since the majority of the population is well above deprivation levels, it is easier to collect support for a model of redistribution which provides allowances for wealthy people.

37 A philosophical case for an unconditional basic income was originally articulated in Philippe Van Parijs, "Why Surfers Should be Fed: The Liberal Case for an Unconditional Basic Income", *Philosophy & Public Affairs* 20 (1991), pp. 101–131. More recent statements include Philippe Van Parijs and Yannick Vanderborght, *Basic Income: A Radical Proposal for a Free Society and a Sane Economy* (Cambridge MA, 2017); and Louise Haagh, *The Case for Universal Basic Income* (Cambridge, 2019). In the next section, I shall address the question of how the duty of democratic redistribution may conflict with egalitarian conceptions which are democracy-independent.

38 The reason to exclude healthcare, education, and due process from the conditionality clauses presented in the previous paragraphs is the particular vulnerability faced by the citizen once deprived of any of these goods. A citizen who faces scarcity of resources due to an unwillingness to work can change their mind and actively look for a job. In opposition, citizens who are sick or charged with a crime may not have a chance to reconsider their decision not to work. Theoretically, education of young adults could be subjected to willingness to work in the future, but this would be very hard to test in the real world and likely undesirable from a normative standpoint. For obvious reasons, children, the disabled, and retired citizens should be exempted from any conditionality regarding willingness to work.

39 Arash Abizadeh, "Cooperation, Pervasive Impact, and Coercion: On the Scope (Not Site) of Distributive Justice", *Philosophy & Public Affairs* 35 (2007), p. 352. In addition, note that immigrants have a general claim to citizenship status and full political participation that is merely delayed until the time when they have established genuine links. In this sense, every immigrant is a potential future recipient of democratic redistribution.

40 G. A. Cohen, "On the Currency of Egalitarian Justice", *Ethics* 99 (1989), p. 907.

41 See, for instance, Pierre Bourdieu, *Distinction: A Social Critique of the Judgment of Taste* (London, 1986).

42 "An *equalisandum* claim specifies that which ought to be equalized, what, that is, people should be rendered equal in". See G. A. Cohen, "On the Currency of Egalitarian Justice", p. 908.

43 Luck neutralizing egalitarianism seems to allow for numerous inequalities, provided that these are the result of individual choices – as opposed to bad brute luck. On this point, see Richard Arneson, "Luck Egalitarianism Interpreted and Defended", *Philosophical Topics* 32 (2004), pp. 1–18. In the next section, I shall claim that, because democratic preferences for equality are both (i) normatively relevant and (ii) context-dependent, the exact measure of equality that should complement sufficiency will vary across democracies.

44 Michael Blake, "Distributive Justice, State Coercion, and Autonomy", *Philosophy & Public Affairs* 30 (July 2001), p. 265.

45 Rainer Forst, "Towards a Critical Theory of Transnational Justice", p. 166 (emphasis in original).

46 Laura Valentini, "Coercion and (Global) Justice", *The American Political Science Review* 105 (2011), pp. 205–220.

47 Michael Hardt and Antonio Negri, *Empire* (Cambridge MA, 2001), p. 282.

48 Joshua Cohen and Charles F. Sabel, "Global Democracy?", *New York University Journal of International Law and Politics* 37 (2006), p. 765.

49 John Keane, *Global Civil Society?* (Cambridge, 2003).

50 Terry Macdonald and Miriam Ronzoni, "Introduction: The Idea of Global Political Justice", *Critical Review of International Social and Political Philosophy* 15 (2008), pp. 521–533.

51 Allen Buchanan and Robert O. Keohane, "The Legitimacy of Global Governance Institutions", *Ethics and International Affairs* 20 (2006), pp. 405–437.

52 Thomas Christiano, "Is Democratic Legitimacy Possible for International Institutions?", in Daniele Archibugi, Mathias Koenig-Archibugi, and Raffaele Marchetti (eds), *Global Democracy: Normative and Empirical Perspectives* (Cambridge, 2011), p. 70.

53 See Jürgen Habermas, "The Constitutionalization of International Law and the Legitimation Problems of a Constitution for World Society", *Constellations* 15 (2008), pp. 444–455.

54 While the term "reciprocity" has its roots in the Latin word *reciprocus*, which meant "moving back and forward", it was used in English for the first time in the mid-eighteenth century. See "Reciprocity", *Oxford English Dictionary*.

55 Raymond de Roover, "The Concept of the Just Price: Theory and Economic Policy", *The Journal of Economic History* 18 (1958), p. 418. Although de Roover is critical of this reading, he acknowledges that it features in "nearly all books dealing with the subject".

56 Notice that the *price* of basic goods such as a meal or a university textbook is not morally relevant *per se* – what is morally relevant is having *access* to such goods, which may happen, respectively, through a decent salary and a good public library.

57 Daniel M. Hausman and Michael S. McPherson, "Economics, Rationality, and Ethics", in Daniel M. Hausman (ed.), *The Philosophy of Economics: An Anthology* (Cambridge, 1994), p. 262.

58 John Rawls, *A Theory of Justice: Revised Edition*, pp. 88–90.

59 A question that may be raised is related to the so-called happy slave problem. What if someone is satisfied with a non-reciprocal arrangement? Would reciprocity still be morally required under such conditions? The answer is that reciprocity, like other moral ideals, is somewhat independent from consent. For instance, one's acceptance to be humiliated does not render a humiliating action respectful.

60 The point that non-coercive, mutually advantageous exchanges may fail to meet the requirements of justice has been made by Chris Meyers in the ongoing debate on the ethics of sweatshops. See Chris Meyers, "Wrongful Beneficence: Exploitation and Third World Sweatshops", *Journal of Social Philosophy* 35 (2004), pp. 319–333.

61 John Rawls, *A Theory of Justice: Revised Edition*, pp. 155–156.

62 Adam Smith, *An Inquiry Into the Nature and Causes of the Wealth of Nations* (Indianapolis, 1993), p. 11.

63 See Robert Nozick, *Anarchy, State and Utopia* (Malden, 1974), pp. 160–164.

64 Iris Marion Young, "A Model of Social Connection", *Responsibility for Justice* (New York, 2011).

65 Ibid., p. 96.

66 Ibid.

67 An issue that may be raised is whether a duty of economic reciprocity conditional upon these two features (i.e. regular exchange and division of labour) applies to self-sufficient economies. However, even in rural contexts, it seems hard to find a modern society where exchange does not happen on a regular basis. Division of labour will become apparent each time the self-sufficient farmer goes to the doctor.

68 See John Rawls, *A Theory of Justice: Revised Edition*, pp. 6–10.

69 Young famously developed her own conception of basic structure in Iris Marion Young, "Taking the Basic Structure Seriously", *Perspectives on Politics* 4 (2006), pp. 91–97.

70 It may be argued that, *given* an unfair economic structure, it may be desirable to fail to reciprocate at the transactional level. This argument is typically employed to justify exploitative relations with the Third World which are, nonetheless, to the advantage of the exploited. Yet, once again, mutual advantage is not to be confused with reciprocity. The former is a necessary but insufficient condition for the latter. An unjust economic order should not, therefore, be taken as given.

71 According to David Hume and John Rawls, limited altruism is one of the "circumstances of justice". See David Hume, *A Treatise of Human Nature* (Oxford, 1896), 3.II.2; and John Rawls, *A Theory of Justice: Revised Edition*, pp. 109–112.

72 Robert Nozick, *Anarchy, State and Utopia*, p. 163.

73 This refers to individuals, and not to companies or states, which may be powerful enough to influence market outcomes on their own.

74 To illustrate this point, consider the following two familiar examples: (i) the young university graduates who made the reasonable choice of pursuing further studies, and now are unemployed due to the oversupply of graduates in the market; (ii) the individuals who lost their jobs after working for decades in industries that became obsolete due to increasing international competition. In

neither of the cases may the present state of affairs be meaningfully linked to poor individual choices.

75 Notice that I equate "discrete transactions" with labour, leaving aside transactions of goods and services. The reason is that, as I have mentioned, the price of labour is not morally neutral, unlike, say, the price of a car – recall that salaries are a barometer of mutual respect. The problem arises as to how this view would suit certain commodity producers, such as small farmers, who do not earn a salary and who depend entirely on the price of the commodity they produce and sell. This point can be addressed by referring to a just economic structure. In a global economy with fair terms of trade, small producers would, in principle, receive a fair share for their commodity. Similar to other workers from democratic states, small producers would be protected from arbitrary changes on the demand side (e.g. nobody buying their commodity any more) by the threshold of basic goods, until they could adapt their production to new market conditions.

76 It might be suggested that, if this line of reasoning were pursued further, the notion of moral responsibility would be altogether undermined. The reason is that not only in the market, but in many other morally relevant settings, outcomes can be shaped by luck. However, the link between the *cause* and *consequence* of human action seems much stronger in certain domains of life than in the context of market exchange. On the role played by luck in moral theorizing, see Thomas Nagel, "Moral Luck", *Mortal Questions* (Cambridge, 1979).

77 Empirical evidence for this claim is presented by Jan Rosset, Nathalie Giger, and Julian Bernauer, "More Money, Fewer Problems? Cross-Level Effects of Economic Deprivation on Political Representation", *West European Politics* 36 (2013), pp. 817–835.

78 In fact, Frederick Solt has established a negative correlation between economic inequality and the level of political engagement. See Frederick Solt, "Economic Inequality and Democratic Political Engagement", *American Journal of Political Science* 52 (2008), pp. 48–60.

79 In 2014, the CEOs of the top 100 companies listed in the FTSE earned 183 times the salary of the average worker in the United Kingdom. See Miles Johnson, "FTSE Chiefs Earn 183 Times Average Salary of UK Workers", *Financial Times* (17 August 2015).

80 While *global* inequality has showed a decreasing trend in the last two decades, particularly due to the economic rise of highly populated countries such as China, India, and Indonesia, *domestic* inequality has been increasing since the 1980s in most developed countries. This is mainly due to a dramatic increase in the share of national income appropriated by the top incomes. See OECD, *Focus on Inequality and Growth* (December 2014) and *World Inequality Database*.

81 François Quesnay, *Tableau Économique des Physiocrates* (Paris, 1969).

82 For the notion of "creative destruction", see Joseph A. Schumpeter, *Capitalism, Socialism and Democracy* (New York, 2008), pp. 81–87.

83 Immanuel Kant, "On the Common Saying: This May Be True in Theory But It Does Not Apply In Practice", in Hans Reiss (ed.), *Kant's Political Writings* (Cambridge, 1991), pp. 61–92.

84 Charles R. Beitz, *Political Theory and International Relations* (Princeton, 1999), p. 145.
85 John Rawls, *The Law of Peoples*, pp. 114–120.
86 Thomas W. Pogge, *Realizing Rawls* (Ithaca, 1989).
87 Andrea Sangiovanni, "Global Justice, Reciprocity, and the State", *Philosophy & Public Affairs* 35 (2007), pp. 3–39.
88 For the figures of Portuguese international trade and foreign investment, see, respectively, Instituto Nacional de Estatística, *Estatísticas do Comércio Internacional* (2014), pp. 28–53; and Aicep, "Fluxos de Investimento Directo de Portugal com o Exterior (1996–2014)".
89 Free trade and investment areas where the terms of cooperation are different from the EU, such as Mercosur, the Association of Southeast Asian Nations, and bilateral agreements, would require separate discussion.
90 The challenges raised by corruption have received growing attention in the last two decades. See, for instance, Transparency International Policy Paper, *Poverty, Aid and Corruption* (2007).
91 In fact, the ILO has created a few important conventions on labour standards, which have been ratified by a considerable number of states and are backed by a supervisory system. In this sense, we may say that a global minimum is already emerging. However, there is much room for improvement. For instance, the *Convention Limiting the Hours of Work in Industrial Undertakings to Eight in the Day and Forty-Eight in the Week* has been ratified by 52 countries, roughly one-quarter of the countries in the world.

2

Democratic redistribution in the EU

I. Introduction

This chapter addresses the question, does the democratic duty to redistribute apply to the EU? Two sub-questions then follow: (i) is the EU sufficiently coercive and democratic to trigger the democratic duty to redistribute? (ii) if so, how should responsibilities to fulfil this duty be allocated amongst the different levels of government in the EU? I begin by developing the concept of "specialized system of coercion", which I define as the capacity to produce generalized compliance in particular domains of policy. I challenge Max Weber's account of the monopoly of force in two ways. First, I claim that certain non-state actors can rely on state-based coercive apparatuses to enforce their commandments – that is, they do not need to have a police force or an army of their own. Secondly, I argue that a coercive system may be domain-specific – that is, the scope of its coercive regulation does not have to be as broad as the state's. This, I argue, is the case for the EU, where supranational institutions rely on national courts and police forces to enforce EU law. In turn, I argue that democracy can be plausibly conceived in terms of a plurality of *demoi* which share common democratic institutions. I claim that, by virtue of its representative institutions and citizenship practices, the EU should be regarded as a "demoicracy". I conclude that the EU fulfils the conditions for the democratic duty to redistribute to apply. I argue that responsibilities for democratic redistribution should be shared by the three levels of government in the Union – local, national, and supranational. I claim that the allocation of responsibilities should follow the principles of proportionality and subsidiarity. In practice, this means that the EU should act as a safety net for domestic social citizenship, supplementing national welfare systems whenever they lack the resources to fulfil the domestic threshold of basic goods.

I begin by summarizing the democratic duty to redistribute advanced in Chapter 1. Subsequently, I introduce the concept of "specialized system of coercion", investigating whether it applies to the EU. I then introduce the notions of demoicracy and multilevel citizenship, discussing whether the latter applies to the EU. I conclude the first part of the chapter by discussing whether the EU is something other than an international organization. In the second part of the chapter, I introduce a crucial problem for multilevel citizenship studies: at what level of citizenship should redistribution take place? To address this question, I compare three ideal-typical models of redistribution in multilevel polities: the first model is based on the nation-state; the second is based on supranational institutions; the third is a mixed model. I explain why the third model is the most desirable one. Then, I discuss the implications of the principles of proportionality and subsidiarity for responsibility sharing amongst levels of government as far as distributive justice is concerned. I discuss the main features of an EU threshold of basic goods, addressing a number of objections against my view. Finally, I briefly explore differences between redistribution in the EU and in other multilevel democratic polities.

II. Why democratic redistribution applies to the EU

In Chapter 1, I argued that the democratic duty to redistribute consists of providing the means for political participation and resistance to power to all the members of a polity. The insights behind this claim of democratic redistribution were twofold. First, to have a *real chance to participate in civic life*, citizens must benefit from a set of material conditions. In the absence of a list of basic goods, their right to participate is merely formal. Secondly, exclusion from participation due to the lack of material resources creates the *risk of arbitrary rule*. If citizens do not have the chance to have a say in the legislative procedure, nor the resources to contest executive and judicial decisions, they become mere subjects to power. In this sense, distributive justice may be regarded as a prerequisite for democratic citizenship. I argued that political institutions should address the threats described previously by assuring that every member of the polity attains a threshold of basic goods. This threshold includes the means of subsistence, access to healthcare, access to education, and resources for due process in court. I claimed that the democratic duty to redistribute may apply beyond borders, but only if both coercive and democratic practices are comprehensively institutionalized.

My subsequent goal is to discuss whether – and if so, to what extent – the democratic duty to redistribute applies to the European Union. To address this problem, both descriptive and normative tasks need to be fulfilled. First, how coercive, and how democratic, are institutions and practices in the EU? It is often pointed out that the EU possesses neither an army nor a police force. Does this imply that coercion is poorly institutionalized at the EU level? Similarly, it is often argued that there is a democratic deficit in the EU. Does this mean that the existing institutions are not good enough for democratic redistribution? A descriptive account is thus needed to assess whether the EU is sufficiently coercive and legitimate to trigger the democratic duty to redistribute. Secondly, normative judgments will be required to understand the implications of this descriptive account. If one concludes that the democratic duty to redistribute applies to the Union, one still needs to specify the principle(s) that should guide the allocation of responsibilities to fulfil the threshold amongst the different levels of government in the EU. This point is crucial, since from competing understandings of the democratic duty to redistribute, very different institutional arrangements will follow – some implying the standardization of social policy, others more akin to a plurality of models. I shall begin the discussion by introducing the concept of "specialized system of coercion".

Specialized system of coercion

By monopoly of force, I mean the capacity to produce generalized compliance through coercive means. According to Max Weber, this capacity is a distinguishing feature of the modern state, which he defines as "the form of human community that (successfully) lays claim to the monopoly of legitimate violence within a particular territory".[1] In turn, by *specialized system of coercion* I mean that such capacity may apply only to particular domains of legislation. In this account, the highest coercive authorities on, say, social policy and trade policy need not be the same, nor does any of them have to be based on the nation-state. This idea is at odds with the Weberian understanding of monopoly of force, which presupposes that the coercive apparatus is ultimately linked to a single political entity: the state. However, does this need to be the case? The link between state and monopoly of force was embedded in a context where all relevant policy areas, as well as the coercive instruments to implement them, were entirely controlled by the state. Yet developments such as globalization and regional integration have undermined the validity of such an assumption.[2] As political power has been shared across different levels of government, often beyond national borders, the idea of a *unified* monopoly became, indeed, problematic. While the state remains the legitimate monopolist of some policy areas, the scope of its monopoly seems to shrink as the degree of political and economic integration grows. Yet how can this be, if only the state has the *means* to enforce the law – namely, a police force and an army?

A first insight behind the idea of specialized systems of coercion is that, to effectively monopolize force, one does not need to possess a police force or an army. Instead, the monopoly can be "indirect", by relying on third-party forces. Surely, armed forces are required for law enforcement and security; my point is that these requisites of public order only need to be *available* for the use of the monopolist, not to be *owned* by it. To illustrate this point, consider three particular types of monopolists: (i) states that do not possess armies, yet benefit from the protection of an army of a neighbour state – this is the case for San Marino and Monaco; (ii) transitional states, as well as states experiencing internal conflict, relying heavily on foreign forces, such as UN peacekeepers, to enforce the law – as illustrated by the cases of Iraq and Timor-Leste; and (iii) states that, despite possessing functioning armies and police forces, would hardly be able to sustain autonomous monopolies if it were not for the backing of another, more powerful army – arguably the case of Taiwan, in relation to the United States. If these three categories of states can be regarded as successful examples of monopolists, this is largely due to means that are beyond their capacity. Hence, when certain conditions are met, a monopolist can rely on the force of other monopolists, without ceasing to be (perceived as) a monopolist or having coercive means at their disposal. This suggests that, to monopolize force, one only needs to effectively employ the threat of using force – and doing so, if necessary – *regardless* of whose force this actually is.

A second insight is that a coercive system does not have to be equated with a single actor – it may, in fact, comprise a variety of actors, which act as monopolists in specific policy domains. The view that a monopoly of force may implicate actors beyond the nation-state challenges the assumption that a monopolist has to be a sovereign, understood in the strong sense of an "absolute and perpetual power of a commonwealth".[3] Surely, the idea of a monopoly of force presupposes a political authority which has the right, as well as the capacity, to say "the last word" in given disputes.[4] However, if a monopolist must be able to say "the last word", it does not have to do so in *all* publicly relevant matters. Historical examples of domain-specific monopolies are the Ottoman Empire and the British East India Company.[5] In fact, once we assume that an (own) police and army are not constitutive of, but are instrumental to, a monopoly of force, it becomes possible to conceive a coercive system in which different layers of power act as monopolists in particular policy areas. Within the realm of its specific competences, each actor will have "the last word", using the coercive means legitimately available to it to enforce compliance. As in the markets of goods and services, where monopolies refer to specific economic areas, one can be the monopolist of a particular policy area – say, energy – while another entity is the monopolist of another policy area – say, agriculture. If this argument is sound, there need not be a single actor that is the ultimate holder of the entire coercive apparatus.

Let me now clarify a few aspects. First, what exactly is the appropriate unit of analysis of coercion? For instance, when I say that I am being coerced to pay my mortgage, who exactly is exercising coercion? Is it the bank, which threatened to press charges against me? Is it the court, which issued an arrest warrant? Is it the police, who are knocking on my door? Or is it the parliament, which enacted the Penal Code? Admittedly, to hold the monopoly of force is to be in charge of two interrelated tasks: specifying what individuals are required to do (or not to do), and enforcing compliance with these specifications.[6] Being authorized to use force does not give one a monopoly of force *per se*. A private company performing security checks at the airport does not hold the monopoly of force, although it has the power to stop me if I do not comply with the rules. Thus a key function of monopolists is to decide the content of the rules to be enforced by the coercive apparatus. In addition, recall that we are only interested in *legitimate* coercion.[7] As we shall see, the process of legitimation of coercion seems to comprise three types of institutions, which constitute, then, the appropriate units of analysis: (i) those *enacting* the law, (ii) those *interpreting* the law and *applying* it to concrete cases, and (iii) those *executing* the law. In fact, in our previous example, the bank can appeal to laws sanctioned by a public authority (but not to the decrees of its CEO); it can press charges in an official court (but not in its own board); and it may expect the police to execute the decision of that court (but not a militia hired by it).

Secondly, it follows from my previous argument that international agencies can be specialized systems of coercion. On this account, the ICC is the highest coercive authority regarding crimes against humanity and genocide in those territories which ratified the Rome Statute, while the WTO is the highest coercive authority regarding trade practices within the members of this organization. This view raises at least two types of objections. The first is that, insofar as cooperation with international agencies is ultimately voluntary, one may not be able to speak of coercion in a proper sense in these cases. An arrest warrant by the ICC always has to be translated into some kind of domestic warrant, sanctioned by domestic courts. In addition, states are always left with an opt-out option. Thus, if a state so wishes, it may withdraw from the Rome Statute or WTO membership and abide exclusively by its own legal standards. A second, interrelated objection is the following: since neither the ICC nor the WTO have their own police force or army, how can they enforce their decisions? What can really happen if a signatory state does not comply with international conventions, besides some diplomatic turmoil? In fact, some states have delayed for many years the extradition of former public officials under international prosecution, and tolerate prohibited trade practices. Do these objections defeat the previous argument?

There are still good reasons to think that the argument is sound. To begin with, the view that *each act* of international cooperation is ultimately voluntary clearly underestimates the exit costs faced by states. In an increasingly interdependent world, the costs of being out of key global institutional networks may be high in terms of the security, economic performance, and reputation of states.[8] Thus, even if states comply with international norms only out of self-interest, they still have strong incentives to do so.[9] It may be suggested that exit costs are not intrinsically coercive, given that the agents facing them preserve their freedom not to comply. Yet exit costs are an important part of the coercive apparatus insofar as they determine whether alternative courses of action are *de facto* available. Exit costs are particularly relevant in the context of EU membership because they make the event of leaving very unlikely. For instance, it is implausible to think that, if the CJEU rules against the interests of a member state regarding, say, environmental policy, this member state will consider leaving the Union to avoid recognizing the verdict. The member state is thus coerced to accept the ruling that it did not want because the alternative of leaving the EU is too costly.

At the same time, the right to the leave the EU does not make EU institutions by definition non-coercive. A few examples can help in illustrating this point. First, consider the case of Scotland in relation to the United Kingdom. The fact that the United Kingdom granted Scotland the right to leave the kingdom does not mean that British institutions ceased to be coercive for Scottish citizens. This could be the case *after* Scotland left the United Kingdom, but not before. Second, the opt-out option also applies to some (admittedly coercive) federations. For instance, according to the US Supreme Court, the states are allowed to leave the union, provided that the other states agree to that.[10] Several other countries specify certain rights of secession for their provinces in their constitutional texts.[11] This formal right to leave does not mean that coercion is absent – it only suggests that coercion will cease *if* a sub-state unit decides to leave the state.

Furthermore, international actors such as the WTO can rely on explicit coercive practices such as the threat of exclusion from membership and economic sanctions. The coercion of the WTO is monopolistic in the sense that it is effectively exercised over *all* member states of this organization – and, ultimately, over their citizens.[12] Furthermore, it has been shown that international norms may transform domestic preferences and expectations, thus creating favourable conditions for compliance.[13] In fact, compliance with international agreements is "relatively good in general".[14] The claim that certain types of infractions of international standards often go without punishment applies not less to the international system than to the domestic level. For instance, most national monopolists lack the capacity to fully enforce the prohibition of marijuana and the payment of taxes. This does not lead us to challenge their coercive status. In fact, tax evasion and illegal consumption of marijuana around the world seem to be much higher than non-compliance with UN resolutions and the warrants of the ICC.

Finally, one may argue that the concept of specialized systems of coercion raises issues of coordination and stability. How will the specialized systems hold together if they are, by definition, fragmented? The answer lies in the scope of the existing institutional arrangements. Specialized systems of coercion presuppose a clear definition of competences for each level of governance, as well as appropriate mechanisms of legitimation, which usually consist of ratified international treaties but can also include more ambitious mechanisms, such as elections. In the cases where an international institution is legally authorized to coerce a state, it may be said that it holds the monopoly of force on the subject of such coercion. This is particularly evident when the international institution is authorized to use the domestic courts and police forces to enforce its commands, as in the case of the European Commission. Surely, this process may generate some turmoil, which again also applies to the domestic level, whenever different state agencies compete for the jurisdiction of a particular matter. Cases in which such tensions *always* lead to the predominance of the state *vis-à-vis* the international agency or agreement, as in the case of the Kyoto Protocol, suggest the absence – and not the ineffectiveness – of a specialized system of coercion. Therefore, the relevant test for the adequate institutionalization of a specialized system will be its capacity to generate compliance amongst the targeted subjects.

The EU as a specialized system of coercion

Within the domains of its regulatory competences, the EU constitutes a specialized system of coercion. The monopolization by the EU is particularly apparent in two legal norms widely accepted by the member states: the principle of *supremacy of EU law* and the principle of *direct effect*. The principle of supremacy states that "European law is superior to the national laws of member states".[15] This norm has two main implications: (i) "the laws issued by European institutions are to be integrated into the legal systems of Member States, who are obliged to comply with them"; (ii) "Member States may not apply a national rule which contradicts to European law".[16] In turn, the principle of direct effect "enables individuals to immediately invoke a European provision before a national or European court".[17] This principle comprises two different aspects: (i) *vertical* direct effect, which applies to relations between individuals and a member state (i.e. "individuals can invoke an European provision in relation to the country"); and (ii) *horizontal* direct effect, which applies to relations between individuals (i.e. "an individual can invoke an European provision in relation to another individual").[18] Note that the principle of direct effect applies even when the EU provision has not been translated into domestic law. Precedence and direct effect – two sides of the same coin – reveal the coercive character of the Union.

At the institutional level, we find more evidence of an EU specialized system of coercion. In fact, the EU architecture comprises the three types of coercive institutions mentioned before: law-enacting (the European Parliament, the Commission, and the Council of the European Union), law-interpreting (the CJEU and national courts), and law-enforcing (national police forces). Regarding law enactment, the competences of the EU are very broad. They are specified in the several treaties which have been ratified by the member states since the founding of the European Community of Coal and Steel. Once an EU act has been passed, it has to be translated into national law, either in its original form (in the case of regulations) or somewhat discretionarily, provided that a particular goal is achieved (in the case of directives). As for the interpretation and application of law, the CJEU is a clear-cut example of a coercive institution. Within the areas of EU competence, the CJEU is the supreme court of Europe, holding the power to contradict the decisions of national courts, which are then forced to reverse their previous rulings. In addition, as already mentioned, national courts are obliged to apply EU law in case this is invoked by any of the conflicting parties. Finally, although the EU does not have its own police, it can rely on the police forces of member states to enforce its commands. Once an EU act has been transposed to the domestic order, it will be duly enforced, as any other piece of legislation enacted by the national legislative bodies.

Hence, the EU passes the test of producing generalized compliance amongst its subjects. To give an illustrative example, all member states with written constitutions had to adapt them to incorporate the principle of precedence, as a result of a decision by the CJEU.[19] This constitutes strong evidence of enforced compliance.[20] One might still argue that the fact that EU legislative and judicial acts have to be translated into national law and national judicial mandates undermines the coercive character of the Union. Ultimately, so the argument will go, the decision to comply remains under national control. However, this requirement of transposition seems to be merely procedural, particularly given the fact that EU law which failed to be transposed into national law can yet be invoked in national courts. In other words, there is not much that a member state can do beyond trying to delay the application of an EU act, within a relatively short period of time. In addition, the TFEU specifies penalties for states which do not comply with an act of EU law.[21] The proceedings for failure to fulfil an obligation implicate the Commission and the CJEU and have been eased with the Lisbon Treaty.[22] In 2012, the Commission brought before the CJEU 35 cases against 12 member states for late transposition of directives, proposing corresponding fines.[23] Given that EU norms, institutions, and practices are coercive, the EU may be rightly regarded as a specialized system of coercion.

Demoicracy and multilevel citizenship

I now turn my attention to another prerequisite of the democratic duty to redistribute: democracy. Recall that in Chapter 1, I defined democracy in institutionalist terms, following closely Robert Dahl's influential account. According to Dahl, democracy comprises seven key institutions: (i) elected officials, (ii) free and fair elections, (iii) inclusive suffrage, (iv) the right to run for office, (v) freedom of expression, (vi) availability of alternative information, and (vii) associational autonomy.[24] Yet what does this approach say about democracy in a context of multiple levels of government, particularly the supranational level? According to Dahl, an international organization "probably cannot be a democracy".[25] However, as I shall claim, the EU cannot be plausibly classified as an international organization precisely because it meets the requirements of democracy that the institutionalist theory postulates. Dahl's typology is particularly useful for assessing the existence of a democracy beyond borders because it sets a common denominator amongst different "patterns" or "models" of democracy.[26] Yet this institutionalist analysis has to address the question of whether a given set of democratic institutions can be linked to a specific body of citizens – that is, a *demos*. As I shall claim, an appropriate test for the existence of a *demos* would not focus on a set of sociological variables such as ethnicity, collective identity, or a sense of shared destiny. These aspects are important, but they are essentially criteria for the feasibility of democracy. Instead, a meaningful understanding of *demos* has to focus on the existing (or emerging) norms and practices of democratic *citizenship*.

Let me clarify two important points. First, to give systematic treatment to the question of whether a *demos* can exist beyond national borders, one must not rely on a definition that is decisively biased in favour of the nation-state. Indeed, to assert that there is a *demos* only when there is a common ethnos, a collective identity, and a sense of shared destiny, is to say that only nation-states can be democracies. However, this is not necessarily the case. Therefore, my definition should be formulated in terms of the constitutional features that make for a *demos* – namely, in terms of subjection to, and right to participation in, common democratic institutions. Admittedly, a degree of shared values is a precondition for democracy to work, if some basic level of consensus is to be achieved.[27] Yet this eventually shifts the burdens of proof that a *demos* exists to the existing democratic institutions. In other words, if democratic institutions are functioning and durable, the presumption should be that the individuals bound by them have enough in common to sustain such institutions. Secondly, the issue of the sociological features that hold the *demos* together must be seen in historical perspective. In fact, the historical experience of most Western European countries where civic bonds are arguably strong shows that any "imagined community" is socially constructed, through a gradual process.[28] In this sense, feelings of belonging and civic friendship have often been the outcome, rather than the origin, of a political community. For these reasons, the prospects of an EU democracy should not be dismissed too quickly on the grounds of a static and nation-state biased "no *demos*" thesis.[29]

In recent years, a number of scholarly accounts have conceptualized democracy and citizenship in a context of multiple levels of government. Amongst the existing frameworks, *demoicracy* and *multilevel citizenship* are of particular interest for my discussion. According to the first approach, democracy does not have to be equated with a single national *demos*; it can instead be conceived in terms of a plurality of national *demoi*, which closely interact with each other. Therefore, in the case of the EU, "the idea of demoicracy resists recourse to a notion of 'European identity' as underpinning the EU polity".[30] This approach has at least two variants, with substantially different implications. On the one hand, it is possible to conceive demoicracy in *horizontal* terms – that is, as a group of states that democratically govern their interdependencies, but where citizens are represented only by their national governments. This scenario is consistent with the absence of a common *demos* and could suit a comprehensive international organization – perhaps the European Community before the first direct elections for the European Parliament were held in 1979. On the other hand, demoicracy can be understood in *both* horizontal *and* vertical terms – that is, in terms of relations not only amongst equal national governments, but also amongst equal citizens of the different *demoi*, through the mediation of shared democratic institutions. This notably implies supranational institutions which directly represent the citizens of the different *demoi*, creating a *de facto* common people. As I shall claim, this is the case for the EU.[31]

The second variant of demoicracy, which combines the horizontal and the vertical dimensions, seems to raise a question about citizenship: how can individuals simultaneously belong to a common *demos* and to their national *demoi*? In fact, this is only problematic if we conceive citizenship as "a unitary and homogeneous legal status granted to an individual by a sovereign state".[32] Alternatively, one may think of different *levels* of citizenship, which include "citizenship not only of the state but also of the sub-state, suprastate, or non-state political communities".[33] This model is helpful because it allows us to accommodate a variety of existing citizenship practices at the local and the supranational level. Once the multilevel model has been adopted, the distribution of rights and duties across different levels of citizenship becomes normatively relevant. As I shall claim, a normatively desirable allocation of rights and duties will have to consider the specific features of the multilevel polity in question. However, a more general proposition can be advanced considering what has been said so far: for a *demos* to exist at any level of government, Robert Dahl's institutions will have to be found at that level. Crucially, citizens will need to have the right to vote for, as well as to hold office in, a representative body that is directly linked to that level of citizenship. This direct link, as well as the citizenship practices that it generates, make demoicracy sufficiently thick to warrant speaking of a *demos*.

The EU as an institutionalized demoicracy

A key issue is, then, whether the EU should be considered a demoicracy, as opposed to an intergovernmental organization.[34] The extent to which member states are politically integrated has been a key, and apparently unsolvable, question for EU studies.[35] This question is crucial for our discussion. If the EU is not more than a politically loose group of states with no serious democratic bonds amongst its citizens, my claim for redistribution may lose much of its strength. Indeed, if the EU is simply an intergovernmental organization, the argument that redistribution applies to the EU *because* the EU is a coercive system may be reversed. In other words, one might claim that that the EU's coercive apparatus is, in fact, excessive – what might be dubbed a "regulatory empire".[36] In this case, the solution would not be *more* integration – including reforms towards distributive justice – but *less*. Indeed, a number of political actors in Europe have recently pursued this line of reasoning. Interestingly, both "pro" and "con" views on EU redistribution seem to imply a similar normative assumption: that the *resources* employed by a given level of government, as well as the scale and scope of its policies, should be proportional to its *goals*. One common strategy amongst the critics of EU redistribution is, precisely, to deny that the EU is *politically* integrated. Hence, the dispute regarding distributive justice in the EU is also a descriptive one: is the EU sufficiently democratic to generate distributive duties?

The institutional architecture of the EU reflects to a great extent that it is a demoicracy in the horizontal and in the vertical sense. To begin with, the treaties establish freedom of speech and autonomy of association as fundamental principles of the Union, being amongst the criteria for accession. In addition, the members of the European Parliament are directly elected by EU citizens through free and fair elections. Every EU citizen has the right to run for office. In turn, the members of the Council, which is regarded by some authors as the upper chamber of the Union, are elected at the state level.[37] If, in the past, an unelected Commission might be rightly charged for holding disproportional powers *vis-à-vis* the Parliament, this state of affairs has been decisively changed after the reforms introduced by the Treaty of Lisbon.[38] Furthermore, EU citizens are entitled to appeal directly to the CJEU for charges related to the breach of fundamental rights, even when performed by their own governments.[39] For these reasons, the EU has been rightly described as a "constitutional order".[40] Given the democratizing potential of the Union, Miguel Maduro has even referred to the "European democratic surplus".[41] A good illustration of this surplus was the consolidation of southern and eastern democracies. The fact that there may be tensions between EU institutions and the national governments does not *per se* undermine the legitimacy of the Union. As Hannah Arendt stressed, the core of democracy is not the absence of ideas and values in tension, but the belief that through such "agonic" confrontation a legitimate outcome may be achieved.[42]

In turn, if the meaning of EU citizenship is far from straightforward, this by no means makes it an empty box. As I have argued, once the unitary model of citizenship is abandoned, we are ready to accommodate the citizenship practices of multilevel structures of government. In the specific context of the EU, Rainer Bauböck has argued for the existence of three levels of citizenship – local, national, and supranational – where EU citizenship is "one layer in a multi-level model of democratic membership".[43] Although EU citizenship is derivative in nature – that is, it is acquired through citizenship of any of the member states – it should be regarded as "potentially coherent and normatively attractive".[44] The importance of EU citizenship becomes clear when we analyse the practices linked to it. The list is far from being parsimonious, including freedom of movement and residence, a uniform passport, direct universal suffrage, the right to vote in municipal elections, and the right of diplomatic protection. Furthermore, it should be noted that this list is not static. Indeed, the *construction* of EU citizenship has been a long and ongoing process.[45] In light of this, it is plausible to conclude that "[t]he reality of European citizenship is not 'either-or', it is 'both/and'".[46]

The claim that an EU *demos* does not exist can only refer, then, to the lack of a common identity, taking the nation-state as a reference point. Yet, as we have seen, the *demos* should be understood in terms of shared democratic institutions and citizenship practices. F. Cheneval and F. Schimmelfennig enlighteningly summarize four key principles underlying the EU demoicracy: (1) sovereignty of national peoples regarding entry, exit, and basic rules of the EU democratic order (i.e. through member state unanimity in treaty legislation); (2) non-discrimination of EU citizens and peoples; (3) equal legislative rights (namely, equal right for EU citizens to vote in EU elections and equal representation in the Commission and Council); and (4) supremacy of EU law and jurisdiction.[47] If it is true that EU membership raises legitimacy disputes in specific policy areas, as well as risks of opportunistic behaviour by member states, including "shifting the burden of making the Union work onto the shoulders (and economies) of other states", this applies not more to the EU than to any (more or less) federalized structure.[48] Surely, the argument presented in this section does not invalidate the claim that the EU demoicracy could (or should) be more democratic in certain respects.[49] However, it leads me to two important conclusions. First, the list of democratic institutions and the citizenship practices presented in the preceding paragraphs make implausible the claim that the EU is just an intergovernmental organization. Second, the EU meets the requirements of Robert Dahl's institutionalist account, fully deserving the label of "demoicracy".

Redistribution in the EU

Let me now return to my initial question: does the democratic duty to redistribute apply to the EU? In Chapter 1, I argued that the democratic duty to redistribute applies whenever coercion and democracy are comprehensively institutionalized. The present chapter has elaborated what the appropriate tests for a coercive system and for democracy would be and applied them to my case study: the EU. As has been shown, the EU comprises a system of coercion that generates the generalized compliance of its members. This is achieved through a complex combination of domestic and supranational institutions with coercive power, from the stage of law enactment to that of law enforcement. At the same time, the EU is a demoicracy, with key democratic institutions, a citizenship status, and a plurality of *demoi*. As we have seen, the institutional architecture and sociological basis of the EU democracy are different from those in the nation-state. For instance, the EU citizenship status is derivative from national citizenship, and the sense of belonging to a common EU project is weaker than membership in national communities. Yet, as I have argued, there is not a single way of realizing democracy; in certain aspects, EU democracy can even be more democratic than the nation-state. Since the EU is both coercive and democratic, we may conclude that the democratic duty to redistribute applies to the EU.

III. Realizing democratic redistribution in the EU

A problem for multilevel citizenship: who owes what, to whom?

I have made a case for a democratic duty to redistribute in the EU, grounded on the coercive and democratic nature of its institutions. Now, recall from Chapter 1 that realizing democratic redistribution implies the attainment by each member of the polity of a threshold of basic goods, which includes subsistence, education, healthcare, and access to justice. In the EU context, the fulfilment of this threshold raises a number of questions. First, who should bear the cost of the provision of these goods to EU citizens who are below the threshold line? Secondly, how exactly should these goods be provided – through domestic institutions, supranational agencies, or both? Thirdly, is the EU threshold exactly the same as its domestic counterparts? What if democracy at EU level raises distributive issues which are different from democracy at national level? Fourthly, is there any room to accommodate the existing differences regarding education and healthcare policy? Or does an EU threshold imply their harmonization? Fifthly, consider the member states where redistribution is, currently, either (i) more comprehensive or (ii) less comprehensive than what the EU threshold prescribes. Are countries within (i) required to lower the level of social provision? Similarly, should countries within (ii) be forced to increase it? Finally, should redistribution in the EU be optional, like membership of the Eurozone, or mandatory? If it is mandatory, should willingness to redistribute become part of the criteria for accession of new member states?

At the heart of alternative answers seems to be a tension between *self-government* and *equality of status*. Which of the two ideals is more important? On the one hand, it seems implausible to think that every EU citizen is entitled to exactly the same social rights, despite their different national affiliations. Firstly, if the autonomy of member states is to be taken seriously, the different types of welfare regimes will have to be accommodated, at least to a certain extent. In fact, even within the borders of the nation-state, local or regional governments tend to maintain a degree of autonomy regarding social provision. Secondly, the strength of social solidarity tends to be much higher amongst national citizens than amongst EU citizens. This would most likely render full equality of status at EU level grossly unfeasible. On the other hand, to deprive EU citizenship of a social dimension, to fully preserve the ideal of self-determination, could mean dooming the former to an irreversible decay. As I have mentioned in the Introduction, as the differences in economic strength and political power to shape the future of the Union grow stronger, so do the risks of having first-class and second-class EU citizens. In other words, a Union without social justice may cease to be a Union at all. Hence, if democratic redistribution is to be realized in the EU, how should responsibilities be allocated amongst the three levels of citizenship?

A set of possible answers

Let us begin by considering three ideal-typical approaches to our questions: (i) distributive justice should be exclusively linked to national citizenship; (ii) distributive justice should be primarily associated with EU citizenship; (iii) distributive justice should take place at each of the three levels of citizenship, according to a given principle of allocation of responsibility across the levels.[50] Notice that two distinct, yet interrelated, issues are at stake: one has to do with the level of government at which distributive justice should be recognized as a matter of right; the other concerns the strategy to fulfil such rights – that is, the welfare model to be adopted. Notice that some welfare models may be normatively more desirable than others. Thus, once it has been established that social rights are linked to one (or more) level(s) of citizenship, a number of alternative models will be available. This diversity of models applies particularly to supranational social rights. For instance, regarding the right to healthcare access, the options will range from a model which is fundamentally based on the domestic healthcare systems and complemented by budgetary transfers across member states whenever needed, to a model whereby every EU citizen has the right to decide the location in the Union where they will receive medical treatment. Since the issues of recognition of rights and welfare model are not identical, I will treat them separately. While this section focuses on the former, the next section will deal with the latter.

In the first chapter, I made a case against the first ideal type. I claimed that, in any context where democracy and coercion are thoroughly institutionalized, every citizen has the right to attain a threshold of sufficiency, which provides the means for political participation and resistance to arbitrary power. Earlier in this chapter, I argued that this threshold also applies to EU citizens. A question which remains to be addressed is whether this understanding of EU social citizenship generates *perfect duties* amongst fellow EU citizens, which ought to be fulfilled by EU institutions. This requirement challenges the status quo which is consistent with the nation-state model of social justice. In an article relevant for this discussion, Dimitry Kochenov has claimed that EU citizenship is "a citizenship without duties".[51] Kochenov argues that the "duties of EU citizenship only exist as one word in the Treaty, which does not happen to correspond to anything in either contemporary legal theory or in practice".[52] If Kochenov's view is sound, the fact that the social rights specified in the EU Charter of Fundamental Rights correspond with imperfect duties will not be a reason for concern. However, as Richard Bellamy has argued, the idea of a citizenship without duties seems both philosophically and empirically implausible.[53] Although the list of duties of citizenship varies across authors, it seems of little controversy that duties as basic as paying taxes and complying with the fundamental laws of the community are implicit in the idea of membership of a polity. If a citizenship without duties is implausible at the level of the nation-state, there is no reason to accept it when it comes to EU citizenship.

In turn, there are good reasons to reject the second ideal type, according to which supranational citizenship should be the core level of social provision. First, the fact that distributive justice historically developed within the nation-state, and is still predominantly linked to national citizenship, suggests that this unit has at least a role to play as far as distributive justice is concerned. In fact, a "third wave" of global justice studies has claimed that cosmopolitan principles of justice are not necessarily incompatible with special duties at the nation-state level.[54] Secondly, this ideal type undermines the prospects of self-government. If deciding the fate of one's community is normatively relevant, we must be ready to allow for a significant variance across member states. As I have argued, democracy within the Union should not be exclusively understood in terms of democratic processes taking place in Brussels, but in the articulation between national democracies and the EU. Thus, although social citizenship is a constitutive element of citizenship, it is not its single component. Finally, the second ideal type would imply an enormous degree of social engineering, which is normatively undesirable.[55] Indeed, the current institutional norms and practices of social justice of EU member states have been accumulated according to different historical experiences and past democratic choices. This suggests that the former could only be undone through a high-scale process of standardization, which would undermine individual liberty.

The third ideal type presents itself as the most promising one, being grounded on the idea of burden sharing. In this account, restraining redistribution within national borders would be problematic, but this does not mean that a full-scale European conception of distributive justice is desirable. Thus, responsibilities to fulfil social rights should be shared by all levels of government involved in the democratic processes of the EU. The reason is that it would be unfair to place all the burdens of social citizenship in one single level, given that democracy is realized by the combination of all the three levels of citizenship. It may be anticipated that the notion of shared responsibility is consistent with a *pluralist* account of distributive justice in the EU. Such pluralism holds that different welfare systems should be allowed to coexist with an EU-level safety net – the threshold of basic goods. While a monist approach would imply a high level of centralization in Brussels, including the harmonization of social policy, the pluralist view preserves the member state's autonomy to define social policy, as long as the basic goods have been provided. Accordingly, the nation-state ought to be regarded as the primary unit for social justice, which should be supplemented by EU budgetary transfers only if a member state does not have the resources to fulfil the threshold of its own citizens. In this sense, a normatively desirable and potentially feasible balance of equality and self-government could, at least in theory, be reached. In the next sections, I shall discuss this notion of shared responsibility in depth.

Proportionality, subsidiarity, and distributive justice

I have suggested that responsibilities to realize distributive should be allocated across the three levels of citizenship. But *how*, and *why*? In fact, it is not enough to claim that responsibilities ought to be shared; we also need to specify the principle according to which the particular duties of each level of government are to be determined. If, at a purely abstract level, there may be compelling arguments in favour of more centralized or decentralized options, a normatively desirable allocation of responsibilities must also consider an empirical dimension. In fact, as I have argued, the *choice* between alternative welfare models is normatively relevant because it translates the value of self-government. Therefore, multilevel polities such as the United States and Switzerland may rightly call for different principles of allocation of responsibility, since they have democratically articulated diverse solutions for the tension between equality of status and self-government. In fact, even within the existing nation-states, the level at which particular social rights are fulfilled varies considerably. For example, while the central government of France has the duty to fulfil the right to affordable housing, this responsibility is regarded as part of the job of local governments in Italy. This suggests that, in order to select a principle of allocation for the EU which is normatively desirable and, as far as we can anticipate, potentially feasible, we will have to take into account the particular features of the EU polity, namely its established practices of distribution of competences across the different levels of government.

Throughout the EU's history, three principles have played a key role in allocating responsibilities amongst national and supranational institutions: the principle of *conferral*, the principle of *proportionality*, and the principle of *subsidiarity*. The principle of conferral determines that "the Union shall act only within the limits of the competences conferred upon it by the Member States in the Treaties to attain the objectives set out therein".[56] In turn, the principle of proportionality states that "the content and form of Union action shall not exceed what is necessary to achieve the objectives of the Treaties".[57] Finally, the principle of subsidiarity establishes that "in areas which do not fall within its exclusive competence, the Union shall act only if and in so far as the objectives of the proposed action cannot be sufficiently achieved by the Member States, either at central level or at regional and local level, but can rather, by reason of the scale or effects of the proposed action, be better achieved at Union level".[58] Insofar as this study presupposes that a change in the content of the treaties may be normatively desirable, the principle of conferral is of little interest to us. By contrast, the principles of proportionality and subsidiarity have much potential to guide reform, while being deeply entrenched in the legal tradition and the institutional practices of the Union. What do these principles say about the allocation of responsibilities to fulfil the democratic duty to redistribute?

If the EU is a demoicracy, proportionality will imply that, under certain conditions, the EU may be responsible for fulfilling the threshold of basic goods. Of course, the meaning of proportionality largely depends on which descriptive account of the EU is adopted. For instance, if the EU were exclusively conceived as an economic association, with the fundamental goal of building an efficient single market, a concern for democratic redistribution would seem clearly disproportional to the goal to be achieved. In this case, a residual conception of "market citizenship", linked to the economic relations between member states, would likely be more suitable.[59] However, if we conceive of the European Union in the terms proposed in this chapter – that is, as a multilevel demoicracy, which pursues political goals such as democratic legitimacy, a common citizenship status, and a set of fundamental rights – then democratic redistribution is not only compatible, but necessary to achieve the goals of the Union. In this case, the principle of proportionality will imply that the EU *may be* required to take action to ensure that every EU citizen has access to the basic goods required for political participation and resistance to arbitrary power within the EU polity. Note, however, that proportionality does not imply that the EU *always has to* take action. Indeed, the conditions under which the EU will be called to act have to be specified by an auxiliary doctrine which clarifies the way in which conflicting interests amongst the different levels of government should be adjudicated – the principle of subsidiarity.[60]

In turn, the implications of subsidiarity for democratic redistribution seem quite straightforward. Indeed, this principle may be plausibly applied to our discussion as follows: *any particular good which is part of the EU threshold of sufficiency should only be provided by the Union if it cannot be satisfactorily provided by the member state.* According to this formulation, the EU will act as a safety net to domestic social citizenship, supplementing national welfare systems whenever they fail to meet the requirements of democratic redistribution. In other words, the basic goods which integrate the threshold will only be provided, or funded, by the EU if a member state does not have the resources to do so. In Chapter 5, I shall discuss the conditions under which a member state is not able to ensure sufficiency for its citizens. It may be anticipated that the institutional design implementing this normative account will have to create effective barriers against free-riding, which would otherwise place unfair burdens on only a few member states. Additionally, the conditions for the economic sustainability of this model will have to be analysed, particularly given the negative correlation between economic performance and social needs. For the moment, this articulation of proportionality and subsidiarity offers a promising answer to the tension which was originally raised, by ensuring equality of status amongst all the citizens of the Union, while preserving the nation-state as the key unit of redistributive practices.

Before discussing the idea of an EU threshold of basic goods in greater detail, it is important to explain how this policy would be funded. One way to achieve this goal would be creating a direct tax to be paid by all EU citizens, such as an EU income tax. This option would strengthen the direct link between the representative institutions at the EU level and EU citizens. The tax rate should then be sufficiently lower than the domestic ones to reflect the subsidiary nature of distributive justice in the EU. An alternative option would be building on the existing model of inter-state transfers proportional to national GDPs, increasing their amount to fulfil the EU threshold. This model is consistent with present-day EU democracy, which is partially mediated by national governments. The second option has the advantage of allowing each member state to decide how to raise the amounts to be transferred to the EU budget. This is desirable because national welfare states have different funding models, which, as I have claimed already, should not simply be harmonized.[61] In addition, the second option requires a lower level of institutional reform, making it likely to be more feasible. In the next section, I shall discuss the meaning and implications of an EU threshold of basic goods and test my argument against a number of important objections.

The EU threshold of basic goods

The idea of an EU threshold of basic goods raises a number of questions. A leading issue of controversy is whether the EU threshold should be equivalent to its domestic counterparts. Since many claim that democracy is thicker at the nation-state than at the EU level, the list of basic goods to be provided at each level may be different. A related objection has to do with the comparability of goods across borders. What does it mean to say that every EU citizen should have access to education and healthcare? How much education and how much healthcare, then? Will an EU threshold of sufficiency not eventually imply the standardization of social policy, which we had previously characterized as undesirable, and most likely unfeasible? Another key set of questions is related to prioritization. First, how should member states prioritize assistance to below-the-threshold citizens? Is it permissible that they assist their own nationals first, or should nationality be morally irrelevant below the threshold line? Secondly, I have suggested that, once the threshold has been fulfilled, it is permissible for each member-state to engage in additional redistribution. Yet will this not undermine the idea of equality of status? Finally, what should be done regarding countries where the domestic conception of distributive justice is *less* comprehensive than the threshold of basic goods? In other words, should a country where, say, healthcare access is not currently provided to national citizens be forced to provide such a good to its own (and other EU) citizens? Or should an exception be granted in such cases, as has been done before in other areas of European integration?

The goods which constitute the threshold should be *qualitatively* similar at the EU and the member states level, not identical. In other words, the list of goods has to be the same (i.e. subsistence, healthcare, education, access to justice), but the exact specification of each good may vary according to contextual reasons. The reasons for this claim are twofold. First, the view that the list of goods should vary according to the comprehensiveness of democratic institutions is unsustainable. Although theoretically possible, adding or supressing goods from the list on the grounds that the parliament is more or less representative, that decision making is more or less consensual, or that the chief of the executive is directly or indirectly elected by the citizens would constitute an arbitrary exercise. Secondly, as I have argued in Chapter 1, the universality of this list does not exclude the need for local (or supranational) *interpretation*. For example, healthcare access will imply different types of provision in tropical countries than in countries with a mild climate. Thus, the health policy of a given state may need to put stronger emphasis on preventive healthcare *vis-à-vis* emergency healthcare. Another example is that the educational contents required for social inclusion may vary from state to state. For instance, certain markets may require a wider offer of vocational training, while others may have greater needs for tertiary education. Therefore, by allowing for different meanings of accessing a similar good, the notion of interpretation assures that a common conception of distributive justice does not imply the standardization of social policy.[62]

The idea of a threshold presupposes that all citizens below the threshold line enjoy absolute priority over those above it. From a normative standpoint, absolute priority is the only means to guarantee equality of status to all EU citizens. Thus, it will only be permissible for a member state to pursue additional redistributive polices aimed exclusively at its nationals once appropriate measures to raise all other EU citizens to the respective level have been taken. In Chapter 5, I shall explain why this requisite is likely not over demanding. In turn, that member states should be allowed to engage with further-than-threshold redistribution within their own borders if they democratically choose to do so is a necessary means for self-government. Notice that this is not inconsistent with the idea of absolute priority *regarding* the threshold line. Within a multilevel polity, there is a diversity of status, and all citizens are said to be equal only with regard to the status which works as common denominator. Thus, a common conception of distributive justice does not imply the levelling down of more generous domestic conceptions of justice, but it does imply the levelling up of more residual ones. A "social Union", which, like the Eurozone, comprises only some of the member states is to be rejected. In fact, the moral hazard of leaving the neediest (or the most prosperous) member states aside is enough to undermine the very idea of social justice in the EU. In Chapter 5, I shall claim that exceptions to this rule can only be justified in transitional terms.

Democratic redistribution in other multilevel polities

Before concluding this chapter, I will briefly address the question of whether the argument presented in the preceding sections applying to the EU could be extended to other multilevel polities. Recall that the two main claims presented in the second part of this chapter were (i) responsibilities to fulfil social rights should be shared by all levels of government which integrate the institutional architecture of a democratic polity, and (ii) the principles of proportionality and subsidiarity offer appropriate guidelines to address the tension between equality of status and self-government. While the first proposition is potentially generalizable, the second claim seems to apply only to the historically situated case of the EU. Regarding the first proposition, it should be noted that equating democracy with different levels of government and citizenship is not an exclusive practice of the EU. In fact, many other polities distribute democratic competences, as well as rights and duties, across multilevel structures. As I have argued, distributive claims grounded in the ideal of democratic redistribution can be plausibly raised at any level of government where democracy is sufficiently institutionalized.

The reason mentioned here – that it would be unfair to place all the burdens of social citizenship in only one of the levels – fully applies to other multilevel polities. Accordingly, proposition (i) applies not only to the EU, but also to Belgium, Germany, Switzerland, the United States, and other federal democracies.

By contrast, the criteria to allocate responsibilities to fulfil the democratic duty to redistribute may vary from polity to polity. As I have suggested, the desirable balance between equality of status and self-government has to take into account the political and sociological features of the polity under consideration. This includes the current distribution of power across different levels of government, the comprehensiveness of coercive and democratic institutions, and the particular features of the *demos/demoi*. When these features are considered, one is led to think that democratic redistribution has different implications in multilevel polities which are clearly dissimilar. The two following aspects are illustrative. First, unlike the EU, some multilevel structures are fully devised states. Consider, for instance, the cases of Belgium and Switzerland. Since a state presupposes a considerable degree of centralization, one may anticipate a bigger distributive role for the federal government when compared to the EU. Secondly, in a few multilevel polities the differences between the various *demoi* are not associated with distinctions between different nations. This is the case of the United States and Germany. Since a nationally unified *demos* typically shows a higher degree of social solidarity than a multiplicity of *demoi*, one may once again expect a more active role of the federal government, *vis-à-vis* supranational EU institutions. All this suggests that proposition (ii) should not necessarily be applied beyond the EU and that the particular features of each multilevel polity will shape the way in which responsibilities for justice should be allocated. Therefore, if democratic redistribution is to be extended to other multilevel polities, further discussion will be in order.

IV. Conclusion

I have argued that the duty of democratic redistribution, in the terms described in Chapter 1, applies to the EU. I claimed that the EU constitutes a specialized system of coercion, within the domains of its regulatory competences. I further argued that the EU is a demoicracy, with key democratic institutions, a citizenship status, and a plurality of *demoi*. I concluded that the EU is not just an intergovernmental organization but a functioning demoicracy. I argued that, in a multilevel polity such as the EU, responsibilities to fulfil the democratic duty to redistribute should be shared by the three levels of government – local, national, and supranational. I claimed that the existing tension between equality of status and self-government can be successfully addressed by relying on the familiar principles of proportionality and subsidiarity. In practice, this means that the EU should act as a safety net for domestic social citizenship, supplementing national welfare systems whenever they fail to meet the requirements of the democratic duty to redistribute. Hence, redistribution across the Union will only happen if a member state does not have the resources to assure the attainment of the threshold by its own citizens. This proposal is consistent with a plurality of welfare models in the EU, which locally interpret what it means to have access to each of the basic goods. Furthermore, each member state will be allowed to pursue redistribution beyond the threshold level amongst nationals, should it decide to do so.

Notes

1 Max Weber, "Politics as a Vocation", in David Owen and Tracy B. Strong (eds), *The Vocation Lectures* (Indianapolis, 2004), p. 33.
2 On this point, see, for instance, William E. Scheurman, "Cosmopolitanism and the World State", *Review of International Studies* 40 (2014), pp. 419–441.
3 Jean Bodin, *On Sovereignty: Four Chapters from the Six Books of the Commonwealth*, ed. Julian H. Franklin (Cambridge, 1992), p. 1.
4 In fact, whenever such right and capacity are absent, one may expect to find the oligopoly of force which was typical of feudalism and can still be observed in a number of post-conflict societies. Amongst the many influential studies on the decentralized structures of power of the Middle Ages, it is worth mentioning Marc Bloch, *Feudal Society* (New York, 2014). For an analysis of the oligopoly of violence in post-conflict societies, see Daniel Lambach, "Oligopolies of Violence in Post-Conflict Societies", *German Institute of Global and Area Studies Working Papers* 62 (2007).
5 Both of these actors acted as monopolists, but their jurisdiction was much more circumscribed than that of the nation-state. Thus the nation-state is not the only form of unrivalled monopolist power one can think of. On this point, see Lauren Benton, *Law and Colonial Cultures: Legal Regimes in World History 1400–1900* (Cambridge, 2002).
6 There is no consensus as to which of these tasks should be the subject matter of specialized literature. For example, while Scott Anderson claims that the study of coercion should focus on enforcement institutions, Grant Lamond argues that "the legal authorization of physical force and sanctions, rather than the existence of enforcement institutions, is the appropriate focus for these enquiries". See Scott Anderson, "The Enforcement Approach to Coercion", *Journal of Ethics and Social Philosophy* 5 (2010), pp. 1–31; and Grant Lamond, "The Coerciveness of Law", *Oxford Journal of Legal Studies* 20 (2000), pp. 39–62.
7 The conditions under which coercion is legitimate have been an issue of much controversy, since the publication of Robert Nozick's seminal article on this topic. In this chapter, I will stress the link between the legitimacy of a coercive *act* and the legitimacy of the *institution* which enacted it. See Robert Nozick, "Coercion", in Sidney Morgenbesser, Patrick Suppes, and Morton White (eds), *Philosophy, Science, and Method: Essays in Honor of Ernest Nagel* (New York, 1969), pp. 440–472.

8 It should be acknowledged that preferences for security, economic growth, and reputation vary across states. For example, a low preference for reputation may help to explain the recent withdrawal of Gambia from the ICC. Notice, however, that this does not necessarily undermine the coercive nature of the ICC. In fact, given that the overwhelming majority of countries stay in the convention when they *could* otherwise leave it, it may be argued that the reputational costs are, indeed, sufficiently high to enforce compliance. On the role played by reputation in international politics see, for instance, Rachel Brewster, "Unpacking the State's Reputation", *Harvard International Law Journal* 50 (2009), pp. 231–269.

9 Andrew T. Guzman, *How International Law Works: A Rational Choice Theory* (Oxford, 2008).

10 See the *Texas* v. *White* decision.

11 Comparative Constitutions Project, quoted by Robert J. Barro, "The Right to Secede", https://scholar.harvard.edu/files/barro/files/secede_ny_daily_new s_032014.pdf (Accessed 8 May 2018).

12 For instance, economic sanctions over the exports of a country will affect its economic performance, ultimately harming its citizens.

13 Michael Tomz, "The Effect of International Law on Preferences and Beliefs", Working Paper (Stanford, 2008).

14 George W. Downs and Michael A. Jones, "Reputation, Compliance, and International Law", *Journal of Legal Studies* 31 (2002), p. S96.

15 EUR-Lex, "Precedence of European Law", http://eur-lex.europa.eu/legal-cont ent/EN/TXT/?uri= URISERV%3Al14548 (Accessed 6 December 2018).

16 Ibid.

17 EUR-Lex, "The Direct Effect of European Law", http://eur-lex.europa.eu/legal -content/EN/TXT/?URL=URISE RV%3Al14547 (Accessed 6 December 2018).

18 Ibid.

19 Judgment of the court of 15 July 1964, *Flaminio Costa* v. *ENEL*.

20 It may be argued that national courts do not always accept the automatic precedence of EU law. For instance, the German Constitutional Court has occasionally disputed such precedence by setting constitutional limits to compliance. Yet in cases of constitutional conflict, member states tend to look for exceptions or opt-outs at EU level, rather than not complying with EU law. In other words, they solve disputes within the framework of EU law.

21 *Treaty on the Functioning of the European Union*, Article 260.

22 The main changes regarding sanctioning procedures introduced by the Lisbon Treaty are discussed in *Communication from the Commission – Implementation of Article 260(3) of the Treaty* (2011).

23 Melanie Smith, "The Evolution of Infringement and Sanction Procedures: Of Pilots, Diversion, Collisions, and Circling", in *The Oxford Handbook of European Union Law* (Oxford, 2015), pp. 372–373.

24 Robert Dahl, *Democracy and Its Critics* (New Haven, 1989), p. 221.

25 Robert Dahl, "Can International Organizations Be Democratic? A Skeptic's View", in Ian Shapiro and Casiano Hacker-Cordon (eds), *Democracy's Edges* (Cambridge, 1999), pp. 19–36.

26 See, respectively, Arend Lijphart, *Patterns of Democracy: Government Forms and Performance in Twenty-Six Countries* (Yale, 1999); and David Held, *Models of Democracy* (Cambridge, 2006).

27 In Chapter 5, I shall discuss whether such consensus exists in the EU as far as distributive values are concerned.

28 Benedict Anderson, *Imagined Communities: Reflections on the Origin and Spread of Nationalism* (London, 2006).

29 For an influential statement of the "no-*demos*" thesis, see Dieter Grimm, "Does Europe Need a Constitution?", *European Law Journal* 1 (1995), pp. 282–302.

30 Kalypso Nicolaidis, "The Idea of European Demoicracy", in Julie Dickson and Pavlos Eleftheriadis, *Philosophical Foundations of European Law* (Oxford, 2012), pp. 256.

31 In light of this distinction, I agree with Miriam Ronzoni's contention that, *at the institutional level*, demoicracy can lead either to a particular form of inter-governmentalism or to a specific type of federalism. However, if demoicracy is not a genuine third way, this does not mean that this conceptual framework is useless, as Ronzoni acknowledges. As we shall see, the version of demoicracy which is both horizontal and vertical is clearly different from the traditional model of federalism. See Miriam Ronzoni, "The European Union as a Demoicracy: Really a Third Way?", *European Journal of Political Theory* 16 (2017), pp. 210–234.

32 Willem Maas, "Varieties of Multilevel Citizenship", in William Maas (ed.), *Multilevel Citizenship* (Philadelphia, 2013), pp. viii–1.

33 Ibid.

34 I share Andrew Moravcsik's assumption that these two concepts are in tension: comprehensive democratic institutions are typical of a polity, not of an international organization. Yet my argument follows a logic opposite to his. While he argues that because the EU is an international organization it does not make sense to speak of an EU democratic deficit, I will claim that, because the EU is vertically demoicratic, it cannot be plausibly regarded as an international organization. See Andrew Moravcsik, "In Defence of the Democratic Deficit: Reassessing Legitimacy in the European Union", *Journal of Common Market Studies* 40 (2002), pp. 603–624.

35 See, for instance, Karen J. Alter, "Who are the 'Masters of the Treaty'?: European Governments and the European Court of Justice", *International Organization* 52 (1998), pp. 121–147; Ernst B. Haas, "Turbulent Fields and the Theory of Regional Integration", *International Organization* 30 (1976); Stanley Hoffmann, "Obstinate or Obsolete? The Fate of the Nation-State and the Case of Western Europe", *Daedalus* 95 (1966), pp. 862–915; Paul Pierson, "The Path to European Integration: A Historical-Institutionalist Analysis", in Wayne Sandholtz and Alec Stone Sweet (eds), *European Integration and Supranational Governance* (Oxford, 1998), pp. 28–59; Andrew Moravcsik and F. Schimmelfennig, "Liberal Intergovernmentalism", in A. Wiener and T. Diez (eds), *European Integration Theory* (Oxford, 2009), pp. 67–87; J. H. H. Weiler, "The Transformation of Europe", *The Yale Law Journal* 100 (1991), pp. 2403–2483.

36 Kazuto Suzuki, "The EU as a Regulatory Empire", *Hokkaido Journal of New Global Law and Policy* 2 (2009), pp. 141–159.

37 An example of such view is Liphjart, *Patterns of Democracy*. It should be noted that, unlike in federal states, elections for this upper chamber are not organized or even harmonized at the EU level. The council represents, therefore, separate

demoi rather than the constitutive units of a federal *demos*. As we shall see, this is one feature that makes it more plausible to describe the EU as a *demoicracy*, not a federal democracy.

38 In fact, the Treaty of Lisbon increased considerably the powers of the Parliament, extending the procedure of co-decision to most of the policy areas within the EU competence range.

39 *Treaty on the Functioning of the European Union*, Article 267.

40 Matias Kumm, "Beyond Golf Clubs and the Judicialization of Politics: Why Europe Has a Constitution Properly so Called", *The American Journal of Comparative Law* 54 (2006), pp. 505–530.

41 Miguel Poiares Maduro, "O Superavit Democrático Europeu", *Análise Social* 35 (2001), pp. 119–152.

42 Hannah Arendt, *Human Condition* (Chicago, 1998).

43 Rainer Bauböck, "The Three Levels of Citizenship within the European Union", *German Law Journal* 15 (2014), p. 751.

44 Ibid., p. 761.

45 Antje Wiener, "Assessing the Constructive Potential of Union Citizenship – A Socio-Historical Perspective", *European Integration Online Papers* 1 (1997).

46 Espen D. H. Olsen, "European Citizenship: Mixing Nation State and Federal Features with a Cosmopolitan Twist", *Perspectives on European Politics and Society* 14 (2013), p. 508.

47 F. Cheneval and F. Schimmelfennig, "The Case for Demoicracy in the European Union", *Journal of Common Market Studies* 51 (2013), pp. 334–350.

48 Jenna Bednar, "Authority Migration in Federations: A Framework for Analysis", *PS* 37 (2004), p. 403.

49 On this point see Thorsten Huller, "Out of Time? The Democratic Limits of EU Demoicracy", *Journal of European Public Policy* 23 (2016), pp. 1407–1424.

50 Since this study is mainly interested in duties between member states, I leave local citizenship aside.

51 Dimitry Kochenov, "EU Citizenship without Duties", *European Law Journal* 20 (2014), pp. 482–498.

52 Ibid., p. 483.

53 Richard Bellamy, "A Duty-Free Europe? What's Wrong with Kochenov's Account of EU Citizenship Rights", *European Law Journal* 21 (2015), pp. 558–565.

54 Laura Valentini, *Justice in a Globalized World: A Normative Framework* (Oxford, 2011), p. 4.

55 In his essay "Utopia and Violence", Karl Popper illustrates the potential illiberal effects of applying a comprehensive blueprint of justice to a given society. See Karl Popper, "Utopia and Violence", in *Conjectures and Refutations: The Growth of Scientific Knowledge* (London, 1989), pp. 355–363.

56 *Treaty on European Union*, Article 5.

57 *Treaty on European Union*, Article 5.

58 *Treaty on European Union*, Article 5.

59 This approach could still give grounds for important reforms, such as a common unemployment scheme and a common pension system, to mention just two outstanding examples.

60 In legal theory, a variety of proportionality tests with multiple steps is currently available. The last stage of virtually every test is typically the one of greatest philosophical interest. At this stage – dubbed "proportionality in the strict sense" (in continental literature), and "balancing" (in Anglo-American literature) – legal theorists apply one or more auxiliary moral principles to give substantive content to the principle of proportionality. In the EU context, this role has mainly been performed by the principle of subsidiarity. A *legal* test of proportionality, involving the interpretation of formal norms, the assessment of states of necessity, and the delimitation of a margin of appreciation for the courts, would be beyond the scope of this book. For an illustrative example of such a test in a global context, see Kai Möller, *The Global Model of Constitutional Rights* (Oxford, 2012), Chapters 6 and 7.

61 For instance, while certain member states rely mainly on general taxation for the funding of social benefits, some rely on specialized social security contributions, and others on capitalization funds.

62 However, this raises a problem of international comparability of the goods that integrate the threshold. One way of performing a cross-national comparison of goods that are, by definition, heterogeneous would be to develop an index that would allow for different modalities of social provision. Member states would then be required to provide their citizens with a certain level of access to each good (rather than an exact specification of each good). If they lacked the resources to do so, they would be assisted by EU institutions. The exceptions to the domestic character of interpretation are some forms of provision that are intrinsically related to EU demoicracy, thus requiring interpretation at the supranational level. The most notorious example is access to justice, which may justify subsidizing travel to the CJEU's headquarters in Brussels. However, these EU-specific forms of provision seem to be rather limited in scope. In Chapter 4, I shall more thoroughly discuss the notion of interpretation.

3

Economic reciprocity in the EU

I. Introduction

This chapter addresses the question, does the duty of economic reciprocity, as discussed in Chapter 1, apply to the EU? If so, to what extent? I argue that claims of reciprocity in the EU are closely linked to the economic structure of the Union, which I discuss in terms of three main features: the common market, the single currency, and freedom of movement. I argue that the patterns of specialization in the common market produced a "distributive vicious circle", which prevents poorly performing states from improving their condition. This state of affairs is reinforced by a fierce competition amongst member states regarding corporate taxes and labour laws. In turn, I argue that poor policy choices can only partially explain the levels of indebtedness of the currently distressed member states. I claim that the design of the Eurozone and the "distributive vicious circle" I just mentioned played an important role in the origins of the Eurocrisis. In addition, I argue that freedom of movement generates two types of distributive obligations. First, EU mobile workers should be protected from the social risks associated with freedom of movement. Second, all EU workers should be given a fair opportunity to seize jobs in other member states. In order to realize reciprocity in the EU, I propose a combination of pre-distributive and redistributive instruments: (i) an EU Fund for Global Competitiveness (FGC), to be funded by (ii) an EU corporate tax; (iii) an EU Labour Code, establishing minimum social standards, particularly regarding minimum wages and severance payments; (iv) a minimum EU corporate tax rate; (v) a fair euro exchange rate; and (vi) the EU threshold of basic goods discussed in Chapter 2, now defended on the grounds of freedom of movement.

I begin by problematizing the application of the notion of reciprocity to the EU. I then review and criticize a few conceptions of EU reciprocity which are available in the literature. I present an alternative approach to why reciprocity applies to the Union, based on three key features of its economic structure. Subsequently, I turn to a detailed discussion of claims of reciprocity in the context of the common market, the single currency, and freedom of movement, respectively. Each section is structured similarly: it begins by identifying unjust states of affairs, then proceeds to discuss assignment of responsibilities, ending with a presentation of the concrete policy instruments that should be used to realize reciprocity in the EU.

II. Why economic reciprocity applies to the EU

Reciprocity in the EU: what does it mean?

In Chapter 1, I argued that economic reciprocity, understood as mutual advantage and mutual respect, is a requirement of a just market. I claimed that, in an economy with division of labour, jobs are a precondition for each other. Such interdependence, allied with our participation in the market as consumers, generates a shared responsibility for market outcomes. Accordingly, I suggested that labour relations should be duly regulated to assure that each worker receives a fair share of the wealth produced by any cooperative scheme. I further argued that reciprocity should be extended to the broader economic structure, which conditions the outcomes of each micro-level scheme of cooperation. Hence, I claimed that public authorities ought to adopt fair economic and monetary policies to promote a morally permissible economic structure. Furthermore, I suggested that the requirements of reciprocity should be proportional to the degree of economic integration – that is, the comprehensiveness of a shared economic structure. Thus, the requirements of reciprocity are expected to be higher amongst two close economic partners than amongst two states which rarely trade with each other. Nevertheless, a global minimum of reciprocity should apply to the international community as a whole. The main goal of this chapter is to investigate whether the duty of economic reciprocity applies to the EU.

At present, the status of reciprocity in the EU is somewhat ambiguous. For much of its history, the European Community has listed socioeconomic cohesion as one of its main goals. For that purpose, a number of structural funds were devised. The purpose of these funds was twofold. First, they were intended to assist member states in developing socioeconomic infra-structure which would allow them to prosper in a common-market context. Second, they were aimed at compensating member states for certain economic costs of EU accession, namely the loss of competitiveness of traditional sectors and the need to adapt human resources to a new competitive context. It was expected that the combined effects of economic integration and structural funds would lead to the convergence of member states concerning the main socioeconomic indicators. Yet although the gap has decreased considerably since accession in all new member states, it has always been far from being eradicated. In fact, it has widened significantly since the beginning of the financial crisis of 2008. The reasons for the poor performance of the relatively worse-off member states are disputed. While some public actors have claimed that the persistence of this gap is explained by the mismanagement of national governments, others have argued that the rules of the common market and the Eurozone are unfair, thus conducing to the widening of the gap. Is the EU basically done with reciprocity, or is reciprocity needed more than ever?

Even if we agree that there should be *some* reciprocity in the EU, what this means is not straightforward. For some members of the Eurogroup, having access to a common market and a single currency area where the rules are the same for everyone seems already good enough as a matter of reciprocity. In addition, EU citizens are equally free to live and work in the entire territory of the Union, which can be regarded as a generous concession by wealthier member states. The consecutive bailouts in Greece, Ireland, Portugal, and Cyprus funded by all the other Eurozone members may be said to constitute an additional and clear demonstration of solidarity amongst member states. However, for many political activists, realizing the ideal of reciprocity requires more than playing by the same market rules; what matters most is the fairness of these rules. Surely, through EU membership, all member states multiply their chances to prosper. Yet if reciprocity is not only about mutual advantage, something is wrong with a Union that fails to produce convergence, despite decades of integration. Furthermore, the terms of the bailouts may be said to be deeply unfair. In addition, they may be regarded as corrosive of a spirit of membership to a fair EU, which, as suggested in Chapter 1, may harm the prospects of the EU democracy. How should reciprocity in the EU be conceived? What are its implications in terms of public policy at both national and EU level?

The economic structure of the EU: three main features

Claims of reciprocity in the EU have been formulated in diverse ways. A first possibility is to claim that the EU constitutes a basic structure in the Rawlsian sense. In this view, the difference principle should regulate the distribution of wealth not only within the borders of the member states, but also throughout the Union. However, if one can (and should) speak of a European structure, the effects of which "are so profound and present from the start", this structure is *qualitatively* different from the Rawlsian one.[1] The argument that member states share a few key political institutions should not lead us to disregard the fact that a number of other institutions remain mainly, or substantially, designed at the national level. This is the case with (i) the *family* (consider, for instance, policies regarding same-sex marriage); (ii) the *legal system* (for example, trial procedures and crime sentences); and (iii) the *political constitution* (namely, the set of rights and goals recognized beyond the prerequisites of EU membership).

These are three key components of a basic structure, according to Rawls.[2] Accordingly, the requirement that economic inequalities should be attached to offices and positions open to all under conditions of fair equality of opportunity seems disproportional to the level of European integration.[3] Therefore, if there is, indeed, a structure in the EU, the latter does not seem to be a *basic* structure in the Rawlsian sense. In turn, leaving "to the voters and their further philosophical arguments" the decision of whether the difference principle applies to the EU, as Rawls himself suggested, seems to fall short of normative guidance.[4]

A second option is to turn the EU into a transfer union, through redistributive mechanisms such as a "Euro-Stipendium" or a "Euro-Dividend".[5] Under these approaches, all EU citizens would be entitled to a social benefit, which would either be means-tested (in the former case) or be an unconditional basic income (in the latter case). Although, as Chapter 1 has claimed, there are good reasons to redistribute in the EU, a view which is exclusively redistributive fails to address economic unfairness at its source – that is, at the level of the rules of cooperation. As I have suggested in Chapter 1, it is morally preferable to prevent an unjust distribution of wealth in the EU through pre-distributive policies than to compensate for it via "massive and systematic transfers across the borders of the member states".[6] In addition, as we shall see in Chapter 5, pre-distribution seems more politically feasible than large-scale redistribution in the EU, particularly given that the bonds of social solidarity are weak. Another variant of the argument in the existing literature states that justice in the EU applies (only) to "the *public goods* generated by participation in European institutions", or "the wealth generated by the process of economic integration".[7] Yet again, improving the distribution of the gains of EU integration *without* changing the unfair rules of the common market and the Eurozone that produce that distribution in the first place seems a second-best remedy for injustice.

Alternatively, I propose that claims of reciprocity in the EU are closely linked to its economic structure, thus mainly requiring pre-distribution. What is an "economic structure"? In Chapter 1, I defined economic structure as the key features of a system of cooperation which pervasively shape its outcomes, regardless of individual efforts. This structure includes features as diverse as patterns of division of labour, conditions of access to capital, endowments of natural resources, terms of trade for goods and services, and formal rules of cooperation, such as taxes and tariffs, exchange rates, and border control regimes. In the context of EU membership, one may think of three structural features with a particularly pervasive impact on the distribution of wealth across the Union: the *common market*, the *single currency*, and *freedom of movement*. If it is true that not all member states belong to the Eurozone, the fate of the euro seems to be shaping the future of the European Union as a whole.[8] On the other hand, the fact that some non-EU members participate in one or more – but not all – aspects of these cooperative schemes does not mean that they are entitled to the *same* type of reciprocity which applies amongst member states. An illustrative example is that Switzerland and Norway do not share their natural resources with the EU member states.[9] Thus this chapter will focus on the three features previously mentioned not because they are the only relevant aspects of the EU economic structure, but because their implications are so profound.

This approach is preferable to the previous alternatives because it allow us to integrate the insight that reciprocity should be proportional to the degree of economic integration and the intensity of economic exchange, as discussed in Chapter 1. In other words, it allows us to distinguish claims of reciprocity in the EU from those more strictly related to the nation-state, on the one hand, and claims of global reciprocity, related for instance to WTO membership, on the other. While differentiating reciprocity claims, the present approach does not exclude any of them. In fact, given that different levels of government presuppose economic structures of different scopes, it is consistent to simultaneously support comprehensive distributive justice at the domestic level and a minimum of reciprocity globally. In addition, the present approach will favour the adoption of pre-distributive policies – namely labour law and economic and monetary policy – which, as I have argued, is more desirable and politically feasible than redistribution. The reason is that the economic structure approach focuses, by definition, on the rules of the game, instead of taking unjust market outcomes for granted. A question which remains to be addressed is how exactly economic structure translates into duties which can be assigned to certain agents. In other words, should this chapter be about individuals, firms, or states? The next section will deal with this and other issues.

Two methodological concerns

A preliminary methodological concern has to do with the relevant unit of analysis for reciprocity in the EU context. Is reciprocity to be realized amongst EU citizens, amongst EU firms, or amongst EU member states? In Chapter 1, I argued that reciprocity applies to both labour transactions and the economic structure more broadly. I then presented two reasons why it is better to think of reciprocity in terms of states than in terms of individuals or firms. First, only states (and some supranational organizations) have the coercive means to enforce reciprocity, through pre-distributive instruments such as labour law and economic policy. In a context of limited altruism, it would be implausible to expect that reciprocity would emerge spontaneously amongst individuals or firms. Secondly, the state corresponds with the most comprehensively institutionalized economic structure currently available. This structure includes features as varied as legal requirements for the licensing of firms, competition and insolvency laws, exchange rate and border control regimes, central banking model, and so on. In addition, this domestic structure constitutes the basis for the relations with other economic structures beyond borders, such as the EU and the WTO. Therefore, claims of reciprocity applied to the EU may be formulated at three different levels: (i) the labour relations within the EU; (ii) the main defining features of the EU economic structure; and (iii) the interplay of national economic structures in a context of freedom of movement of people, goods, and capital. This chapter will address all three dimensions.

Another important concern is how to reconcile reciprocity-based claims which seem to point in opposite directions. On the one hand, one may argue that poorly performing member states should assume responsibility for the mismanagement of their resources. This means not only that they are not entitled to any sort of assistance, but also that they may be called to answer for the negative externalities that their economies have caused in the "well-behaved" member states. On the other hand, one may claim that both labour relations and the economic structure of the Union are unfair. This suggests that the rules of cooperation should be changed, and that compensation may be due for the harmful effects of unfair rules in countries such as Greece. Which of the two types of claim is foremost? To address these and other claims, one needs to unpack the many issues which are at stake. As I have argued in Chapter 1, injustices may be caused by a variety of actors and may require different types of remedies. For instance, the claim that member states should be held responsible for their policy choices in the past says very little about the fairness of the exchange rate of the single currency. Thus reciprocity-based claims should not mix different types of problems but address them separately. This is why this chapter is organized around three key components of the economic structure of the EU: common market, single currency, and freedom of movement. In what follows, I shall discuss them in turn.

III. Reciprocity in the common market

The Ricardian hypothesis

Liberal trade policy is grounded on a very simple idea: that through international trade, every country becomes better off. An explanation for this hypothesis was advanced for the first time by economist David Ricardo.[10] Ricardo claims that, when two countries trade with each other, their aggregated wealth increases. The reason is that in the long run, each country specializes in the goods which it produces *relatively* more efficiently – that is, where it has *comparative advantage*. Ricardo's key finding is that, even when one country is much more productive than another in absolute terms, both will become better off if they trade with each other. When each country focuses its resources on what it does best, the amount of goods that they can produce – that is, their *production possibility frontiers* – expands significantly. As the New Trade Theory pioneered by Paul Krugman has observed, this comparative advantage is reinforced by *returns to scale*, as further efficiency gains arise from an increase in the scale of production.[11] Thus, consider a world where countries A and B are isolated, with each producing both goods 1 and 2. As they open their economies to international trade, A will gradually specialize in, and export much of, say, good 1, while B will specialize in, and export much of, good 2. (How much will be exported depends on the relative prices of the goods – that is, the *terms of trade*). The resulting equilibrium is better than the one without trade, since many more units of each good are produced and consumed overall. If later models have certainly increased in sophistication, Ricardo's critical insight that international trade increases "the size of the pie" remains at the heart of international trade theory.[12]

Ricardo's hypothesis has critical distributive implications. Indeed, while improving the size of the pie is certainly a positive aspect, the effects on the size of each slice also must be taken in account. Thus, international trade changes domestic distributions of income mainly for two reasons.[13] First, trade has a significant impact on employment. In fact, international trade not only creates and destroys jobs, but it also changes relative wages. As has been suggested, "the efficiency gains caused by trade liberalization are expected to lead to positive overall employment effects, in terms of quantity of jobs, wages earned or a combination of both".[14] Yet, in the absence of appropriate distributive policies, this may not apply to everyone. In fact, "[a]verage wage increases may [...] hide distributional changes that affect some workers negatively".[15] International trade theory has assumed that, in the long run, the short-run "losers" of international trade will become "winners" by moving to flourishing industries and services. However, in recent years, many of the individuals who have lost jobs due to fierce international competition seem unable to return to the job market, having thus become *structurally unemployed*.[16] This is a reason why a number of recent proposals of social policy have focused their attention on the "activation" of workers, mainly by improving their skills.[17] Yet this approach begs the question of who should fund a large-scale, and continuous, requalification of human capital. This question is critical for the EU, since certain member states lack the resources to fund such reforms.[18]

Secondly, international trade impacts the productive pattern of each country, shaping its position in the international value chain. As I have mentioned, whenever two countries engage with international trade, their production shifts to the goods which they can produce relatively more efficiently. Now, under certain conditions, such as pronounced asymmetries of technology and skills, a country may end up by specializing in goods of *low* added value – say, cheap clothing – while the other specializes in goods of *high* added value – say, automobiles.[19] In fact, it has been demonstrated that "the quality a country tends to export depends positively on its level of development, as it is correlated with per capita GDP".[20] From a distributive standpoint, this imbalance of the terms of trade is problematic. One reason is that goods of higher added value generate higher income. Theoretically, this effect would be compensated via quantity of production. Thus, country A would produce enough cheap clothing to afford a car produced by country B, and both would be equally better off through trade. However, globalization has made competition in low added value sectors typically much fiercer than in the high added value ones. Thus, countries which had managed to position themselves at higher stages of the value chain have become relatively much better off than others. Another reason for concern is that, once comparative advantages are established, it can be very hard for a country to move up the value chain. This, as we shall see, is particularly true for the EU common market.

A distributive vicious circle in the common market

While the common market has been a source of prosperity for all EU member states, certain aspects of economic integration have rendered it unfair.[21] A primary problem is related to the patterns of specialization within the Union. Thus "the 'richer', northern countries tend to export higher quality products than the 'poorer', southern countries".[22] As I have suggested, these patterns might not have raised distributive issues if the EU did not trade so intensively with the rest of the world. In that case, southern member states might have been able to sustain their competitive advantages, since northern states would still need the goods they produced. Yet with increasing competition at the global level resulting from trade liberalization, the competitive position of member states that had specialized in the "low-cost" segment gradually deteriorated.[23] In fact, "economic liberalizations have added to the global market place countries that have vast supplies of labour but very little capital".[24] Thus Germany and France could now buy even cheaper clothing from the rest of the world, while their technology-based exports remained highly competitive. This did not apply to most of the cheap exports of southern countries, which lost much of their competitiveness.[25] In addition, they faced hardship in shifting their production towards "high-quality" segments, where northern member states had developed pronounced comparative advantages, given that protectionist policies are not available.[26] In certain aspects, the divide between the north and south "is more evident than it was 10 or 20 years ago".[27] This suggests that the chances to prosper in the common market became uneven.

This state of affairs is self-reinforcing. As real income in "low-cost" member states decreases with the loss of competitiveness, so do salaries. This means less savings, which, in turn, means less capital available for investment. At the same time, as opportunities become so unequal amongst member states, many of the highly skilled workers of poorly performing economies migrate to the better performing ones, in a quest for better jobs. This further widens the gap by transferring innovation potential from the worse-off countries to the better-off ones. Being left with virtually no chance of moving up the value chain, these member states are under pressure to become more competitive at its bottom. With this goal in mind, they lower real salaries, decrease the level of social provision, and relax labour laws again and again.[28] The result is a lower equilibrium, where workers of "low-cost" economies are in a much worse "starting" position than those of the wealthier member states. Given the decisive role of technology in achieving sustainable comparative advantages, cutting salaries and social benefits may not be enough to solve the problem – in fact, it may make things worse.[29] The real source of the problem is that "most high technology activities are unevenly distributed across the regions of EU-27".[30] Thus the southern barista may serve more and more coffees, do extra hours of work, and experience a loss of their social rights, but, if their coffee machine is slower, they may never be a match for northern productivity standards.[31] In this sense, the different outcomes achieved by member states are structural and, to a certain extent, independent of individual efforts.

This distributive vicious circle has been deepened by the increasing level of tax competition within the EU, with serious implications for the sustainability of the EU welfare systems. In fact, "because the EU is not a federation and because its national governments worry more about their national balance of payments and export earnings, their policies are often highly competitive with one another".[32] This notably applies to corporate taxes, where competition amongst member states is fierce. Thus, in recent years, many EU firms have delocalized their headquarters to the territory of other member states for the sole purpose of paying less tax. This practice is unfair because it constitutes a form of free-riding.[33] Although tax competition can also be disadvantageous for well-performing member states, it is particularly harmful for those which are already burdened by high levels of unemployment or public debt and cannot afford to play the fiscal game. Indeed, these states are faced with a dilemma: on the one hand, they are pressured to follow the tax cuts elsewhere to contain their loss of competitiveness; on the other, doing so may put their welfare systems at risk and may prevent them from complying with the conditions of the Stability and Growth Plan, which would trigger excessive deficit procedures. This puts them into a fiscal deadlock that they cannot exit on their own.

A similar reasoning applies to labour markets, where the incentives to liberalize have raised a collective action problem. Given that each member state is competing against its neighbour, it has a strong incentive to relax its labour laws to attract more investment. At the same time, the opportunity cost of preserving high labour standards becomes higher as the other member states liberalize their labour markets. This process has the potential to bring all member states to social equilibria that they did not desire in the first place.[34] As I have claimed, the pressure to liberalize is typically stronger in labour-intensive economies, where the source of comparative advantage is the low cost of labour. This particularly applies to small member states, which "have greater trade vulnerability than large countries".[35] Thus in a number of peripheral member states, minimum wages are not high enough to cover living expenses, or are even far below this level.[36] This is tragic, since large segments of the population of these states earn the minimum wage.[37] And yet, since the EU is now a global player, labour may never be sufficiently cheap and flexible. In fact, member states are not only competing amongst each other, but also against countries that do not have a welfare state and where firms have, by definition, lower cost structures. This is not to suggest that European labour markets should not be modernized, but any reform should take distributional goals into account. In other words, the European Social Model should not simply "be dropped as a competitive liability".[38]

Reciprocity in the common market

The problems previously listed ought to be addressed at the EU level for at least two reasons. First, most policy instruments which were routinely used to deal with external shocks challenging domestic social models have been ruled out by EU law.[39] Currently unauthorized practices include the following: (i) tariffs on the imports from other member states; (ii) increases in public spending beyond the limits set by the Stability and Growth Plan; (iii) the use of publicly owned enterprises as an employment buffer; (iv) the use of state aid and public procurement as instruments of regional and sectoral policy; (v) controls of capital movements; and (vi) depreciation of the national currency.[40] This lack of means suggests that any effective escape from the distributive vicious circle can no longer be found (at least exclusively) at the national level. Second, given that "the whole process of integration is fundamentally dynamic, it constantly develops a situation in which benefits and losses are created and distributed unevenly".[41] However, this distribution should not be taken for granted. According to Iris Young's model of social connection discussed in Chapter 1, a scenario of economic integration, such as the common market, generates responsibilities for distributive justice. Along Ricardian lines, the point is not to renounce free trade but to improve the distribution of its outcomes. Any instrument intended to achieve such a goal will require coordination at the EU level.

I will now turn my attention to possible remedies for the present state of affairs. For that purpose, it is important to recall the arguments of Chapter 1. There, I claimed that there are two fundamental types of solution for distributive unbalances: pre-distribution – that is, equalizing opportunities, mainly by adjusting the rules of the market; and redistribution – that is, transferring wealth from some individuals (or states) to others through fiscal and social policy. I further argued that there should be a preference for pre-distribution, since it is better to prevent an evil than to compensate people for it. This claim is particularly pertinent to the common market. Breaking the distributive vicious circle described in the previous sections seems much more promising than compensating the worse-off via welfare transfers. If "low-cost" member states manage to improve their competitive position, they will need to rely less and less on other member states. In that case, any move below the EU threshold of basic goods presented in Chapter 2 will likely be temporary, as member states will in principle be able to provide decent social welfare to their national citizens. This will make EU redistribution merely residual. In addition, pre-distribution seems much more feasible than large-scale redistribution, as we shall see in the last two chapters of this book. However, I have also claimed that redistribution will be needed in cases in which pre-distribution is neither possible nor effective.

I propose the following two strategies to achieve stronger reciprocity in the common market: (i) *establishing minimum standards* that limit competitive practices in the EU; and (ii) *improving the competitive position* of the member states that are being left behind. I shall introduce each strategy in turn. The first strategy is entirely pre-distributive and aims at levelling the playing field in the EU. It could be put in practice through two key policy instruments: a *minimum EU corporate tax rate* and an *EU Labour Code*. What would these instruments entail? The minimum corporate tax rate would have straightforward implications: member states would not be allowed to charge the firms operating under their jurisdiction with rates lower than the EU minimum.[42] However, member states would be free to set higher rates. In turn, an EU Labour Code would imply that certain basic parameters of the labour market would be regulated at the EU level – most notably, minimum wages and severance payments.[43] Here, the idea would be to coordinate minimum levels of social protection for EU workers adjusted to purchasing power parities.[44] This would again leave member states free to set higher-than-minimum levels of protection for their workers. This proposal would imply the extension of the existing legal framework at the EU level, which regulates issues such as working conditions and child labour, but leaves matters of social inclusion aside. These two instruments would help the EU move from a competitive to a more cooperative paradigm of the common market.

The rationale behind these instruments is threefold. First, they are intended to solve the collective action problem described previously. Given the intensity of international competition, fair labour laws are only possible if member states coordinate with each other – otherwise, any failure to liberalize will have overly high costs in terms of competitiveness. Although this argument primarily applies to labour-intensive states, coordination at EU level would also empower the technology-intensive member states to protect the workers in their (relatively small) labour-intensive sectors through pre-distributive policies. Secondly, disabling "social dumping" as a systematic economic policy would protect poorer member states from the unfair and often coercive behaviour of the wealthier ones.[45] Through a variety of institutional channels, wealthy member states have continuously pushed for the liberalization of labour markets as a strategy to correct the imbalances of southern economies, excusing themselves from taking part in a more sustainable solution for the distributive vicious circle.[46] Thirdly, a fair EU Labour Code setting common minimum standards would ensure a basic degree of reciprocity amongst all EU workers, while empowering them to resist arbitrary power, in line with the argument of Chapter 1.[47] This is consistent with the very high degree of economic integration of the common market. In addition, there is no reason to regulate goods, services, and capital while leaving labour and corporate taxes aside. Regulating labour and corporate taxes would complete the single market and level its playing field.

The second strategy to achieve reciprocity in the common market is to improve the competitive position of the worse-performing member states. This could be done by creating an EU FGC to be funded by a small EU corporate tax rate. The goal would be to give member states the budgetary capacity to execute structural reforms that create technological advantages and readjust the skills of their workforce to the market needs. This proposal goes beyond the current state of affairs in two ways. First, the continuing call for structural reforms in the EU has been strikingly detached from any distributive considerations. It is not enough to say that Greece must invest much more in innovation and training – the question is how any substantial spending in such areas could be afforded by a state that clearly lacks the resources to do so.[48] This would then be the purpose of the FGC. Secondly, unlike the existing structural funds and the European Globalization Adjustment Fund, the FGC would have its own source of revenues – a dedicated EU corporate tax, which would be collected by national authorities and transferred to the EU budget.[49] This tax would establish a direct link between the wealth generated by the common market and the mechanisms to assist member states where the burdens of integration are heavier.[50] The combined effect of the two strategies would offer a desirable "balancing of market-enhancing and market-correcting concerns at the European level".[51]

A number of difficulties arise for the views presented here. First, part of my claim has emphasized the north–south dichotomy in the EU, rather than that of west–east. Does my argument apply to the eastern region, too? Secondly, it may be argued that these proposals would imply a significant loss of competitiveness in the global market for a number of countries in the Union – particularly, the most distressed ones. This would only reinforce the struggle to return to growth that the EU has experienced in the last few years. Thirdly, it may be claimed that legislating welfare at the EU level would constitute an undesirable loss of sovereignty for its member states. Social policy rightly is a competence of the nation-state, and there are no provisions in the EU treaties which would allow for such reforms. Fourthly, there is an issue of national responsibility. Why should some member states pay for the inefficiencies and bad choices of others? If a member state made the right policy choices, if it managed to move up the value chain, if it saved enough resources to face adverse times, why should it be called to share its gains? Finally, it may be argued that this ambitious combination of pre- and redistribution would only be feasible if there were a strong sense of social solidarity across the Union. However, such solidarity is largely absent. Indeed, citizens of many member states seem to be eager to reduce their bill of EU membership, rather than increase it. How can these objections be addressed?

First, let me clarify the implications of my argument for eastern Europe. I have focused my attention on the north–south divide for two reasons. One, the long-term consequences of economic integration can be better assessed in those member states which have been part of the Union for a longer period. For instance, it may be argued that the economic imbalances of Hungary and Romania will be healed by the ongoing transition process – a claim that hardly applies to Greece and Portugal, which have been part of the Union for more than 30 years. Two, the current economic crisis has hit the south more harshly than the east, leading most public debates on the social consequences of economic integration to focus on that region. However, it can be anticipated that the argument presented so far will suit the eastern member states in the near future. Eastern economies "are now increasingly specialized in labour-intensive export industries", being entirely dependent on foreign capital.[52] Their comparative advantage lies on a combination of relatively cheap and skilful workforce. The existing innovation is, in fact, "rather limited in scale".[53] If the eastern states lose their current comparative advantage – which does not seem so unlikely given that Asia is catching up in education and has lower salaries – the transnational companies that contribute strongly to their growth will most likely delocalize their production. This indicates the extreme vulnerability of the eastern model to changing investment decisions by other member states and global actors, in a way which is analogous to southern Europe.

A few remarks should be made regarding the remaining objections. First, the claim that distributive justice would leave the EU in a worse competitive position is disputable. In fact, several authoritative studies have shown that decent labour regulation and lower levels of inequality are not necessarily bad for growth – in fact, they may be a precondition for it.[54] The key question is, rather, how exactly each distributive policy should be devised to minimize efficiency costs and to allow for a reasonable degree of flexibility at the state level. For instance, in the case of an EU minimum wage, this could be achieved through a coordination policy which would preserve the wage-setting system of each member state and would be supported by sustained productivity gains resulting from the investments by the FGC. This issue, as well as the question of whether distributive justice is compatible with the existing degree of social solidarity in the EU, will be discussed in Chapter 5. Secondly, even if distributive justice turned out to be economically costly, that does not mean that it should be rejected. Undoubtedly, it was immoral to advocate against the abolition of slavery in the United States on grounds of its implications for the cotton industry. As I have argued in Chapter 2, the claim that distributive justice should remain within the exclusive domain of the nation-state is flawed. Given the current level of integration in the EU, justice claims are stringent. Yet the principle of national responsibility has, as we shall see, a role to play in the configuration of a just Europe, thus deserving careful treatment. Since this principle has often been evoked in the context of the sovereign debt crisis, I shall discuss it in the following section, which addresses claims of reciprocity in the Eurozone.

IV. Reciprocity in the Eurozone

Holding nations responsible … for what?

In recent years, a number of claims of national responsibility have marked the debate on the sovereign debt crisis. One of the main arguments is that member states that are highly indebted owe their position to poor policy choices in the past. They were living high for many years, surfing the wave of cheap credit of the pre-crisis period, spending more than they could afford. Thus, their economies developed a number of imbalances, including chronic deficits in the external accounts, dysfunctional monopolies in key economic sectors, and incentives for rent-seeking. In contrast, relatively well-performing member states have saved in times of prosperity, reformed their public sectors, and wisely invested their resources in research and innovation, as well as in their human resources. It is therefore not surprising that some member states are doing much better than others. Accordingly, "[f]or all the brave talk about solidarity among euroland member states, their taxpayers don't want to put on the table the money which might keep their badly behaved and undisciplined neighbours afloat".[55] These taxpayers "believe that this is not *their* cause and the nations which misbehaved should pay for the effects by themselves".[56] In political theory debates, David Miller has been the most influential voice defending the thesis that past policy choices are critical for present-day distributive assessments, which he famously illustrates through an analogy to the story of the ant and the grasshopper.[57]

I shall take no issue with the general principle that states should be ready to face the consequences of their choices. My questions, rather, will touch on (i) the range of public choices to which this principle applies and (ii) the extent to which it applies *absolutely*, that is, without having to be balanced against competing principles. Regarding the first question, the principle of national responsibility seems to apply only to policy domains controlled by a given state. In other words, a state can be deemed responsible for a certain state of affairs only if, by engaging with different policies, an alternative state of affairs could have been produced. For instance, it would seem odd to blame Chile for the escalation of tensions in the Middle East, or Botswana for the global financial crisis. As far as the second question is concerned, collective responsibility can only apply in absolute terms in the presence of an exclusive causal link between a certain policy choice and a given consequence. Instead, if policy X is only one amongst other conditions that produced the result Y, then national responsibility will have to be balanced against other principles, such as economic reciprocity. For example, corruption is one of the causes of the underdevelopment of a number of states, yet other historical factors, such as colonialism, have also played a very important role. These two nuances regarding national responsibility will be critical for our discussion on the Eurozone.

How far in the past should we look to assess national responsibility? This question has been symbolically put on the table by the Greek government. State officials have suggested that if Greece's poor policy choices in the 1990s and 2000s need to be taken into account for present distributive purposes, what about German war debts? In other words, do unfulfilled duties fade as time passes by, or do they "accumulate with compound interest the longer they remain undischarged"?[58] Since it seems clear that a look back into the past has to stop somewhere, the issue is one of criterion. The key question is, how can we link past wrongdoing with present justice claims? A plausible answer may be formulated as follows: *past wrongdoing may give rise to justice claims whenever the harm caused in the past is reproduced in the present.*[59] Note that by "reproduced" I do not mean the somewhat trivial proposition that the present reality is different from what it would have been if the wrongdoing had not been perpetrated. There is not much to compensate on this grounds, particularly given the absence of a counterfactual scenario.[60] Even if such counterfactual information was available, it would be hard to explain why the present-day individual would have to rectify a past action done by someone else if there was no reference to a lasting benefit of such action. Therefore, by "reproduced" I mean the *continuation* of the perpetration of the harm, even if in modified terms, by contemporary agents. The link between past and present – which generates moral responsibility – lies, then, in the participation of the present agent in an order of things which actualizes the past harm.

Let me clarify my view with a few examples. From the standpoint of distributive justice, the problem with colonialism is not only the historical exploitation of former colonies but primarily the fact that the coercive economic system resulting from colonialism has not been fully overcome. In fact, the perpetuation of an exploitative international division of labour and disadvantageous terms of trade continue to harm the citizens of former colonies. Thus injustice can cast a long shadow, injuring not only whoever suffered it but also the prospects of their descendants.[61] Likewise, the problem with slavery and racial segregation in the United States is not only the violence that it originally produced, but the fact that many individuals are still victims of racial discrimination. The latter keeps shaping the life chances of every new-born based on race, from the likelihood of landing a job to the chances of accessing credit.[62] In the same way, the moral issues raised by the fact that many of the Ancient Egyptian treasures are currently exhibited in Western museums is not so much the original theft, but the fact that Egyptian citizens would have to travel to Paris or London to see many of the masterpieces of their culture and history, as the Louvre and the British Museum (respectively) systematically refuse restitutions. Therefore, it seems possible to link past injustice with the present by looking at the harm that injustice is still producing today. In this sense, it may be rightly said that reparations are "not for the sake of the past, but for the sake of the future".[63]

Revisiting the origins of the Eurozone crisis

In this section, I discuss the origins of the sovereign debt crisis and its impacts on the current functioning of the Eurozone from a normative perspective. I have already deconstructed the simplistic narrative of "well-behaved" and "misbehaved" member states. As I have argued, the dynamics of the common market, pushing some member states up the international value chain and others down, have also contributed much to the collapse of once fast-growing economies. It has been empirically demonstrated that "the large current account imbalances of individual Eurozone countries reflected to an important extent the asymmetric impact of trade shocks originating outside the Eurozone, as well as sustained cheap financing from core Eurozone countries to the largest net debtors".[64] More specifically, "the rise of China generated strong demand for machinery and equipment goods exported by Germany while exports from Eurozone debtor countries were displaced from their foreign markets by Chinese exports".[65] In turn, this vicious circle has been aggravated by the rules of the Eurozone. As has often been reported, the single currency has not allowed the fragile economies of the Eurozone to perform monetary devaluation, which could have helped them regain competitiveness and alleviate their debts. In the absence of any monetary instrument, the options left for the financially distressed states were raising taxes and issuing debt, leaving their economies under even higher pressure.[66] At the same time, capital was gradually relocated to the strongest economies in the Eurozone, namely Germany, whose treasury bonds had, at times, negative return rates.[67] These dynamics of trade and investment have led a scholar to describe Germany as "the Eurozone's biggest free-rider".[68]

One may be sceptical that wealthier member states bear responsibility for this state of affairs. While I have been referring to the costs of the Eurozone for the periphery, there are also many benefits to be listed. These include price stability and the reduction of transaction costs. In addition, a number of generous measures have already been adopted, namely the restructuring of Greek debt in 2012 and the bond-buying programme of the European Central Bank, which may be regarded as a "hidden redistributive mechanism".[69] Furthermore, the impact of poor policy choices should not be underestimated. First, the lack of adequate reformist agendas to deal with unsustainable pension systems, oversized public sectors, and large-scale tax evasion was noticeable at least since the early 2000s. Secondly, distressed member states clearly spent more than they could. This is not only true for the public sector, but also for the private sector, where companies and families accumulated large amounts of debt. Thirdly, after having hidden the truth regarding its public accounts, the Greek government basically triggered the Eurozone crisis when the real figures came out in 2009.[70] Fourthly, poorly performing member states had a chance to improve their condition, since they received large sums through the European Structural Funds. If they did not use the money wisely, this is certainly not the fault of the currently better-off states. All things considered, are the outcomes of the single currency fair? Or is it rather the case that a "number of factors converged to produce the Euro crisis"?[71]

In fact, responsibility for the crisis has to be shared by all member states.[72] Surely, most indebted countries have spent more than they should. Equally clear is their postponement of much-needed structural reforms. Yet poor policy choices went along with the poor design of the Eurozone. First, the fact that member states have to issue their debt in a currency they have no control over triggered the so-called *self-fulfilling liquidity crisis*, which occurs when investors lose confidence in one country – "[t]his is exactly what happened in countries like Ireland, Spain and Portugal".[73] Secondly, the lack of *macroeconomic stabilizers*, such as redistributive transfers and highly mobile workers, prevents governments from compensating for the imbalances resulting from a currency that is too strong for some member states and too weak for others.[74] These stabilizers have been critical to sustain the US dollar for so long in a country with as many economic asymmetries as the United States.[75] It is true that poorly performing member states have gained much from their membership of the Eurozone and that a limited number of policies with redistributive effects have already been put into practice. Yet this is different from saying that the Eurozone is just as it stands. Furthermore, certain acts of misbehaving behind the current state of affairs – such as lying about public accounts and conceding unpayable credit – seem not to belong properly to the domain of *collective* responsibility; indeed, they refer to the unauthorized actions of private agents. How could reciprocity be achieved in the Eurozone, then?

Reciprocity in the Eurozone

There are at least three critical steps to create a more reciprocal Eurozone. The first is to allow for the devaluation of the euro. The key idea behind this claim is that the interests of *all* member states should be considered when setting targets for the euro exchange rates, which clearly does not apply to the strict prohibition of devaluation in the Eurozone.[76] Note that, as an alternative to monetary devaluation, one could recommend redistributive transfers between member states. Yet, as I have argued before, there are good reasons to favour pre-distribution, whenever the corresponding policy instruments are available and effective. Thus, devaluation may be rightly regarded as a pre-distributive instrument, preferable to alternative tools such as Eurobonds and facilitated access to loans, which would only reinforce a state of affairs where poorer member states are unable to stand on their own feet.[77] A related second step would be making the institutions of the Eurozone more accountable. In fact, though it makes decisions on matters which critically shape the future of the EU, the European Central Bank is hardly subjected to scrutiny. Even more problematic is the lack of democratic control of the Eurogroup. In fact, the reunion of the ministers of finance of the Eurozone does not even have the status of a formal EU institution. Decisions within this body have often been described as undemocratic. Unlike the spirit of the Treaty of Lisbon, the Eurozone is governed almost exclusively on an intergovernmental basis, where the most powerful states tend to set the rules, with limited room for negotiation. The prospects of a reciprocal Union critically depend on the inclusion of the Parliament within the negotiation processes, as happens in other areas of EU integration.[78]

At the same time, reciprocity implies a strong commitment to structural reforms aimed at ensuring the sustainability of member states' public debts. Most importantly, under the principle of reciprocity, each member state should do its best to improve the efficiency of its public institutions, in a way nevertheless consistent with the standards of social provision defended in this book. One reason is that it would be unfair to ask for the assistance of other member states (through either pre- or redistribution) to cover inefficiency costs which could be reasonably avoided. For example, if a member state can save substantial amounts of money by centralizing the procurement of medical equipment for its hospitals, it is morally required to do so.

In addition, it would be unfair for a member state to expect assistance if it is living more excessively than other member states. A frequently mentioned example is the retirement age. As has rightly been noted, if the retirement age is 62 in Greece and 66 in Germany, there is something wrong about transferring German funds to the Greek welfare system.[79] Another reason why structural reforms are implied by the principle of reciprocity is the negative externalities of non-reforming. In fact, within a single currency area, all member states may be significantly affected by the instability of just one of the states. In this sense, it is fair that all member states be called to ameliorate their position as far as they can.

Yet a red line for how much reform one may demand from a particular member state is implied in the discussion held in the previous chapter. In Chapter 2, I argued that, insofar as the EU comprises a coercive system with democratic legitimacy, all of its citizens are entitled to access a set of basic goods, which gives them the chance to participate in democratic life and to resist arbitrary power. Thus, reforms should never go as far as to undermine the capacity of each member state to ensure the achievement of this threshold. In other words, the formula "assistance for reforms", widely applied in the context of the adjustment programmes implemented in Greece, Ireland, Portugal, and Cyprus, can only be fair if the required reforms do not imply unacceptable social costs. Yet a humanitarian disaster was at least partially politically induced in Greece, as illustrated by virtually every social indicator.[80] It is true that alternative solidarity measures have already been adopted, particularly the pardon of a part of Greek debt in 2012. However, these seem to have been painkillers rather than actual cures. What a reciprocal Eurozone needs is not simply the renegotiation of debts; it needs rules of cooperation which prevent member states from becoming highly indebted in the first place. To achieve this purpose, it is not enough to set debt targets. It is also critical that the chances to play fairly in the single currency area are not undermined from the outset for some member states – and, consequently, for their citizens.

V. Reciprocity in freedom of movement

Distributive consequences of freedom of movement

Migration may have important distributive consequences, which vary according to its extent and type. By letting foreign individuals participate in its job market, a given society shares with them its opportunities for wealth and success. These opportunities for a better life can then be extended to the families of migrants, through their remittances to the countries of origin. Indeed, it is worth noting that some of the poorest countries in the world are amongst the top receivers of remittances.[81] The benefits of migration go both ways. By employing a foreign workforce, a receiving society can produce more and more efficiently. Amongst other reasons, this is explained by "a 'brain gain' of innovation and creativity".[82] Hence, in the long run, migration has the potential to be a win-win game.[83] However, migration may also imply certain distributive costs. For instance, if the number of immigrants is too high, the supply of labour may turn out to be excessive, potentially resulting in lower real wages and increasing unemployment. The opposite reasoning applies to the sending country. If a state loses much of its qualified workforce, and if remittances are not enough to offset this effect, emigration will have a negative impact on the economy.[84] This is notably the case for a few developing countries.[85] Thus the distributive consequences of migration seem to depend on the scale, length, and qualifications at stake.

In the specific context of a free-movement area, such as the EU, a number of other distributive issues arise. A principal problem has to do with the set of social rights that, if any, mobile workers are entitled to. This question is particularly relevant for two reasons. First, mobile workers are particularly vulnerable to certain social risks. For instance, if EU citizens have worked in more than one member state, they may fail to meet the conditions for accessing certain types of pensions and unemployment benefits in any of the countries where they worked, given that they contributed to different social security systems.[86] This exclusion is arbitrary, leaving mobile workers in a much worse position than their non-mobile counterparts. Secondly, the risks for mobile workers have become higher in recent years. In fact, there have been numerous attempts to restrain the access to non-contributory social benefits by EU citizens who are not nationals of the member state where they live. This is apparent in the increasing evidentiary requirements demanded from EU citizens applying for social benefits in member states such as Germany and Austria, as well as in the growing number of cases in the CJEU on this matter.[87] These developments seem to be triggered by the fear of social welfare seeking in the free-movement area. Yet they seem incompatible with a reciprocal free-movement area.

Another distributive concern has to do with the chance to capture the economic potential of free movement. In 2015, only 3.6% of all EU active citizens worked or searched for a job in a member state other than their country of origin, a figure considerably lower than that of inter-state migration in other multilevel polities, such as the United States.[88] Yet one must ask – who are these 3.6%? In the period between 2011 and 2015, the percentage of high-skilled workers working in another member state was consistently above 40% of the total number of intra-EU migrants, which compares to figures always below 20% for low-skilled workers.[89] Although this discrepancy may in part be explained by the composition of the demand for migrant labour, distributive issues are likely to play an important role. First, many low-skilled workers lack the financial resources for subsistence on their own in another member state in search of a job. As an illustration, a report issued in 2016 indicated that, amongst recent EU movers of working age, only 10% were unemployed.[90] This figure is strikingly low, given the high domestic unemployment rates in southern and eastern Europe.[91] Secondly, finding a job in a foreign country may require upfront costs related, for instance, to additional training to meet local needs or to the recognition of qualifications. Again, these costs are only affordable for certain groups of individuals. These features challenge the view that freedom of movement realizes *per se* the ideal of equality of opportunity in the EU.[92] The redistributive potential of freedom of movement seems quite significant, but it can only be realized when everyone has a *chance* to use it. At present, "*spatial* mobility for the sake of *social* mobility is not attainable for all EU citizens".[93]

A final issue shows another face of the distributive vicious circle of the common market. As the gap between wealthier and poorer member states increases, particularly regarding job opportunities and salaries, the incentives for citizens of poorer member states to search for better jobs elsewhere in the EU become higher. However, as I have mentioned, highly qualified workers are better able to use such opportunities. Thus, we may obtain a perverse effect whereby part of the most highly employable workforce in one member state moves to another one, leaving behind unemployed and low-skilled compatriots. This poses a problem of sustainability for the domestic welfare systems, which then see their number of contributors decreasing in relation to the numbers of recipients. It addition, it raises a normative concern that individuals may simply withdraw their distributive obligations towards deprived compatriots.[94] As I have suggested before, this pattern of migration may also help to perpetuate the imbalance by transferring knowledge and innovation potential from southern and eastern to northern Europe. In addition, since highly skilled labour typically implies substantial educational costs for the state, free movement of people, as it stands, leads to the odd result that peripheral member states have been partially funding the growth of more prosperous ones. Thus, like the common market and the single currency, freedom of movement implies a range of benefits and costs, which do not seem to be evenly shared by different agents in the present-day EU.

Reciprocity in freedom of movement

In a context of freedom of movement, workers have both to be *protected* against the social risks raised by mobility and *empowered* to enjoy the benefits of the common market. This can be achieved by implementing an instrument already presented in the previous chapters: the EU threshold of basic goods. Recall that the idea of a threshold presupposes that every EU citizen attains a basket of basic goods, which consists of the means of subsistence, and access to education, healthcare, and the judiciary system.

Furthermore, recall that sufficiency can be attained either through a fair salary or through a combination of social benefits. In the previous chapters, I have justified this policy on grounds of democratic redistribution: I argued that the threshold provides the means for political participation and resistance to arbitrary power to all the members of the EU polity. Yet the threshold can also be justified on grounds of reciprocity, in a context of free movement of people. Indeed, if mobile workers are to take their chances in the job market of another member state, they must possess the means to afford the many transitional costs associated with this move. In the absence of appropriate social protection, mobile workers in search of a new job are exposed to risk of falling below the sufficiency line. As I have mentioned, this applies particularly to low-skilled workers, who typically have limited resources. This state of affairs is unfair, because it leaves both high-skilled mobile workers and resident nationals in a much better position to enjoy the benefits of the market of a given member state.

A free-movement area equipped with the threshold of basic goods would substantiate the EU principle of non-discrimination. EU citizens would more easily be allowed to search for opportunities in other member states, and they would have the time to adapt their skills to the requirements of local markets. In Chapter 1, I argued that pre-distribution should be prioritized over redistribution, given that it is better to prevent an evil than to attempt to correct it. Yet I also claimed that, in certain circumstances, it may be impossible to prevent injustice just by changing the rules of cooperation. This fully applies to freedom of movement since, as I have suggested, realizing *fair* equality of opportunity requires a degree of redistribution. If my argument is sound, non-discrimination should not be equated with a residual account of rights of "hospitality", as proposed by Maurizio Ferrera.[95] Ferrera draws on a long-standing intellectual tradition ranging from Homer to Kant to claim that "the most promising normative framings for the contentious politics of pan-European solidarity should rest on the norms of 'sober brotherhood' (for cross-national solidarity) and 'non-dominating hospitality' (for transnational solidarity)".[96] In my understanding, his proposal amounts to a defence of the status quo – if anything, "[t]he balance now existing between opening and closure should be recalibrated to take account of the sensitivity of certain countries' public opinion and of the demands of their governments".[97] Yet, if, as he recognizes, "non-discrimination, as enshrined in the treaties, should certainly remain the 'first principle' to defend free movement from a legal and moral point of view", then this principle should not simply be abandoned due to realistic concerns.[98]

In addition, minimalistic accounts of social rights for mobile workers may be inconsistent with the equal status of all EU citizens and the requirement of mutual respect. Even if unwillingly, minimalistic accounts treat mobile Europeans as second-class citizens, reinforcing a problem already discussed in Chapter 2. This becomes particularly apparent when, following the suggestion of Andrea Sangiovanni, one analyses the *social meaning* of the recent efforts by a number of member states to exclude non-nationals from comprehensive access to social rights.[99] The case of the United Kingdom, enlighteningly discussed by Sangiovanni, is illustrative: against plentiful empirical evidence that EU migrants have been net contributors to the British economy, as well as to the British treasury, the UK government endeavoured to restrain their access to the welfare system. As Sangiovanni puts it, this is to say, "We don't care what the facts are, and are willing to proceed merely on the basis of widespread beliefs about recent EU migrants as mainly benefit frauds and exploiters".[100] If, as I argued in Chapter 1, reciprocity implies not only mutual advantage, but also mutual respect, EU workers ought to be treated in a dignified and truly non-discriminatory manner. This means acknowledging their contribution to the economies of the member states and providing them with substantial protection against social risks. Surely, the idea of a threshold of basic goods raises a number of practical concerns, such as free-riding and welfare tourism, which may require non-ideal solutions. In Chapter 5, I shall thoroughly discuss the feasibility conditions of my proposal.

Reciprocity towards workers from the rest of the world

Although the research questions of the present study focus on the duties of EU citizens towards each other, a few words should be said about migrants who work in the common market. What sort of social rights are these workers entitled to? I cannot aim to address this question in depth, but only to provide general guidelines which seem consistent with the argument presented here. In short, I do not find any compelling normative reason for third-country nationals who have been admitted to the common market to be discriminated against. It seems highly unfair to have two workers performing the same job but letting only one of them acquire the rights associated with that job, simply on grounds of nationality. This is not to say that nationality is morally irrelevant. In an international system where the nation-state is a key unit of self-determination and democracy, nationality, even if arbitrarily acquired by birth, is an indispensable predicament. Yet the moral worth of nationality is not absolute. Against what has been suggested by a number of authors, nationality is not relevant in itself, but only in respect to certain features that can be plausibly linked to the functioning and flourishing of institutions and practices of self-government.[101] Therefore, nationality is morally *irrelevant* when it comes to types of judgements that have little or nothing to do with civic life, such as an objective assessment of the work done by someone. This suggests that, once they have been admitted to the common market, citizens of third countries should be entitled to social rights similar to those of native EU workers.

A more difficult question would be, to what extent is the EU morally required to open its borders to foreign workers? For instance, it might be argued that, in a globalized economy, reciprocity requires that borders be open, both to ensure equality of opportunity and to compensate for the continuous delocalization of capital. Notice, however, that this chapter has taken the circumstances of justice for granted. This means that a nation-state system where the power to control territorial borders remains at the discretion of domestic authorities is not being challenged. Although a case for open borders may be made on distributive grounds, my endeavour has been to deduce the distributive implications of the EU free-movement zone. A comprehensive treatment of this question – how many labour immigrants should be admitted into the EU – which assesses the merits of a substantial reform of the current border control regimes of developed countries is not possible in this chapter. It may be anticipated, however, that reciprocity has to be balanced against other important values such as self-determination, which may require at least a degree of border control. In light of these considerations, I shall rely on the minimalistic principle that non-EU citizens who are already working in the common market are entitled to the same reciprocity claims as EU citizens.

VI. Conclusion

I have argued that the duty of economic reciprocity applies to the EU. I claimed that the common market, the Eurozone, and free movement of people generate claims of justice amongst member states. I asserted that justifications of the status quo grounded on the principle of national responsibility have to be balanced against the "distributive vicious circle" which currently affects a number of member states. Accordingly, I suggested that the socioeconomic costs of the current crisis ought to be shared by all member states. I argued that these problems should be addressed primarily by pre-redistributive mechanisms, such as an EU Labour Code setting minimum social standards, and a minimum EU corporate tax rate. Yet this ought to be complemented by redistributive mechanisms such as an EU FGC, funded by an EU corporate tax, and the EU threshold of basic goods.

Notes

1 John Rawls, *A Theory of Justice: Revised Edition* (Cambridge MA, 1999), p. 7.
2 Rawls discusses the components of the basic structure in John Rawls, *A Theory of Justice: Revised Edition*, pp. 6–10.
3 The difference principle is presented in John Rawls, *A Theory of Justice: Revised Edition*, pp. 52–57.
4 John Rawls, "Deuxième Lettre", in John Rawls and Philippe Van Parijs, *Three Letters on* The Law of Peoples *and the European Union*, https://ethics.

harvard.edu/files/center-for-ethics/files/2003.rawlsvanparijs.r.phil_.econ_.pdf (Accessed 16 December 2017).

5 See, respectively, Philippe C. Schmitter and Michael W. Bower, "A (Modest) Proposal for Expanding Social Citizenship in the European Union", *Journal of European Social Policy* 11 (2001), pp. 55–65; and Philippe Van Parijs and Yannick Vanderborght, "From Euro-Stipendium to Euro-Dividend", *Journal of European Social Policy* 11 (2001), pp. 342–346.

6 Philippe Van Parijs, "Must Europe Be Belgian?", *Just Democracy: The Rawls-Machiavelli Programme* (Colchester, 2011), p. 114.

7 See, respectively, Andrea Sangiovanni, "Solidarity in the European Union: Problems and Prospects", in Julie Dickson and Pavlos Eleftheriadis (eds), *Philosophical Foundations of European Union Law* (Oxford, 2012) (emphasis in original); and Miguel Poiares Maduro, "A New Governance for the European Union and the Euro: Democracy and Justice", *RCSAS Policy Papers* (2012).

8 Jürgen Habermas, *The Crisis of the European Union: A Response* (Cambridge, 2012), pp. 119–126.

9 In fact, the reason why natural resources are not included in the following discussion on the economic structure of the EU is that their current open-access status already seems fairly egalitarian in prohibiting discrimination in access to these resources on the grounds of nationality. For instance, the citizens of all member states are equally entitled to fish in each other's waters and to cultivate each other's soils.

10 David Ricardo, *On the Principles of Political Economy and Taxation* (Indianapolis, 2004).

11 Paul Krugman, "Increasing Returns in a Comparative Advantage World", in *Comparative Advantage, Growth, and the Gains from Trade and Globalization: Festschrift Papers in Honor of Alan V. Deardorf* (Ann Arbor, 2010).

12 See Alan V. Deardorff, "General Validity of the Law of Comparative Advantage", *Journal of Political Economy* 88 (1980), pp. 941–957.

13 These two reasons are mentioned by Paul R. Krugman, Maurice Obstfeld, and Marc J. Melitz, *International Economics: Theory and Policy* (Essex, 2015), pp. 83–115.

14 International Labour Office and the Secretariat of the World Trade Organization, *Trade and Employment: Challenges for Policy and Research* (2007), p. 2.

15 Ibid.

16 Structural unemployment is the share of total unemployment which cannot be explained by (temporary) economic recession. In Portugal, Spain, and Greece, structural unemployment consistently increased in the period 2002–2015, reaching alarming levels – respectively, 12%, 16%, and 17%. See OECD, "Structural Unemployment" (2002–2015).

17 This is notably the case of the so-called Social Investment paradigm. For an overview, see Anton Hemerijck, "The Quiet Paradigm Revolution of Social Investment", *Social Politics* 22 (2015), pp. 242–256.

18 In a proposal for a "Social Investment Pack" for the EU, focused on improving the skills of EU workers, Frank Vandenbroucke, Anton Hemerijck, and Bruno

Palier only marginally address the issue of funding. In a single paragraph dedicated to the topic, they suggest that each member state should be responsible for funding its social investment, with two compensation mechanisms on the EU side. The first is Eurobonds, aimed at stabilizing the Eurozone; the second is the familiar structural funds. In my reading of their proposal, there would be few changes to the rules governing the EU, and inter-state transfers would not be significantly increased. Thus, assuming that social investment is an effective policy, it would imply that member states which are already wealthy would be able to improve the skills of their citizens at a much higher pace than the poorer member states, which have less resources to do so. This would only reinforce the gap amongst them. Yet the authors strikingly claim that "[s]uch a reform-oriented, forward-looking deal may contribute to creating a real sense of 'reciprocity' in the EU". See Frank Vandenbroucke, Anton Hemerijck, and Bruno Palier, "The EU needs a Social Investment Pack", *OSE Opinion Paper 5* (2011).

19 The Heckscher-Ohlin model emphasizes the importance of the relative endowments of capital and labour for the resulting patterns of international trade. Thus, a country where capital is relatively abundant will specialize in capital-intensive industries, while a state where labour is relatively abundant will specialize in labour-intensive sectors. Later models have pursued a similar argument, but using three factors – capital, high-skilled labour, and low-skilled labour. The Stolper-Samuelson Theorem that results from this model anticipates that the effects of trade liberalization for low-skilled workers may be dramatic in the absence of appropriate distributive instruments. For an overview, see Edward E. Leamer, "The Heckscher-Ohlin Model in Theory and Practice", *Princeton Studies in International Finance 75* (1995).

20 Marion Jansen, "International Trade and the Position of European Low-Skilled Labour", *World Trade Organization Staff Working Paper* (2000), p. 6.

21 See, for instance, Gianmarco Ottaviano, "European Integration and the Gains from Trade", in Harald Badinger and Volker Nitsch (eds), *The Routledge Handbook of European Integration* (New York, 2016), pp. 181–182. Ottaviano shows both that the common market benefits all member states and that the distribution of these gains is very unequal.

22 Ibid.

23 Notice that trade liberalization did not happen by accident. It is, indeed, the outcome of a variety of trade and investment deals with third-party states. The power of establishing such deals lies entirely with the EU.

24 Edward E. Leamer, "The Heckscher-Ohlin Model in Theory and Practice", p. 39.

25 Of course, globalization also affected the workers of certain economic sectors in Germany and France. The point is that Germany and France can redistribute their enormous gains from global trade through domestic social policies. Such instruments are largely unavailable at the EU level.

26 A number of economists have argued that protectionist policies may be justified in the context of infant industries. If this argument is sound, the fact that protectionist instruments are not available within the EU will favour the most advanced economies in the Union in relation to the less developed ones. On

this issue, see Marc J. Melitz, "When and How Should Infant Industries Be Protected?", *Journal of International Economics* 66 (2005), pp. 177–196.

27 John Bradley, George Petrakos, and Iulia Traistaru, "Integration, Growth and Cohesion in an Enlarged European Union: An Overview", *Integration, Growth, and Cohesion in the European Union* (New York, 2004), p. 8.

28 This tendency is illustrated by the widening of the gap of labour costs per hour in the EU15 during the period 2004–2016. In this period, the difference between the average cost of one hour of labour in Denmark (the highest hourly cost in the EU15) and Portugal (the lowest) increased by more than 50%. In fact, it is possible to identify two contrasting groups of member states: one where the costs of labour are situated above 30 euro/hour and have increased consistently since 2004, and another where one hour of labour costs less than 15 euro and has remained virtually stagnant since 2004. Amongst the first group of countries are Germany, France, Luxembourg, Belgium, the Netherlands, and Denmark; amongst the second group are Greece and Portugal. See Eurostat, "Hourly Labour Costs" (2004–2016), http://ec.europa.eu/eurostat/statistics-explained/index.php/Hourly_labour_costs (Accessed 1 December 2017).

29 For instance, Jörg Huffschmid claims that "as far as the flexibility agenda has been realized it has been damaging for the innovation performance in Europe". See Jörg Huffschmid (ed.), *Economic Policy for a Social Europe: A Critique of Neo-liberalism and Proposals for Alternatives* (New York, 2005), p. 82.

30 Stilianos Alexiadis, *Convergence Clubs and Spatial Externalities* (New York, 2013), p. 191.

31 Michael E. Porter has argued that the microeconomic foundation of a country's competitiveness is its productivity. Thus, the way for a country to move up the international value chain is to become more productive. This, however, should not lead one to conclude too quickly that the disadvantaged position of certain member states is due to the lack of effort of their workers. Notice that productivity is measured as a ratio which compares a given amount of labour to its output (i.e. added value). The problem is that, as illustrated by the barista example, such output is shaped by exogenous variables, which are beyond the control of microeconomic agents. This is notably the case of the technology employed in the productive process and the terms of international trade. See Michael E. Porter, *The Competitive Advantage of Nations* (New York, 1998).

32 Susan Strange, *Mad Money* (Manchester, 1998), p. 104.

33 Consider a firm that produces and sells shoes in Spain but declares the profits of its operation in a Dutch holding. This practice can be regarded as free-riding on at least two accounts. First, one may say that this firm is operating in the Spanish market at the expense of the firms that consent to pay their taxes there. In fact, a substantial amount of state revenue is needed to cover the costs of a functioning market, which include property rights enforcement, the infrastructure for mobility of people and goods, and so on. Second, the Dutch state is also free-riding on the Spanish state, since it seizes Spanish fiscal revenues without sharing any of the costs described here.

34 An overview of the ways in which liberal labour market reforms in Europe have challenged the specific pattern of social citizenship in each member state

is provided by Silke Bothfeld and Singrid Betzelt (eds), *Activation and Labour Market Reforms in Europe: Challenges to Social Citizenship* (New York, 2011).

35 Snorri Thomas Snorrason, *Asymmetric Economic Integration: Size Characteristics of Economies, Trade Costs, and Welfare* (New York, 2012), p. 160.

36 Brian Fabo and Sharon Sarah Belli, "(Un)believable Wages? An Analysis of Minimum Wage Policies in Europe from a Living Wage Perspective", *IZA Journal of Labour Policy* 6 (2017), pp. 1–11.

37 In 2014, the proportion of workers on minimum wage was higher than 7% in seven member states. This figure would be higher if workers earning above the minimum wage but below the subsistence level were considered. See Eurostat, "Proportion of Employees Earning Less than 105% of the Minimum Wage" (2014), http://ec.europa.eu/eurostat/statistics-explained/index.php/Minim um_wage_statistics (Accessed 1 December 2017).

38 Claus Offe, "Social Protection in a Supranational Context: European Integration and the Faces of the 'European Social Model'", in Pranab Bardhan, Samuel Bowles, and Michael Wallerstein, *Globalization and Egalitarian Redistribution* (Princeton, 2006), p. 56.

39 Fritz W. Scharpf, "The European Social Model: Coping with the Challenge of Diversity", *Journal of Common Market Studies* 40 (2002), p. 646.

40 Ibid.

41 András Inotai, "The Check Republic, Hungary, Poland, Slovak Republic, and Slovenia", in *Winners and Losers of EU Integration: Policy Issues for Central and Eastern Europe* (Washington, 2000), p. 19.

42 Notice that this proposition would also imply the extinction of the existing tax havens, which are unfair in the context of a common market, for the free-riding reasons previously presented.

43 Notice that, along the lines of the argument presented so far, an EU Labour Code would also be required to set minimum standards regarding other important variables, such as weekly working hours, days of holidays, duration of contracts, and so on. In this book, I focus on minimum wage and severance payments given their direct impact on the distribution of income amongst EU workers.

44 Note that a coordination policy differs from one that sets absolute minimums. For instance, a coordinated minimum wage could be set at $x\%$ of the median income of each member state. Similarly, coordinated severance payments could be set at y monthly salaries of compensation. On this point, see Enrique Fernández-Macias and Carlos Vacas-Soriano, "A Coordinated European Union Minimum Wage Policy?", *European Journal of Industrial Relations* 22 (2016), pp. 97–113.

45 Social dumping can be defined as set of practices aimed at improving the competitiveness of a country by worsening the contractual conditions (e.g. remuneration, working hours, contract duration, and so on) and restraining the social rights of workers.

46 This coercive behaviour became particularly apparent during the negotiations of the adjustment programmes in Greece, Portugal, and Cyprus. Consider, for instance, the cut of the minimum wage in Greece by 22% in 2012.

47 Recall that in Chapter 1, I defined reciprocity not only as mutual advantage but also as mutual respect amongst the participants of an economic exchange. As I argued, this concern may justify establishing low and high caps on wages when the level of economic integration is very high. It is true that setting limits to top salaries at the EU level would be normatively problematic since, as I explained before, any understanding of proportionality of wages is strongly context-dependent. Yet this argument does not apply to minimum wages, which are more easily calculated in terms of access to certain basic goods, adjusted to the costs of living. Note that this minimum level of welfare allows citizens to resist not only arbitrary acts of public institutions, but also the potentially harmful outcomes of asymmetrical labour relations.

48 This is illustrated by the sharply decreasing amounts of public investment (measured as a percentage of GDP) in southern economies in recent years, in opposition to central and northern European member states, where public investment has remained relatively stable. This situation can only be worsened by an expected reduction of structural funds for the southern region in the years to come. See "Public Investment in Europe", *ECB Economic Bulletin 2* (2016).

49 Notice that the idea would not be to replace structural funds, which could still be regarded as an instrument of basic convergence after accession, but to complement them. As to the existing Globalization Adjustment Fund, my proposal would dramatically extend its rather limited scope and budget.

50 The reason to target profitable firms is that they are, by default, the winners of economic integration. Although it would be plausible to differentiate firms according to the amount of their exports, as suggested by Miguel Maduro, it seems fairer to tax all firms, given the spillovers of the exporting industries for the economy as a whole. Recall that in Chapter 2, I argued that the threshold of basic goods should be funded through inter-state transfers. The reason why I proposed a different funding model has to do with the nature of the duties at stake. In fact, the democratic duty to redistribute is a duty of citizenship, which should then refer to the income/wealth of citizens. As such, it is not directly linked to the wealth produced by firms. See Miguel Poiares Maduro, "A New Governance for the European Union and the Euro: Democracy and Justice".

51 Fritz W. Scharpf, "The European Social Model: Coping with the Challenge of Diversity", p. 658.

52 Andreas Nölke and Arkan Vliegenthart, "Enlarging the Varieties of Capitalism: The Emergence of Dependent Market Economies in East Central Europe", *World Politics* 61 (2009), p. 691.

53 Ibid., p. 690.

54 See, for instance, Joseph Stiglitz, *The Price of Inequality* (New York, 2013); and Daron Acemoglu, "Good Jobs Versus Bad Jobs", *Journal of Labor Economics* 19 (2001), pp. 1–21.

55 Dimitris N. Chorafas, *Sovereign Debt Crisis: The New Normal and the Newly Poor* (New York, 2011), p. 8.

56 Ibid (emphasis in original).

57 David Miller, *National Responsibility and Global Justice* (Oxford, 2007), pp. 69–76.

58 Lea Ypi, Robert E. Goodin, and Christian Barry, "Associative Duties, Global Justice, and the Colonies", *Philosophy & Public Affairs* 37 (2009), p. 125.

59 A similar thesis is presented in George Sher, "Ancient Wrongs and Modern Rights", *Philosophy & Public Affairs* 10 (1981), pp. 3–17.

60 Jeremy Waldron, "Superseding Historical Injustice", *Ethics* 103 (1992), pp. 4–28.

61 Janna Thompson, "Historical Injustice and Reparation: Justifying Claims of Descendants", *Ethics* 112 (2001), p. 117.

62 For different aspects of racial discrimination in the United States, see, for instance, Devah Pager and Hana Shepherd, "The Sociology of Discrimination: Discrimination in Employment, Housing, Credit, and Consumer Markets", *Annual Review of Sociology* 34 (2008), pp. 181–204.

63 Leif Wenar, "Reparations for the Future", *Journal of Social Philosophy* 37 (2006), p. 396.

64 Ruo Chen, Gian Maria Milesi-Ferretti, and Thierry Tressel, "External Imbalances in the Eurozone", *Economic Policy* 73 (2013), p. 104.

65 Ibid.

66 In a paper where he compares the public debts of the United Kingdom and Spain, Paul De Grauwe identifies the following paradox: despite the fact that, in 2011, the United Kingdom's public debt as a percentage of GDP was 17 percentage points higher than that of Spain's, the markets put a much higher premium on Spanish government bonds than on British ones. This paradox is even stronger given that the trend of Spanish public debt had always been better than the United Kingdom's in the 10 years before the beginning of the crisis (Spain consistently decreased its debt from 2001 to 2007, while the United Kingdom consistently increased its own in the same period). De Grauwe shows that the only plausible explanation for this phenomenon is membership of the single currency. In the absence of the option of devaluation, "financial markets acquire the power to force default" on more fragile states. See Paul De Grauwe, "The Governance of a Fragile Eurozone", *CEPS Working Document* 346 (2011), pp. 1–25.

67 According to the neoclassical models of economic growth, the accumulation of capital "is the key to international differences in economic growth". This leaves countries which are able to attract foreign capital in a much better competitive position. For the quote, as well as an overview of the prominent theories of economic growth, see N. Gregory Mankiw, "The Growth of Nations", *Brookings Papers on Economic Activity* 1 (1995), pp. 275–326. The objection that, by virtue of membership of the Eurozone, southern states had access to much (cheap) capital in the pre-crisis times has a point, but it may also be reversed: since the money inflows to southern Europe were mainly aimed at boosting consumption (consider the case of the real-estate bubble), and not at promoting productive investment, they produced perverse incentives which severely harmed southern countries.

68 Pavlos Eleftheriadis, "Why Germany is the Eurozone's Biggest Free-Rider", *Fortune* (22 October 2014).

69 Klaus Tuori, "Has Euro Area Monetary Policy Become Redistribution By Monetary Means? 'Unconventional' Monetary Policy as a Hidden Redistributive Mechanism", *European Law Journal* 22 (2016), pp. 838–868.

70 Peter A. Hall, "Varieties of Capitalism in Light of the Eurocrisis", *Journal of European Public Policy* (2017), p. 1.

71 Ibid., p. 2.

72 At the global level, the claim that the responsibility for the financial crisis should be shared by wealthy and poor countries has been advanced by Matt Peterson and Christian Barry, "Who Must Pay for the Damage of the Gobal Financial Crisis", in Ned Dobos, Christian Barry, and Thomas W. Pogge (eds), *Global Financial Crisis: The Ethical Issues* (New York, 2011), pp. 158–184.

73 Paul De Grawe, "Design Failures in the Eurozone: Can They Be Fixed?", *LSE Europe in Question Discussion Paper Series* 57 (2013), p. 9.

74 The importance of stabilization policy in a context of a single currency area has been stressed in a seminal article by Robert A. Mundell, "A Theory of Optimum Currency Areas", *The American Economic Review* 51 (1961), pp. 656–665. In a recent article, Paul Krugman has argued that Mundell's theory "suggested serious concerns about the euro project". Krugman suggests that a "transfer union" would be an effective solution to the Eurocrisis, but he deems it politically unfeasible. See Paul Krugman, "Revenge of the Optimum Currency Area", *NBER Macroeconomics Annual 2012* 27, pp. 439–448.

75 Philippe Van Parijs and Yannick Vanderborght, *Basic Income: A Radical Proposal for a Free Society and a Sane Economy* (Cambridge MA, 2017), pp. 232–233.

76 It has been empirically demonstrated that a marginal depreciation of the euro would have a significant impact on the exports of the Eurozone members. See Nahid Kalbasi Anaraki, "Effects of Euro Devaluation on Eurozone Exports", *International Journal of Economics and Finance* 6 (2014), pp. 19–24.

77 In a setting where one needs to decide between launching Eurobonds and maintaining the status quo, Eurobonds would certainly be a positive development. Yet here I am assuming that the available options are wider than the ones usually discussed in the public debate. At a normative level, it is better to address the imbalances that create debt than trying to make debt more sustainable.

78 The fact that the Eurozone comprises only 19 out of 28 EU member states could be overcome through extraordinary sessions of the Parliament, where only the Members of the European Parliament (MEPs) of the Eurozone states would be allowed to vote.

79 Notice the question of *how* these reforms should be conducted is a different one. The rather coercive model adopted during the Eurocrisis, particularly regarding the negotiations of the adjustment programmes, is hardly consistent with a democratic polity.

80 For instance, in the period 2010–2013, Greece's public expenditure with social protection, healthcare, and education fell, respectively, by 18%, 40%, and 9%. See Directorate-General for Internal Policies, *Employment and Social Developments in Greece* (2015), p. 21.

81 World Bank, *Migration and Remittances Factbook: Third Edition* (2016), Table 14.

82 Darell M. West, "The Costs and Benefits of Immigration", *Political Science Quarterly* 126 (2011), p. 428.

83 The long run caveat has to do with possible adjustment costs, such as frictional unemployment.

84 Nigel Harris, "The Economics and Politics of the Free Movement of People", in Antoine Pécoud and Paul de Guchteneire (eds), *Migration Without Borders: Essays on the Free Movement of People* (2007). p. 44.

85 For instance, in 2010/2011, 75% of the individuals with tertiary education in Haiti had emigrated; in Zimbabwe, 44% had done so; in Congo, 37% had left the country. Amongst the top 10 senders of tertiary-educated citizens as a percentage of the total, eight states are underdeveloped. See World Bank, *Migration and Remittances Factbook: Third Edition*, Figure 11.

86 Accessing social benefits of these kinds typically presupposes a period of contributions in that member state. In recent years, the EU has attempted to tackle this issue through a degree of social security coordination amongst member states. Yet coordination currently excludes a variety of social benefits, such as supplementary pensions and unemployment benefits.

87 Michael Blauberger and Susanne K. Schmidt, "Welfare Migration? Free Movement of EU Citizens and Access to Social Benefits", *Research and Politics* 1 (2014), pp. 1–7.

88 European Commission, *Annual Report on Intra-EU Labour Mobility 2016: Second Edition* (2017), p. 10. This figure would certainly be higher if we considered all the workers who have worked in another member state at a certain point in their careers. Yet the point that mobility of labour is lower than in other multilevel polities still holds.

89 European Commission, *Annual Report on Intra-EU Labour Mobility 2016: Second Edition*, Table 9. The difference between high- and low-skilled refers to the category of medium-skilled workers.

90 Ibid., Table 10.

91 There are important non-economic barriers to mobility, such as language. Yet, again, low-income workers seem to be in a more vulnerable position to face them.

92 In fact, such a claim misses the distinction between "formal" and "fair" equality of opportunity. According to John Rawls, "[t]he thought here is that positions are not only open in a formal sense, but that all should have a fair chance to attain them". See John Rawls, *A Theory of Justice: Revised Edition*, p. 63.

93 Christof Roos, "Freedom of Movement in the EU and Welfare State Closure: Welfare Regime Type, Benefit Restrictions, and Their Implications for Social Mobility", in Melike Wulfgramm, Tonia Bieber, and Stephan Leibfried (eds), *Welfare State Transformations and Inequality in OECD Countries* (2016), p. 285 (my italics).

94 Anna Stilz has made this point forcefully through a thought experiment dubbed "Elite Escape", which discusses the scenario where the top 1% permanently leaves a state, withdrawing any distributive duties towards fellow citizens. Amongst other reasons, this would be unfair since escapers have received necessary benefits from the state, such as national security. See Anna Stilz, "Is There an Unqualified Right to Leave", in Sarah Fine and Lea Ypi (eds), *Migration in Political Theory: The Ethics of Movement and Membership* (Oxford, 2016).

95 See Maurizio Ferrera, "The Contentious Politics of Hospitality: Intra-EU Mobility and Social Rights", *European Law Journal* 22 (2016), pp. 791–805.

96 Ibid., p. 804.
97 Ibid., p. 803.
98 Ibid., p. 804. Although Ferrera may be right that his account is the most "real-istic" for the present-day EU, this should not prevent us from looking into the future. In Chapter 4, I shall discuss the relevant time horizon for normative proposals.
99 Andrea Sangiovanni rightly argues that, to understand whether a given prac-tice implies discriminatory behaviour, "we need to examine the broader social context" in which it takes place. See Andrea Sangiovanni, "Non-discrimination, In-work Benefits, and Free Movement in the EU", *European Journal of Political Theory* 16 (2017), p. 154.
100 Ibid., p. 155.
101 See, for instance, David Miller, *On Nationality* (Oxford, 1997).

4

A moderate feasibility test
for normative theory

I. Introduction

This chapter addresses two questions. How can we assess the feasibility status of a theory of distributive justice? What should a feasibility test for the proposals presented in the previous chapters look like? I claim that feasibility debates by political theorists should focus on practical restrictions that human agency cannot reasonably be expected to overcome, leaving aside feasibility barriers which are presumably temporary. I argue that a pervasively feasible theory of justice has at least four key features. It must (i) fit, to a certain degree, the political culture of a given community; (ii) be economically sustainable; (iii) be translatable into policies and institutions that have a reasonable prospect of delivering the goals underlying the policy; and (iv) be consistent with the degree of social solidarity amongst the citizens to which the policy is to apply.

I begin by identifying a key question in the research agenda of non-ideal theory. Subsequently, I discuss the concept of feasibility, introducing two conceptual distinctions: "constrained" versus "unconstrained" feasibility, and "pervasive" versus "temporary" feasibility. I then turn to the main features that a test for pervasive feasibility will display, and I discuss the types of reasons that can be plausibly presented to justify a charge of unfeasibility. Finally, I turn to a detailed discussion of four key feasibility requirements of a liberal democratic theory of distributive justice.

II. The concept of feasibility

A problem for non-ideal theory

In recent years, a growingly body of literature has stressed the importance of feasibility constraints in normative theory. Central to this claim is a particular view on the role of facts in political theory.[1] In fact, a number of non-ideal theorists have argued that "[g]reater concern for the facts, either in relation to implementing the recommendations of ideal theory in the real (non-ideal) world or through incorporating those facts into normative theorising itself, will produce a theory more suited to guiding action here and now".[2] A failure to take feasibility constraints into account inhibits political theory from guiding political action, and it may even result in the dismissal of alternative non-ideal, yet justice-enhancing reforms.[3] This applies stringently to the EU, where the barriers against social reforms seem to be multiple. Although the extent to which feasibility constraints should apply has been a matter of dispute, there seems to be an emerging consensus that a compelling political theory should offer considerations regarding the way in which it is to be realized.[4] Hence, non-ideal theorizing "is not just a question of testing our 'principles' against the 'facts'", but is a matter of "seeing political theory as part of a process we call 'politics' and that process is one of change, of engagement, and of drama".[5] This does not imply a dismissal of utopian theorizing, but it does suggest that utopias must be somewhat realistic if they aim to be realized.[6]

Yet, if both ideal and non-ideal theory have a role to play, what exactly should this be? In my view, each of these approaches is linked to a particular type of research agenda. To illustrate the point, recall the first research question of this study. I have asked, does the political and economic configuration of the EU generate distributive duties amongst EU citizens, and/or between member states? This question takes the political and economic configuration of the Union as given. It thus explores the normative consequences of an existing, and possibly non-ideal, order. Here, the goal is to advance proposals for *incremental* (though possibly ambitious) change. Ideal theory, instead, would be particularly useful if our goal were to develop a conception of a just Europe, which is independent from its current configuration. For instance, one might have asked, "How should the EU be configured economically and politically to fully realize the ideal of distributive justice?"[7] Here one might argue, for example, that an EU federation would be the best means to realize distributive justice in the EU. Therefore, the research goals are key to decide which approach should be adopted. Since the starting point of this enquiry is existing institutional arrangements, the non-ideal approach is more suitable.

However, an important difficulty arises when one tries to apply the non-ideal approach. What exact types of feasibility constraints should be considered, and why? According to Laura Valentini, "[t]he key to a successful theory would be to make sure that its factual input is in some sense 'appropriate' to the particular question it aims to answer".[8] Valentini is sceptical that we may "come up with a general rule", the reason being that "facts will vary on a case-by-case basis".[9] However, this legitimate resistance to generalization leaves the non-ideal position in a somewhat precarious situation. Advancing compelling reasons why feasibility constraints should be considered, while leaving them undertheorized, may result in a failure to realize the primary goal of non-ideal theory: guiding political action.

Is there a way to attain a reasonable degree of generalization regarding feasibility constraints? If so, what should a moderate feasibility test look like? Although a number of variables have been identified by the existing literature, they often suffer from a considerable degree of vagueness. Alternatively, more comprehensive lists may be either too abstract to be effectively applied or too broad to exclude more than grossly unfeasible policies.[10] To address this problem, I shall begin by discussing what feasibility means.

What does feasibility mean?

Defining "feasibility" is a complex task. On the one hand, as John Rawls famously put it, distributive justice seems to be conditioned by a number of constraints – the "circumstances of justice" – such as limited altruism of individuals and moderate scarcity of resources.[11] In fact, for Rawls, the circumstances of justice are not only constraints that shape the structure of normative arguments but also conditions under which distributive justice is unescapable. Given that these constraints influence the reasonableness and importance of a justice claim, they should be considered by political theorists.[12] On the other hand, if a wider set of constraints, including redistributive preferences and public culture, are taken into account, the discussion may abandon its original purpose. In fact, if feasibility is too narrowly defined in terms of endorsement by public opinion and current political institutions, political theory will end up merely replicating the status quo. Public opinion can tell us something about the feasibility of implementing a given policy, but it cannot decide on the moral status of that policy.[13] What do we mean by saying that a given political theory is feasible?

In a first sense, a political theory is feasible only if it is *possible* to implement it in a *sustainable* way. This condition translates the well-known Kantian maxim that "ought" implies "can".[14] Thus, a theory is feasible "if and only if the effective implementation of its principles is compatible with human psychology, human capacities generally, the laws of nature, and the natural resources available to human beings".[15] For instance, a theory prescribing work days of 20 hours for highly talented individuals for the sake of their communities is likely unfeasible, given the limitations of the human body. Similarly, a theory requiring all new-borns to be taken away from their families and educated by the state is highly unfeasible, considering the importance of emotional ties between parents and children to the well-being of both.[16] Notice that any meaningful understanding of feasibility has to equate possibility with sustainability. Thus, perhaps the 20-hour working day *could* be implemented for a short period of time, and babies *could* be taken from their parents through a discretionary decree. Yet the resulting state of affairs would likely be, respectively, so unendurable and so unstable that a long-lasting implementation of the theories would be undermined.[17]

In turn, what *can* be done for the sake of distributive justice varies according to time and place. This becomes particularly clear when we analyse the history of redistribution as a concept and a practice. In fact, only within a mature capitalist economy was the problem of economic inequality systematically formulated for the first time.[18] Once widely spread, the sense that the new possibilities of industry and trade would allow everybody to live a better life if wealth was properly redistributed positioned social justice as a topic of rising interest for philosophers, and a motive for enduring political struggle. By the same token, the expansion of the welfare state in the second half of the twentieth century overlaps with the period of the highest economic growth in world history.[19] The outcomes of such processes varied significantly from country to country, partially as a result of local constraints.[20] A more recent illustration of the way in which context shapes the prospects of distributive justice is the discovery of oil in Alaska, which eventually allowed for a generous basic income policy. All these historical examples suggest that feasible policies should, indeed, be fact-dependent, that is, they must to be sensitive to basic facts about human beings and the world they live in.[21]

However, the propositions that (i) "ought" implies "can" and (ii) "can" is context-dependent do not clearly specify which types of facts are relevant for a feasible theory of justice. For sure, these propositions would recommend the rejection of principles which contravene the laws of science or require amounts of resources which are currently unavailable. Yet once we move away from these types of "technical" constraints, we may run into serious trouble.[22] The reception of the work of John Rawls is illustrative of this point. Rawls states that, under the conditions of impartiality devised by the veil of ignorance, the parties "understand political affairs and the principles of economic theory; they know the basis of social organization and the laws of human psychology".[23] However, there is much disagreement within the realms of economic theory and moral psychology, and Rawls's accounts of economics and psychology have been challenged accordingly.[24] This gives to the Rawlsian "general facts about human society" a status of hypotheses, not proper facts. More generally, it raises doubts that feasibility tests may achieve a significant degree of consensus. Can we hope to agree on a basic outline for the test?

"Constrained" feasibility tests

Feasibility tests which attempt to go beyond "technical" constraints seem to entail a set of assumptions. Consider the following example. It has been asserted that it may be psychologically impossible to comply with certain moral rules.[25] This suggests that, whenever moral principles are advanced, one should make sure "that the character, decision processing, and behaviour prescribed are possible, or are perceived to be feasible, for creatures like us".[26] However, what is deemed psychologically possible is, at least to a certain extent, conditioned by our normative worlds. While a policy which would require every citizen to transfer all their wealth to a fund run by the state would seem unfeasible in capitalist societies, it constitutes an ordinary practice in communities of Franciscan friars. This indicates that doing so *is* indeed psychologically possible.[27] Therefore, the claim that a policy of this sort is unfeasible should not simply refer to a descriptive account of psychology; it also implies the *normative* assumption that individuals should not be obliged, nor forced, to hand over all of their income to assist other people. In this and other cases, typically described as over demanding, what is at stake is not impossibility but a conception of negative freedom and negative rights on the grounds of which the notion of feasibility is developed.

Similarly, economic feasibility is usually subjected to normative assumptions. When institutions develop economic models to assess the feasibility of social policy, they typically assume that some things are *not* to be changed.[28] Most notably, they assume that a given policy is to be delivered under a capitalist system, which comprises a particular way of organizing production, remunerating capital and labour, and setting the prices of goods and services. This practice implies pre-empirical assumptions regarding which types of action and of social organization are desirable, and which are not.[29] Thus Keynes's proposal of a 15-hour working week may not be feasible under capitalism, but it might be achievable under an entirely different way of organizing our society and the economy, as the one famously advocated by Thomas More.[30] Although being far from present-day reality, an economic order of a different kind is not necessarily unfeasible. In fact, the emergence of a number of hippie communes since the 1960s suggests that the conditions of modern capitalism are not unescapable.[31] Of course, there are good reasons to reject the claim that individuals should be obliged or forced to join small communities to live an allegedly better life. Indeed, this is why the structure of feasibility statements tends to be of a conditional type: the 15-hour working week is unfeasible *assuming* a market economy and a set of basic liberal freedoms.

The critical question is whether this sort of conditionality renders feasibility testing redundant. If, when testing the feasibility of a set of options, we adopt *normative* assumptions that, by definition, imply that some of these options are unfeasible, will the test be meaningful? The answer is affirmative. It is not inconsistent to perform "constrained" feasibility tests, which equate feasibility with the basic requirements for a project to be deemed acceptable in a given society. For instance, we can consistently say that project X is unfeasible *within* a liberal democratic order. This type of assessment provides practical guidance both to (i) a society that is deeply committed to a particular type of social order, thus promptly rejecting any project which is incompatible with it, and (ii) a society that considers project X especially compelling, yet needs to understand the scope of reform required for its implementation. As we shall see, "constrained" feasibility tests – that is, tests that incorporate some basic normative assumptions regarding what types of results are acceptable – refer not only to a political and economic order, such as liberal democracy and market economy, but also to culture and history.[32]

"Constrained" feasibility tests seem preferable to "unconstrained" ones, which assume that the potential of social engineering is unlimited, once "technical" feasibility has been assured. The "unconstrained" approach has at least three shortcomings. First, "unrestrained" tests seemingly operate under the assumption that, with the appropriate degree of social change, any project can be realizable.[33] This assumption is flawed, since it is clear that some theoretical models do not work in practice for a number of reasons, including non-compliance and social instability.[34] Secondly, "unrestrained" tests may be simply unmanageable. Any feasibility test presupposes that one can make predictions about the impact of a given project. Yet as the number of variables increases, the degree of uncertainty regarding the results grows. For example, it would be difficult to operationalize feasibility tests for highly disruptive political projects such as Tomas Campanella's City of the Sun and Francis Bacon's New Atlantis.[35] Finally, "unrestrained" tests do not provide much practical guidance. Insofar as they assume virtually unlimited social change, "unconstrained" tests can only indicate that any project which respects the most basic laws of science is feasible. This seems rather insufficient. All this suggests that the "constrained" approach is, indeed, preferable.

"Constrained" feasibility tests may be exposed to a charge of path dependency. If the test refers only to a particular type of social order, will it not immediately discard processes of radical change, which may yet prove to be feasible, as in the case of the abolishment of slavery? This objection underestimates the potential of reform associated with "constrained" tests. "Constrained" feasibility does not imply that a radical change such as the abolishment of slavery would be deemed impossible before it happened. Alternatively, "constrained" analysis would typically suggest that slavery could have only be abolished *if* a slavery-based economic order had been abandoned.[36] Feasibility tests assess whether we can do X within a certain type of social order, yet they do not say that such an order cannot be changed at all. In fact, the main risk that is at stake is failing to acknowledge that the test is "constrained", treating undesirability as gross unfeasibility.[37] In addition, one should note that radical change may be feasible without fundamentally changing the social order. An illustrative example is the impressive progress in environmental regulation since the 1970s. In this sense, "constrained" feasibility tests do not protect the status quo; rather, they show the price at which change may be attained.

Pervasive and temporary feasibility

An additional problem is the relation between individual preferences and feasibility. On the one hand, it seems politically unfeasible to implement a policy package which does not gain a minimum degree of acceptance by the citizens. In the absence of a basic threshold of support, non-compliance, as well as more or less radical forms of protest, will likely defeat the project. This suggests that individual preferences and public opinion are important dimensions of feasibility. On the other hand, a few critical steps in the history of Western democracies have been made against a background of fierce opposition to change. Consider the cases of the end of slavery in the United States and the decolonization of Africa. These examples show that crucial processes of change may, at a first stage, come up against the preferences of the majority. What was once politically unfeasible may become feasible under different circumstances or after a number of intermediate steps have been made. Hence, to what extent should current preferences be considered when feasibility is being tested?

A helpful way of proceeding will be to consider different types of feasibility. Some policies seem to be *pervasively* unfeasible, that is, they face practical restrictions that human agency cannot reasonably be expected to overcome, at least within a particular type of social order. Consider, for instance, the economic costs, in terms of taxation and efficiency, of implementing a principle of justice which prescribes the fulfilment of highly expensive tastes, within a market economy.[38] On the other hand, the implementation of a few other principles seems to be *temporarily* unfeasible: their unfeasibility status results from circumstances that could arguably be overcome. Consider, for instance, the preferences of voters in times of a deep economic recession or an international security crisis. As mentioned previously, feasibility tests usually entail a number of normative constraints regarding what is to be deemed feasible, and they are based on the information available at the specific moment of time in which they are performed. Thus, it will be consistent to say that a particular policy is *pervasively* unfeasible *within* a liberal democratic order, *given* the technology currently available and the resources presently known to the world.

The intuition behind this prospects-based classification of feasibility is simple. For any plan in life, we can ask two different types of questions: (i) can we do it *now* (i.e. in the near future)? and (ii) could we do it *one day*? Both questions are crucial in the political realm. As mentioned already, history provides plenty of examples of achievements which were regarded as unfeasible for a period of time. This suggests that we need to look beyond the question of what can be done right now. Yet the converse is also true:

some projects may be politically feasible only at a specific moment in time in which particular circumstances are combined. If we disregard issues of timing, we may miss exceptional chances to achieve change. What is the role of feasibility testing, then? While politics must address the first question, political theory should be mainly interested in the second question. For non-ideal political theory, it is critical that a given policy be politically feasible; yet it does not have to be feasible *immediately*.[39] Hence, the definition of feasibility that better suits normative theorizing is one that considers pervasive unfeasibility but ignores temporary unfeasibility.

This conceptual framework raises at least two difficulties. First, how far in the future should we look when pervasive feasibility is under assessment? Should a policy that will only be implemented in, say, 200 years from now be labelled as pervasively feasible? And if so, of what use is this distinction? Pervasive feasibility abstracts from time: whether a goal is to be achieved in 2, 200, or 2,000 years is not relevant. What really matters is whether it is reasonable to seek a certain goal, considering a number of constraints. Recall that the purpose of feasibility testing is providing practical guidance. In other words, we are interested in knowing whether a particular project is worth fighting for, even if it is not immediately feasible. One may ask whether a distant state of affairs is capable of motivating agents to act in a certain way. From the study of history, it becomes apparent that many individuals are ready to act, and even to die, for an ideal which is far from being immediately realizable. While temporary feasibility will be more useful for individuals who have a preference for short-term goals, pervasive feasibility shall provide guidance to those who feel the appeal to pursue an ideal of justice which may yet seem rather distant.

A second objection goes as follows: how can we distinguish what is merely temporarily unfeasible from what is pervasively unfeasible? For instance, how can we plausibly say that, although X cannot be done right now, it may be done in the future? In the next section, I shall attempt to address this question in a systematic manner by discussing types of reasons for which a project may be charged with being pervasively unfeasible. A short answer to the question will emphasize distinguishing political preferences and processes, which are dynamic and subject to continuous change, from more structural barriers to the implementation of a given project, such as political culture and historical context. Thus, while a temporary feasibility test discusses the appropriate *circumstances* for doing X (whether that be peace or war, economic growth or recession, powerful or weak trade unions, and so on), a pervasive feasibility test analyses whether it is possible and sustainable to implement X within a particular social order, by referring to the expected *consequences* of so doing. To further object that every temporarily unfeasible project is potentially pervasively feasible if we look sufficiently far ahead would mean adopting the "unrestrained" approach, which has already been rejected here. In what follows, I shall discuss these issues in greater detail.

III. A moderate test of pervasive feasibility

Key features of the test

I am now ready to discuss the specific requirements of a pervasively feasible theory of distributive justice in a liberal democracy. I argue that a policy is pervasively feasible if it combines at least four key features: (i) it matches, to a certain degree, the political culture of a given community; (ii) it is economically sustainable; (iii) it can be translated into concrete institutions and policies, with a reasonable prospect of delivering the social goals underlying the policy; and (iv) it is compatible with the degree of social solidarity amongst the individuals to which the policy is to apply. I argue that each of these criteria is a necessary condition for pervasive feasibility. Although it may be reasonable to think of different degrees of (un)feasibility, where some projects are more or less feasible than others, the four requirements establish a binary setting whereby a given policy can either meet or fail to meet them, with the purpose of providing action-guidance.[40] Before discussing each of the requirements in detail, let me provide a few preliminary clarifications regarding the nature and goals of the test.

By "moderate" test I mean an analysis of critical dimensions of feasibility that focuses on plausibility and likelihood, and not on proper demonstration. The test asks whether a world in which theory X is implemented is possible and speculates about how such a world would look. It does so by drawing on thought experiments and historical analogies.[41] Admittedly, there is no way of being entirely sure of what the impacts of applying X would be. In fact, "[a]nswers to questions about humanly plausible worlds are not given by the social scientists' generalizations, or the philosophers' possible worlds, or by any other method or model. They are given by judgment, in particular, by practical judgment".[42] Thus we may reasonably claim that individuals would not comply with a policy which is entirely detached from their political culture. This type of qualitative exercise is not scientific in a narrow sense, but it can be systematic, if the types of reasons on which a charge of unfeasibility can be grounded are carefully identified and problematized. Therefore, although we may never know for sure whether a policy is pervasively feasible, "we can make more or less educated guesses".[43]

It should be emphasised that the test is to be performed at a specific moment of time, based on the knowledge available at that moment.[44] In this sense, it may need to be revised in the face of new developments, such as technological improvements. As I have suggested, it is not inconsistent to say that a policy is *pervasively* feasible *under* certain conditions, namely a particular production function and a given stock of natural resources, which may change as time passes. Hence, the results of the test should be regarded as provisional. As I have noted, the test which is being outlined refers to the liberal democratic order, which, for simplicity, is here understood in terms of four main institutions: (i) free and fair elections; (ii) responsive government; (iii) respect for human rights; and (iv) a market economy. Testing policies meant for a different type of institutional network may imply other feasibility requirements than the ones listed. Since my main concern is the EU, it is sensible to focus on liberal democracy. Finally, notice that my purpose is not only to identify sources of unfeasibility, but to indicate strategies to enhance the feasibility potential of a given project. This is why, while formulating four feasibility requirements, I shall discuss ways in which policies can be adapted to overcome their unfeasibility status.

A question that remains to be addressed is whether the type of predictions offered by the test are good enough for our purpose. I believe this to be the case for three reasons. First, if the main goal of the test is to provide practical guidance, we only need to understand the big picture, with a limited amount of detail. To return to my previous example, anticipating that non-compliance would be "very high" would be enough for a sound feasibility assessment. We do not need to know what the exact non-compliance rate would be. Secondly, it is true that this exercise requires us to engage with a considerable deal of speculation regarding the hypothetical impacts of different options. Yet what choice in life does not require us to do so? Whenever we consider alternative courses of action, we speculate about the *likely* consequences of our actions. Yet most individuals would agree that epistemic uncertainty about the future should not allow us to act without thinking first.[45] Thirdly, the four requirements allow for a constructive dimension in the test. Insofar as the test identifies a differentiated set of sources of unfeasibility, it fosters the understanding of ways to improve the prospects of feasibility of a given policy. For these reasons, and despite its limitations, the test may be regarded as a useful toolkit for political action.

Before analysing four key feasibility requirements for a theory of distributive justice in detail, I should overview what *types of reasons* can be plausibly employed by my argument. The need to take this preliminary step is twofold. First, if I am interested in obtaining a non-arbitrary and consistent set of constraints, I must first identify the social mechanisms behind unfeasibility. For sure, it is not enough to say that X is a feasibility constraint; I also have to explain *how* exactly X works as a prevalent barrier to change. Second, I need to explain what makes a feasibility constraint pervasive, and not merely temporary. Again, doing so systematically requires a reflection on the kind of reasons which may be plausibly advanced to support charges of pervasive unfeasibility. In what follows, I shall introduce four types of justification for pervasive unfeasibility: (i) high levels of non-compliance; (ii) erosion of social stability; (iii) weakening of trust in institutions; and (4) lack of means for implementation.

The first type of reason is that the implementation of theory X would be followed by broad-based refusal to comply. The basic idea is that, if too many individuals fail to comply with a certain policy, this will eventually undermine its effectiveness.[46] Non-compliance can assume many different forms, from mere inertia to acting in a certain way, to organizing a strike or engaging with violent protest. An illustrative example of the potential impact of non-compliance is former British prime minister Margaret Thatcher's attempt to launch a poll tax, eventually blocked by a massive wave of protests, riots, and refusals to pay the tax. If massive non-compliance can be anticipated, based on good reasons to think that the failure to comply will be pervasive, and not merely circumstantial, one may appeal to this argument.[47] In turn, non-compliance can be expected based on a variety of features of a policy that implements a principle, such as gross violations of self-interest, incompatibility with the basic preferences of the citizens of liberal democracies, historical precedents of non-compliance, and so on. Thus understood, non-compliance is one source of pervasive unfeasibility.

The second type of reason is that theory X would generate much instability. If the resulting state of affairs were one of intense social conflict, dysfunctional political institutions, or even chaos, the policy would not be sustainable.[48] To illustrate this point, and to understand how it differs from non-compliance, imagine a society in which Robert Nozick's principle of legitimacy is fully applied. Nozick suggests that to be legitimate, private property must have been rightfully acquired in the first place, and rightfully transmitted from owner to owner until the present day.[49] If we were to challenge the legitimacy of the ownership of each piece of land on the grounds of past wars, robberies, or other forms of injustice, the result would very likely be chaotic. In such a context, every individual could have claims on each other's property, raising generalized uncertainty. In addition, it would be very hard to adjudicate who was right, due to the lack of historical sources. Therefore, a principle of justice that creates generalized instability is self-defeating, insofar as it undermines the basic conditions for its implementation.

The third type of reason is that theory X would disrupt trust in the institutions of a given political community. A type of trust that is particularly relevant for feasibility assessments in liberal democracy is linked to the fulfilment of a sense of justice. By sense of justice I mean the widespread perception that political institutions realize, to an acceptable extent, a set of public values and beliefs, which themselves constitute the essentials of a social order and without which such order could not subsist.[50] Notice that non-compliance is not the only social mechanism potentially triggered by a sense of injustice. If a sense of injustice is sufficiently widespread, citizens will eventually call either for the replacement of the policy or for the reinvention of the institutions, as in the case of the collapse of the French Fourth Republic. It seems hardly possible to effectively rule a modern country if citizens radically distrust the capacity of political institutions to deliver basic standards of justice, such as rule of law enforcement. This is particularly true for democracies, where the expected standards of justice can be higher than in other regime types.

Finally, the test assumes that theory X can only be realized if there are the means to do so. The intuition behind this argument has already been discussed and is somewhat trivial: we can only do things that can actually be done. A less obvious task will be defining what can and cannot be done. For instance, there is reasonable disagreement about ways to promote economic growth and to reduce unemployment. This information will shape the feasibility status of a number of redistributive policies. An illustration of this point is the discussion on whether a basic income policy would lead to an unsustainable decrease in a country's workforce by creating incentives not to work. In other cases, however, it is easier to anticipate that a given principle cannot be realized under conditions of resource scarcity. An appeal to an argument of this kind is also plausible whenever there is no agent who can legitimately be called to realize a given principle, or any known policy or institution that can deliver the goals of the principle. I shall return to this point later on.

The reasons just presented can be evoked to charge normative theories in multiple domains of pervasive unfeasibility. In what follows, I shall focus my attention on theories of distributive justice. The next sections will present four feasibility requirements that are justified on the grounds of one or more of the reasons previously presented. These four requirements may not be exhaustive, but as Chapter 5 will demonstrate, they are crucial in the context of EU membership.

Fitting in the political culture

Consider the following question: to what extent must a distributive policy fit the political culture of a specific polity in order to be feasible? On the one hand, it seems hard to implement a principle that does not match at all the beliefs, customs, and public values of the society that is required to comply with it. For instance, polities hosting dissimilar ethnic or religious groups have often developed differentiated laws and institutions to achieve political stability. This practice goes back at least to the Roman Empire and is still observable in strongly regionalized states such as Switzerland and the United Kingdom. The lack of such adjustment to local beliefs and practices has arguably been the reason why a few attempts to export Western democracy to other regions of the world failed dramatically. On the other hand, a great deal of change throughout history has been counter-cultural. The emancipation of women, decolonization, and globalization happened against a background of male predominance, Western imperialism, and nationalism, respectively. This suggests that culture is not the ultimate obstacle to change. Hence, is political culture a pervasive constraint or just a temporary barrier to change?

To begin with, I should clarify what I mean by culture. In a context of high mobility and intense exchange at a global scale, it is problematic to refer to culture in a unified sense. While states are gradually becoming multicultural in their demographic composition, identities are increasingly situated at the intersection of different cultures. However, this important development does not imply the abandonment of the concept of culture, understood as a system of symbols and meanings which shape (but do not determine) human practices.[51] In this account, "[t]o engage with cultural practice is to make use of a semiotic code to do something in the world".[52] Once internalized, the code has the dual function of providing meaning to the reality in which individuals are embedded and to their own behaviour. Indeed, "[p]eople who are members of a semiotic community are capable not only of recognizing statements made in a semiotic code [...] but of using the code as well, of putting it into practice".[53] Thus the fact that "different worlds of meaning" can be found within the same state does not render the concept of culture obsolete. When we talk about *political* culture we are not assuming cultural uniformity; in fact, we are referring to a particular way of organizing difference.[54]

Let me illustrate the significance of political culture as a pervasive feasibility constraint with a concrete example. Consider the different levels of social provision across liberal democracies. A few authors have systematized these differences in welfare state typologies, which typically include a northern or social democrat model, a Christian democrat model, and a liberal model.[55] It is true that much of these differences may be explained by the historical experience of each country, but political culture has also played an important role. According to the European Social Survey, people living in eastern and southern Europe ask, on average, for more comprehensive social provision than do people in central Europe.[56] Easterners and southerners assign more responsibilities to the government in ensuring a high level of employment, a reasonable standard of living for the unemployed and the elderly, and adequate healthcare and childcare services.[57] In turn, Europeans tend to be considerably more supportive of social provision than North Americans, and less supportive than Japanese and South Koreans.[58] Would it be feasible to standardize the level of social provision across these countries based on a demonstrably sound principle of distributive justice?

The answer would likely be negative. The first reason is that the perceptions of what is just are highly contextual. As a number of communitarian authors have pointed out, all conceptions of justice emerge within specific communities.[59] A public conception of justice is a repository of local concerns, collective experiences, and specific anxieties about the future. Any attempts to impose policies that do not fit the political culture of the community risk undermining the general sense of justice which characterizes well-ordered societies, raising serious issues of political stability and compliance. In addition, any conception of justice comprises particular causal explanations of the world. For instance, if we were to ask western Europeans or North Americans why certain individuals are poor while others are rich, we would typically receive different answers. Accordingly, the perceived degree of individual responsibility for one's success or misfortune, the amount of inequality which is deemed acceptable, and the role assigned to the state in fighting poverty seem to be correlated to political culture.[60] Even the content of basic concepts in distributive justice seems to vary across political cultures. For instance, most liberal democracies recognize equal opportunity as a central social and political value; yet what France takes this to mean is considerably different from how it is understood in the United States. All this suggests that it is insufficient for a feasible distributive policy to be normatively compelling and to work nicely elsewhere.

It should be noted that the political culture of a given society may change considerably. In fact, "worlds of meaning" are "contested, mutable and highly permeable".[61] However, it would be a mistake to think that we could simply get rid of the political lexicon of a society, at least in the absence of the use of force. Revolutionary experiences of social engineering from scratch are always either tyrannical or unsustainable.[62] Whomever wants to achieve political change in a liberal democracy has to engage with the meanings and symbols of a particular society, even if the ultimate goal is to reform them. In the process of creating new meanings and symbols, it is not only the older ones that are subjected to change; the aimed principle of justice is also adapted, and even reformulated. As Fred Dallmayr points out, "[e]ven assuming widespread acceptance of universal norms, we know at least since Aristotle that rules do not directly translate into *praxis* but require careful interpretation and application".[63] This suggests "that it is insufficient [...] to throw a mantle of universal rules over humankind without paying simultaneous attention to public debate and the role of political will formation".[64]

What, then, are the requirements of a feasible distributive policy concerning culture? I propose the following formulation: to originate pervasively feasible policies, a principle of justice has to be able to be *interpreted* within the terms of the particular culture to which it is to be applied. By interpretation I mean the process by which concrete meaning is given to an abstract statement. This process includes a number of tasks, namely, (i) *making the principle intelligible* to the members of a given society, by referring to local beliefs, public values, and history; the principle may be presented either as a corroboration of these older codes or as a critique of them; (ii) *ensuring a degree of consistency* between the principle at stake and the other principles endorsed by that society; this may be achieved either by adjusting the new principle or by reformulating the older ones; (iii) *filling in the gaps* resulting from the abstract and general character of the principle; notably, this includes defining the exact amount of a certain good which is to be provided to the citizens; and (iv) *designing the specific institutions and policies* which are to deliver the principle, in accordance with the institutional network currently available and the specific needs of the population. If any of the steps (i) to (iv) is not satisfactorily addressed in a given society, the principle will likely be pervasively unfeasible in this society.

This approach raises at least two difficulties. First, who is to interpret the principle? Second, what if the principle is not at all compatible with a given culture? To answer the first question – the principle should be interpreted through democratic processes. It will be the task of political institutions to discuss the possible nuances of the principle, to design specific policy instruments, and to work out solutions to concrete problems raised by its implementation. The answer to the second question is somewhat more complex. A principle which strongly goes against the political culture of a given society seems to be pervasively unfeasible. This is exasperating, since it may mean the perpetuation of injustice. However, it does not dismiss the possibility that less ambitious progress might be achieved. One may lower the original goal, trying to achieve change little by little. In these cases, the main challenge seems to be establishing precedents. This may happen somewhat spontaneously, as a result of unforeseen circumstances, but it usually requires a timely seizing of opportunities by the relevant social actors, as well as the ability to create new and powerful symbols.

Being economically sustainable

The second feasibility requirement is that the implementation of a principle be economically sustainable. By economical sustainability I mean that the principle can be implemented without interruption for a theoretically unlimited period of time. More specifically, this means that realizing the principle at a moment of time t will not hamper the chances of realizing it at $t+1$. Why should political theorists care about sustainability? Under conditions of resource scarcity, the prospects of normatively defensible principles of justice are limited.[65] Redistribution is further conditioned by the inefficiency costs it generates. Each additional unit of tax produces a dead-weight loss, which implies a decrease in the potential GDP. If the redistributive effort is too heavy, it may become self-destructive, in the sense that there will be fewer and fewer resources left to redistribute.[66] Thus implementing Singer's strong principle of redistribution is pervasively unfeasible insofar as it would imply a level of taxation so high that it would seriously undercut the creation of wealth. As John Rawls has suggested, feasibility requires a compromise between fairness and efficiency.[67] The task of finding the right balance can only be performed empirically, by referring to each particular production possibility frontier and each potential GDP.

A context of particular relevance for economic feasibility is economic crisis. To what extent can crisis shape the feasibility status of a given principle of justice? One could assert straight away that, since most crises are temporary, they are not relevant for pervasive feasibility assessments. Yet an important challenge arises from the cyclical nature of business within capitalist economies. If the implementation of a principle of distributive justice has to be suspended every x years – whenever growth slows down, unemployment rises, and public revenue falls – can it be appropriately deemed pervasively feasible? The answer depends on whether it would have been possible to avoid such suspension, by means of precautionary measures. In fact, saying that a certain level of social provision is unfeasible due to bad economic performance constitutes an *ex post* judgement. The fact that it is impossible to afford a given policy *now* does not exclude the possibility that, had enough public savings been made, the policy could still be realized. This suggests that pervasive feasibility should refer to a long-term resource management strategy, a topic that I shall develop in Chapter 5. Therefore, the key question for pervasive feasibility will be, is it possible for a given principle to accommodate the fluctuations of the business cycle through any specific policy mechanism? If it is, implementing the principle may be feasible; if not, the principle should be rejected.

The problem is what should be done regarding compelling principles which fail to be economically sustainable once translated into policies. Should we simply abandon sound ideals of justice which fail to meet the requirement of economic sustainability? In these cases, the appropriate procedure will be trying to adjust the principle to the available resources and efficiency constraints. Thus, Singer's strong principle could be tentatively reformulated as follows: utility-equalizing redistribution is required up to the point at which each additional unit of equality represents an unbearable cost in terms of efficiency. However, it is important to stress that this strategy of searching for a proxy to the ideal case will not always lead to satisfactory results. As R. G. Lipsey and Kelvin Lancaster have noted in "The General Theory of the Second Best", "if there is introduced into a general equilibrium system a constraint which prevents the attainment of one of the Paretian conditions, the other Paretian conditions, although still attainable, are, in general, no longer desirable".[68] In other words, the process of adjusting a principle to feasibility constraints may require substantial deviation from its original goals. If the final result is unacceptable from a normative standpoint, the principle should then be abandoned.

Being translatable into institutions and policies

A third requirement of pervasive feasibility is related to the prospects of operationalization of a given principle of justice. Under this requirement, the implementation of a principle is only pervasively feasible if there are – or will be in a conceivable future – *policy instruments* which can effectively realize it, and if there is – or will be in a conceivable future – any *agent* which can be called to realize such policies. To illustrate the point, consider a principle of justice which requires citizens to give a certain amount of love to their fellow citizens. How could such a principle be institutionalized? What kind of policy device could enforce a specific pattern of distribution of a good as spontaneous as love? Because there is no policy and no agent that is capable of applying it, either now or in the foreseeable future, the principle implies pervasive unfeasibility. Another example is a principle of justice which requires that politicians should abstain from populist promises and that citizens should vote wisely. What kind of policies could prevent politicians from being populists in a liberal democracy? And how could the content of a "wise" vote be defined? Of course, one may argue that education policies would decrease the likelihood of certain types of populism and establish procedural criteria to achieve an informed vote. Yet these policies are far from giving us any strong reason to think that the principle would be realized. Therefore, in the absence of appropriate policy instruments and agents to deliver it, a given principle cannot be more than a philosophical ideal.

An agency-related issue of great importance for feasibility assessments is the dynamics of politics. This includes the political incentives posed by particular party and electoral systems, the relative strength of trade unions, the types of compromise required to form government coalitions, and so on. The key question would be, are they temporary or pervasive constraints? Although very powerful, these constraints should be regarded as temporary. A future in which a reform blocked by electoral incentives is eventually implemented may not be foreseeable, but it is certainly conceivable. In politics, circumstances change dramatically, while political incentives vary accordingly. In the EU, the banking union looked unfeasible before, and in the early stages of, the crisis that started in 2008. Similarly, a European Defence Union seemed very far away before Donald Trump won the elections in the United States. Financial crisis, the international context, and changing preferences rendered these temporarily unfeasible projects at least partially realizable. Their previous unfeasibility status resulted from barriers that could be overcome – although, before being overcome, these barriers may have seemed quite definitive. It is true that some of the features of a political system are indeed pervasive, but these have already been incorporated in the political culture requirement. Translatability into institutions and policies only requires the possibility of democratic agency.

Being consistent with the degree of social solidarity

Finally, a pervasively feasible distributive policy must be minimally consistent with the degree of social solidarity amongst the individuals which are to be bound by it. The requirement of "minimal consistency" takes two different insights into account. On the one hand, social solidarity, at least to a certain extent, can be constructed and extended beyond its existing limits. Historically speaking, both deliberated action and unintended events have produced higher solidarity bonds between individuals. Consider, for instance, the bonds created by the nationalist campaigns and state-building policies of the nineteenth and early twentieth century and through participation in the Second World War. This suggests that solidarity is not static and that "avant-garde" political agency can be effective.[69] Therefore, a principle of justice which requires a level of social solidarity higher than the existing one should not be immediately discarded on grounds of being over demanding. On the other hand, the extent to which social solidarity can be extended to additional groups of people seems to be limited. Individuals are always willing to do more for certain groups of people than for others. Accordingly, a cosmopolitanism that presupposes that redistribution towards fellow citizens and towards distant foreigners should be exactly the same seems grossly unfeasible. Hence, to be feasible, distributional principles seem to presuppose a degree of social solidarity that is somewhat proportional to their degree of demandingness.

A helpful way to conceptualize how much social solidarity is needed to realize a given principle of justice is to think in terms of a scale or a continuum. For instance, different amounts of redistribution presuppose different levels of social solidarity to be pervasively feasible. This approach is preferable to a binary account, which simplistically assesses social solidarity as either "existent" or "inexistent". It is right to think that individuals are willing to do more for the people to whom they feel morally closer than for others. Yet this does not exclude that they might still be willing to do *something* for distant strangers, particularly if the costs of doing so are relatively low. For instance, many individuals voluntarily contribute to remote humanitarian causes, but typically lesser amounts than the taxes that they pay for domestic redistribution. If a principle of justice is not consistent with the differentiated degrees of social solidarity, it will most likely face a high degree of non-compliance and generate much political instability. Thus, a feasible distributive policy has both to be open to a possible increase of social solidarity and to be minimally consistent with limited altruism. It is worth noting an important implication of what has been said. On this account, social solidarity is not simply a function of ethnicity, culture, and shared history. Although these aspects are very important, solidarity is a complex and dynamic variable. Therefore, the existing social and political arrangements should not be used too quickly to dismiss the prospects of social reform.

IV. Conclusion

I have argued that it is possible to outline a moderate feasibility test for a theory of distributive justice. I suggested that, to be manageable, the test has to be "constrained" to a particular paradigm of social order, such as liberal democracy. I have also argued that the test should focus on assessing pervasive feasibility, understood as practical restrictions that human agency can reasonably be expected to overcome. In addition, I have claimed that a pervasively feasible distributive policy presents at least four key features: (i) showing a degree of adherence to the political culture of a given community; (ii) being economically sustainable; (iii) being translatable into policies and institutions, which have reasonable prospects of delivering the social goals of its underlying principle(s); and (iv) being proportional to the degree of social solidarity amongst the individuals bound by that policy.

Notes

1 A concern for facts is typical of both "non-ideal" and "realist" political theorists. These terms are overlapping but not synonymous. As Matt Sleat puts it, "[w]hereas the ideal/non-ideal theory debate consists of a series of methodological issues that take place squarely within the liberal framework, and hence retains many (if not all) of its assumptions regarding the purpose of politics and the ambitions of political theory, realism is a competing theory of politics in its own right that presents a radical challenge to those liberal assumptions". Since the account of distributive justice presented in this study is predicated on liberal assumptions, in what follows I shall focus on the insights of the non-ideal position. See Matt Sleat, "Realism, Liberalism and Non-Ideal Theory or, Are There Two Ways to do Realistic Political Theory?", *Political Studies* 64 (2016), p. 27.

2 Matt Sleat, "Realism, Liberalism and Non-Ideal Theory or, Are There Two Ways to do Realistic Political Theory?", p. 29. As A. John Simmons has noted, the distinction between "ideal" and "non-ideal" theory is not a straightforward one. For simplicity, I shall assume that the main distinguishing feature of the non-ideal approach is the emphasis put on feasibility constraints, such as Rawlsian non-compliance with what justice requires and unfavourable conditions. See John A. Simmons, "Ideal and Nonideal Theory", *Philosophy & Public Affairs* 38 (2010), pp. 5–6.

3 Amartya Sen, "What Do We Want from a Theory of Justice", *The Journal of Philosophy* 103 (2006), p. 217. Sen gives the example of the reform of the healthcare system in the United States to illustrate the point that significant advancements of justice would often be impossible in the absence of non-ideal commitments.

4 While a few theorists with non-ideal concerns are ready to incorporate facts both when they define an abstract conception of justice and when they discuss the means for its implementation (John Rawls), others take facts into account only at the implementation stage (Robert Goodin). The principles advanced in the previous chapters have taken basic facts into account. In this chapter, I shall suggest that the implementation stage requires a much more comprehensive set of constraints than the initial level of abstract theorizing. See, respectively, John Rawls, *A Theory of Justice: Revised Edition* (Cambridge MA, 1999); and Robert E. Goodin, "Political Ideals and Political Practice", *British Journal of Political Science* 25 (1995), pp. 37–56.

5 Marc Stears, "The Vocation of Political Theory: Principles, Empirical Enquiry and the Politics of Opportunity", *European Journal of Political Theory* 4 (2005), p. 347.

6 As suggested by David Eastlund, it is critical for non-ideal theorists that their approach does not turn into a prima facie objection against ideal theory. Utopian thinking has its own role to play, as attested by the enduring presence of a number of utopian works in the canon of political philosophy. Therefore, I must stress the point that my preference for "realistic utopias", to use John Rawls's expression, results from a concern with action-guidance, not a full rejection of utopianism. See David Eastlund, "Utopophobia", *Philosophy & Public Affairs* 42 (2014), pp. 113–134; and John Rawls, *The Law of Peoples* (Cambridge MA, 2001), pp. 11–22.

7 This question has notably been raised by Philippe Van Parijs. See, for instance, Philippe Van Parijs, "Must Europe Be Belgian?", *Just Democracy: The Rawls-Machiavelli Programme* (Colchester, 2011).

8 Laura Valentini, "Ideal vs Non-Ideal Theory: A Conceptual Map", *Philosophy Compass* 7/9 (2012), p. 660.

9 Ibid.

10 For instance, Michael Phillips attempts to derive "principles adequate to historical circumstances", yet he only refers to the criteria of logical consistence and psychological possibility. In turn, Mark Jensen suggests that any principle is practically possible if "(a) it is logically consistent (b) it conforms to physical laws (c) it presumes our world history (d) it reflects natural human abilities". While the former list seems incomplete (consider, for instance, economic and cultural constraints), the latter seems underspecified (what does "presuming our world history" specifically mean?). See Michael Phillips, "Reflections on the Transition from Ideal to Non-Ideal Theory", *Noûs* 19 (1985), pp. 561–562. Mark Jensen, "The Limits of Practical Possibility", *The Journal of Political Philosophy* 17 (2009), p. 172.

11 John Rawls, *A Theory of Justice: Revised Edition*, pp. 109–112.

12 It has been rightly observed that desirability is independent from feasibility status. The cure for cancer is desirable, even if it cannot be achieved. Yet to act to achieve a desirable end that is nevertheless unfeasible seems unreasonable. In the previous example, this would mean, for instance, performing a surgery that has no chance of being successful. Although desirability is a relevant moral category, it is not directly linked to moral obligation. I may be able to identify a moral ideal such as equality, yet I can only be bound by it to the extent that equality can actually be achieved.

13 Adam Swift, "Public Opinion and Political Philosophy: The Relation between Social-Scientific and Philosophical Analyses of Distributive Justice", *Ethical Theory and Moral Practice* 2 (1999), pp. 352–353.

14 Immanuel Kant, "On the Common Saying: This May Be True in Theory But It Does Not Apply in Practice", in Hans Reiss (ed.), *Kant's Political Writings* (Cambridge, 1991), pp. 61–92. Although the validity of this axiom has been under scrutiny in recent years, there are good reasons to adopt it. These are helpfully listed in Steve F. Sapontzis, "'Ought' Does Imply 'Can'", *The Southern Journal of Philosophy* 29 (1991), pp. 383–393.

15 Allen Buchanan, *Justice, Legitimacy, and Self-Determination* (Oxford, 2004), p. 61.

16 As proposed in Plato, *The Republic* (Oxford, 2008), Book V.

17 There are obvious epistemic difficulties in making predictions about the future, particularly regarding unprecedented events. As I shall argue later in the chapter, a satisfactory account of the types of reasons to justify a charge of unfeasibility is needed for that purpose.

18 The first systematic account of redistribution in the modern sense (i.e. understood as a right, as opposed to charity, or hospitality) is François-Nöel Babeuf's, in the last years of the eighteenth century. See Samuel Fleischacker, *A Short History of Distributive Justice* (Harvard, 2004), pp. 75–79.

19 Thomas Piketty, *Capital in the Twenty-First Century* (Cambridge MA, 2014), Figure 2.4.

20 Compare, for instance, the early development of the welfare state in England to its relatively late development in France and very limited development in the United States. See, respectively, Bernard Harris, *The Origins of the British Welfare State: Society, State and Social Welfare in England and Wales* (Basingstoke, 2004); Paul V. Dutton, *Origins of the French Welfare State: The Struggle for Social Reform in France 1914–1947* (Cambridge, 2002); and Walter I. Trattner, *From Poor Law to Welfare State: A History of Social Welfare in America* (New York, 1999).

21 On the distinction between fact-dependent and fact-independent principles see G. A. Cohen, "Facts and Principles", *Philosophy & Public Affairs* 31 (2003), pp. 211–245.

22 The term "technical feasibility" is used by David Miller to refer to gross forms of unfeasibility such as contravening "physical laws or rock-bottom social or psychological laws". He gives the example of a project "that required all citizens to have advanced mathematical skills or to be able to recall every transaction they had made over the last twelve months". See David Miller, *Justice for Earthlings: Essays in Political Philosophy* (Cambridge, 2013), p. 37.

23 John Rawls, *A Theory of Justice: Revised Edition*, p. 119.

24 See, for instance, Benjamin R. Barber, "Review: Justifying Justice: Problems of Psychology, Measurement, and Politics in Rawls", *The American Political Science Review* 69 (1975), pp. 663–674; Michael S. Pritchard, "Rawls's Moral Psychology", *The Southwestern Journal of Philosophy* 8 (1977), pp. 59–72; Joseph H. Carens, *Equality, Moral Incentives, and the Market: An Essay in Utopian Politico-Economic Theory* (Chicago, 1981); and G. A. Cohen, "The Pareto Argument for Inequality", *Social Philosophy and Policy* 12 (1995).

25 The notion of psychological impossibility in moral theory has notably been discussed by R. M. Hare. Hare suggests that it may be impossible for an individual to act in a certain way for purely non-physical reasons. These psychological constraints downgrade the level of moral responsibility of the individual and may result in disobedience of rules. As Galen Strawson has noted, the pursuit of this type of argument may eventually lead one to challenge the very notion of moral responsibility, considering that individuals cannot choose who they are. See R. M. Hare, *Freedom and Reason* (Oxford, 1963), pp. 67–84; and Galen Strawson, "The Impossibility of Moral Responsibility", *Philosophical Studies* 75 (1994), pp. 5–24.

26 Owen Flanagan, *The Varieties of Moral Personality: Ethics and Psychological Realism* (Cambridge MA, 1991), p. 32. An alternative view, carefully articulated

by Lisa Tessman, suggests that some moral principles are non-negotiable, that is, they hold even when it is psychologically not possible to fulfil them. See Lisa Tessman, *Moral Failure: On the Impossible Demands of Morality* (Oxford, 2015).

27 The objection that this level of generosity may be psychologically possible for some individuals but not for others, even if sound, would render the application of psychology to moral theory unhelpful. Following this logic, there may always be someone for whom a particular moral principle is psychologically impossible due, for instance, to personal history.

28 Most consultancy firms and government bodies operate under a *ceteris paribus* assumption. Policy is evaluated from the perspective of incremental change, in relation to the best available alternative. Yet "the best available alternative" typically excludes radical change. Think tanks can sometimes constitute an exception to this way of proceeding. On the standard proceeding to assess public policy see David L. Weimer and Aidan R. Vining, *Policy Analysis: Concepts and Practice* (New York, 2011).

29 Elizabeth Anderson, "Ethical Assumptions in Economic Theory: Some Lessons from the History of Credit and Bankruptcy", *Ethical Theory and Moral Practice* 7 (2004), p. 347.

30 See John Maynard Keynes, "Economic Possibilities for Our Grandchildren", in Lorenzo Pecchi and Gustavo Piga (eds), *Keynes Revisited: Economic Possibilities for Our Grandchildren* (Cambridge MA, 2008); and Thomas More, *Utopia* (Cambridge, 1989).

31 For instance, communes such as "Twin Oaks" (Virginia) and "The Farm" (Tennessee), founded in 1967 and 1971, respectively, have existed for more than 40 years. There are many other examples.

32 By social order I mean a relatively stable and large-scaled system of cooperation, which coordinates individual goals and allocates resources. The nouns "economic" and "political" put emphasis on particular dimensions of social order. The adjective "liberal democratic" refers to a particular type of social order. For a brief discussion of social order as the solution to the problems of cooperation and coordination, see Michael Hechter and Christine Horne, "The Problem of Social Order", in Michael Hechter and Christine Horne (eds), *Theories of Social Order* (Stanford, 2003), pp. 27–32.

33 This assumption echoes the philosophy of the Enlightenment, particularly René Decartes' goal of "bâtir dans un fonds qui est tout à moi", and builds from there. See René Descartes, *A Discourse on the Method* (Oxford, 2008).

34 On this point, see Karl Popper, "Utopia and Violence", in *Conjectures and Refutations: The Growth of Scientific Knowledge* (New York, 1989).

35 Tommaso Campanella, *The City of the Sun* (Berkeley, 1981); Francis Bacon, "New Atlantis", in *Three Early Modern Utopias* (Oxford, 2008).

36 A branch of historiography has highlighted the role played by the industrial revolution in the ending of slavery. It was not only a humanitarian awakening that allowed for the abolishment, but also a comprehensive process of industrialization, which made the economy less dependent on an agricultural workforce. On this view, see especially Eric Williams, *Capitalism and Slavery* (Chapel Hill, 1994).

37 This confusion is apparent in many political debates. For instance, the advocates of austerity in Greece often employ the argument that there is no alternative to

this economic strategy (i.e. "non-austerity" is unfeasible). However, as many renowned economists, including Paul Krugman, Joseph Stiglitz, and Thomas Piketty, have suggested, there are credible alternative paths. Thus, the argument should be that austerity is desirable (or preferable to other options), not that other strategies are unfeasible. On the way in which economic theories may become self-fulfilling prophecies, see Fabrizio Ferraro, Jeffrey Pfeffer, and Robert I. Sutton, "Economics Language and Assumptions: How Theories Can Become Sell-fulfilling", *Academy of Management Review* 30 (2005), pp. 8–24.

38 On expensive tastes, see G. A. Cohen, "Expensive Tastes Rides Again", in Justine Burley (ed.), *Dworkin and His Critics* (Malden, 2004), pp. 3–29.

39 Juha Räikkä, "The Feasibility Condition in Political Theory", *The Journal of Political Philosophy* 6 (1998), p. 29.

40 Holly Lawford-Smith has suggested that the binary approach "makes feasibility all but useless in politics". The reason is that in politics "[w]e don't want to rule options off the table entirely". However, it seems critical both for the manageability of the political debate and for the sake of political stability that some options be (democratically) ruled out. This does not exclude the theoretical point that some projects may be more unfeasible than others. A project which does not meet any of the four requirements is more distant from reality than one which fails to meet only one. See Holly Lawford-Smith, "Understanding Political Feasibility", *The Journal of Political Philosophy* 21 (2003), p. 244.

41 Although thought experiments and historical analogies can reveal the implausibility of a given scenario, each of these methods has its own limitations. See Tamar Szabo Gendler, *Thought Experiment: On the Powers and Limits of Imaginary Cases* (New York, 2013), pp. 18–24; and Peter N. Stearns, "Forecasting the Future: Historical Analogies and Technological Determinism", *The Public Historian* 5 (1983), pp. 30–54.

42 Geoffrey Hawthorn, *Plausible Worlds: Possibility and Understanding in History and the Social Sciences* (Cambridge, 1991), p. xi.

43 Holly Lawford-Smith, "Understanding Political Feasibility", p. 243.

44 Mark Jensen helpfully distinguishes two types of possibility. One thing is to say that an event is possible *per se* (first-order possibility); another thing is to say that an event would be possible if certain conditions, currently impossible, were brought about (second-order possibility). Due to epistemic uncertainty about the future, the test must take the world as it is now (for instance, it should refer to currently existing resources). Accordingly, it focuses on first-order possibility. See Mark Jensen, "The Limits of Practical Possibility", pp. 168–184.

45 In fact, recent research has shown that our imaginative thought is much more reliable than one would think at a first glance. On this point, see Ruth M. J. Byrne, *The Rational Imagination: How People Create Alternatives to Reality* (Cambridge MA, 2005).

46 The importance of the prospect of compliance by "ordinary men" has been highlighted by Henry Sidgwick. See Henry Sidgwick, *The Methods of Ethics* (Cambridge, 2012).

47 Notice that the consequences of launching the tax where not unforeseeable. For instance, Nigel Lawson, Thatcher's chancellor of the Exchequer, warned that her controversial poll tax would be "completely unworkable and politically catastrophic". See Matt Chorley, Claire Ellicott, and David Wilkes,

"Thatcher's Chancellor Nigel Lawson warned Tory PM Her Poll Tax was 'Completely Unworkable and Politically Catastrophic'", *The Daily Mail Online* (30 December 2014).

48 Sune Lægaard has helpfully distinguished stability as a normative ideal from stability as a feasibility constraint, referring to the seminal work of John Rawls, and focusing on the debate on liberal nationalism. See Sune Lægaard, "Feasibility and Stability in Normative Political Philosophy: The Case of Liberal Nationalism", *Ethical Theory and Practice* 9 (2009), pp. 399–416.

49 Robert Nozick, *Anarchy, State and Utopia* (Malden, 1974), pp. 150–182.

50 The concept of a sense of justice, as well its relevance for liberal societies, was first discussed by John Rawls. See John Rawls, "The Sense of Justice", *The Philosophical Review* 72 (1963), pp. 281–305.

51 William H. Sewell Jr, "The Concept(s) of Culture", in Victoria E. Bonnell and Lynn Hunt (eds), *Beyond the Cultural Turn: New Directions in the in the Study of Society and Culture* (Berkeley, 1999), p. 51.

52 Ibid.

53 Ibid.

54 Ibid., p. 56.

55 See, for instance, Gøsta Esping-Anderson, *The Three Worlds of Welfare Capitalism* (Cambridge, 2004).

56 European Social Survey, *Welfare Attitudes in Europe: Topline Results of Round 4 of the European Social Survey* (November 2012), p. 5.

57 Ibid., p. 4.

58 World Values Survey, "Government Responsibility", *Wave* 6 (2010–2014).

59 See Alisdair McIntyre, *After Virtue* (London, 2013); and Michael Walzer, *Spheres of Justice: A Defence of Pluralism and Equality* (New York, 1983). Communitarians argue that one-size-fits-all principles are not only unfeasible but also normatively undesirable.

60 See, for instance, Alessandro Alessina and Nicola Fuchs-Schündeln, "Good-bye Lenin or Not? The Effect of Communism on People's Preferences", *American Economic Review* 97, pp. 1507–1528.

61 William H. Sewell Jr, "The Concept(s) of Culture", p. 53.

62 On this point, see the distinction between "grown order" and "made order" observed by Frederik Hayek. See Frederik Hayek, *Law, Legislation and Liberty* (London, 1998).

63 Fred Dallmayr, "Cosmopolitanism: Moral and Political", *Political Theory* 31 (June 2003), p. 434.

64 Ibid.

65 Pablo Gilabert has rightly pointed out that "[e]conomic feasibility depends not only on the presence of resources, but also on the willingness of agents to create or use them in certain ways". Yet the *empirical* claim of resource scarcity should not be challenged, as illustrated by the limited amount of natural resources in the world. See Pablo Gilabert, "The Feasibility of Basic Socioeconomic Human Rights: A Conceptual Exploration", *The Philosophical Quarterly* 59 (2009), p. 667.

66 On this point, see the discussion in A. B. Atkinson and Joseph Stiglitz, "The Structure of Indirect Taxation and Economic Efficiency", in *Social Justice and Public Policy* (Cambridge MA, 1983).

67 This concern is implicit in his formulation of the difference principle. For his discussion of efficiency, see John Rawls, *A Theory of Justice: Revised Edition*, pp. 57–65.

68 R. G. Lipsey and Kelvin Lancaster, "The General Theory of the Second Best", *The Review of Economic Studies* 24 (1956/1957), p. 11.

69 See Lea Ypi, *Global Justice and Avant-Garde Political Agency* (Oxford, 2011), especially Chapter 6.

5

Realizing distributive justice in the EU

I. Introduction

This chapter addresses the question, is distributive justice in the EU a feasible project? I apply the feasibility framework developed in the previous chapter to the reforms proposed in Chapters 2 and 3. I argue that, when the long run is taken as the relevant time frame, distributive justice in the EU is feasible. At the same time, I claim that this conclusion is subject to a number of conditions. First, I argue that, to be feasible, the scheme has to be consistent with a plurality of welfare regimes in the Union. This can be achieved by ensuring that the goods which integrate the EU threshold are part of a broad cross-national consensus regarding primary goods. In addition, this requirement can be met by allowing member states to diverge above the sufficiency level, instead of attempting to harmonize all social policies. Secondly, I claim that a feasible scheme must imply a limited amount of inter-state transfers. This can be done by focusing on pre-distribution, which is expected to considerably reduce the level of deprivation in the EU, thus tackling the distributive issues at their source. Thirdly, I argue that the scheme needs to be backed by a doctrine of public finance management that anticipates increasing social needs in times of crisis. This can be achieved through a policy of public savings based on marginally higher contributions to the EU budget. Fourthly, I claim that distributive justice requires a new institutional framework at the EU level. This includes a change in the treaties and the creation of an EU agency for social justice, with the task of dealing with the main budgetary and operational challenges raised by the new policies. I claim that, although ambitious, these reforms are within the Union's reach, and they may significantly increase its cohesion and stability. I conclude by claiming that this study has succeeded in addressing the three tensions raised in the Introduction.

I begin by reviewing the four criteria of feasibility discussed in the previous chapter. Subsequently, I apply these criteria to the case of distributive justice in the EU, discussing each of them in turn. In doing so, I explore ways in which the feasibility prospects of this project could be ameliorated, and I discuss major objections to its implementation. In the second part of the chapter, I offer an overview of the findings of this study. First, I revisit the research questions and explain why they have been successfully addressed. Second, I describe what would change in the EU if my proposal was implemented. Third, I discuss issues of timing and agency concerning the implementation of this proposal in the near future. I conclude by offering my view on what can be expected regarding social reform in the Union.

II. Is distributive justice in the EU feasible?

In the previous chapter, I argued that normative theories should be tested against pervasive unfeasibility – that is, implementation barriers which cannot, most likely, be superseded, under the constraints of a liberal democratic order. Accordingly, I listed four main feasibility requirements: (i) fitting the political culture; (ii) being economically sustainable; (iii) being translatable into functioning institutions; and (iv) being consistent with the degree of social solidarity amongst individuals. The next sections will investigate whether the policy proposals advanced in this book meet these requirements. Recall that the main policy proposals discussed previously were an EU threshold of basic goods, consisting of the means of subsistence and access to healthcare, education, and the judiciary system; an EU Labour Code, setting minimum social standards, namely a coordinated minimum wage; an EU minimum corporate tax rate; an EU Fund for Global Competitiveness (FGC); and a fair euro exchange rate. In the previous chapters, I claimed that these policies are desirable; in what follows, I will argue that they are feasible, at least in the long run.

A few preliminary remarks are in order. To begin with, note that the purpose of the following discussion is *not* to produce a generic judgement about the feasibility status of distributive justice in the EU as whole. Even if we have listed a particular set of public policies, there are different ways in which the latter can be realized, some being more feasible than others. To illustrate the point, consider that the aforementioned threshold of basic goods could be funded in a variety of ways, ranging from an EU value-added tax to budgetary transfers amongst EU member states. Therefore, it is useful to compare different courses of action through which similar policy goals could be achieved. Accordingly, the argument of this chapter is frequently formulated in terms of conditional statements: *if* we do X, the feasibility prospects of a given policy are higher than if we do Y. This way of proceeding shall, at times, lead me to propose certain non-ideal caveats and transitional measures. In addition, note that the following discussion is structured around the four feasibility criteria, rather than around the policies. The reason is that similar feasibility objections often apply to different policies. It should be anticipated that certain policies will be more thoroughly discussed than others, given that the degree of controversy they raise varies from case to case. Let me now address the feasibility criteria in turn.

Fitting the political culture

In the previous chapters, I have anticipated a few challenges to the belief that a common conception of justice could be achieved in the EU. A first difficulty is that each member state has its own conception of justice, translated into its institutional norms and practices, and presumably shared by a considerable proportion of the population. This means that EU citizens from different member states may regard certain socioeconomic arrangements in very different ways. For example, Latvian and Greek citizens tend to be more supportive of government intervention in market outcomes than do their Dutch and French counterparts.[1] A similar cross-national variance can be found at the level of the causal beliefs regarding one's fortune or misfortune. While in some countries "hard work" is perceived as the main source of wealth and success, in other states prosperity is associated with more structural factors, such as unequal opportunities and corruption.[2] Given the contrasting preferences and beliefs in the Union, it is not clear whether a scheme of social justice at EU level would collect broad support (or, at least, avoid fierce opposition) from each of the member states. Are common social policies compatible with the current diversity of world-views? In other words, can a Rawlsian "overlapping consensus" be found in the EU?[3]

The difficulties raised by political culture can be applied to the proposal of an EU threshold of basic goods. First, why should we think that all member states would agree that any specific list of goods is *good enough*? For example, the Nordic welfare systems tend to be more generous than this threshold. Would then redistribution at EU level imply a levelling down of redistribution at the national level? If so, is it plausible to assume that every member state could be on board to pass such a proposal? Secondly, how could member states agree on *how much* of each good is to be provided? Notice that member states have different levels of mandatory schooling and that certain medical services are part of healthcare access only in a few member states. If distributive justice in the EU were to imply harmonizing education and health policy, would such project be feasible? Thirdly, *through which means* should the goods be provided? Once again, there is much variation across borders. For instance, healthcare access in France is realized through a comprehensive network of public hospitals and general practitioners, directly funded by the state. In contrast, in Germany access to healthcare is achieved mainly through mandatory private insurance, funded by the state in the case of insufficiency of financial resources. Is it possible to foresee an EU scheme of social justice in which one size fits all?

The answers to these questions depend on how exactly the scheme is conceived. As I suggested in Chapter 2, the implementation of a European safety net does not necessarily imply the levelling down of domestic welfare provision. The main reason for this claim lies in distinguishing between a *common* conception of justice for the EU – advocated in this book – and a *single* conception of justice. Common justice presupposes that a given ideal of justice could be shared by all member states, but it leaves room for additional, and more comprehensive, ideals at the national level, provided that the national and the supranational conceptions are not fundamentally incompatible. Instead, single justice holds that there can only be *one* understanding of justice in Europe. Thus, while single justice seems pervasively unfeasible, particularly due to the political instability and distrust in EU institutions that such a rigid blueprint would generate, common justice presents itself as a plausible scenario. Under appropriate conditions of temporary feasibility – such as significant economic growth and greater stability of the EU borders – it seems plausible to think that member states *could* agree on a common safety net, which would still allow them to pursue further distributive policies at home and to maintain their domestic welfare regimes. Yet what if the EU threshold proves to be incompatible with the domestic conception of justice of one or more member states?

The current institutional norms and practices of the 27 member states suggest that such fundamental conflict does not exist. In fact, despite a variety of practices regarding the amount and method of social provision, all member states subscribe to some type of social safety net policy.[4] National policies have, in fact, shown a moderate trend of convergence in recent years, reducing the institutional cleavages amongst member states.[5] Moreover, all member states identify similar circumstances of vulnerability under which social benefits are due, including unemployment, retirement, maternity, and childhood. Notice that, if the proposal of a fair minimum wage were implemented, this list would cover the overwhelming majority of cases where public authorities could be called to fulfil the threshold of basic goods. Hence, the EU threshold of basic goods does not seem too far from the domestic conceptions of justice.[6] An apparent overlapping consensus can also be found at the level of labour law. According to the European Commission, "the EU complements policy initiatives taken by individual EU countries by setting *minimum standards*".[7] As far as political culture is concerned, the proposal of more dubious feasibility is perhaps an EU minimum wage, adjusted to the national level of prices. Yet notice that the majority of the member states have now established a minimum wage.[8] Indeed, the recent adoption of a minimum wage policy in Germany – a state in which such a policy had never collected much support – illustrates that, under the appropriate political and economic conjuncture, a minimum wage policy may, indeed, become feasible.

As I argued in Chapter 4, a critical step to assure the feasibility of a project that has a universalistic scope, in a context of multiple political cultures, is allowing for *local interpretation*. By interpretation, I mean the process by which concrete meaning is given to an abstract statement, including specifying how much of each good is to be provided, and selecting concrete institutions and policies to deliver them. On this account, if social justice implied the harmonization of social and educational policy, it would be pervasively unfeasible. It seems, indeed, implausible to think that 27 member states would one day democratically agree on providing *exactly* the same education and healthcare services to their citizens. By the same token, the idea that the strategies to deliver social goods (e.g. welfare regimes and institutions) could be standardized seems highly implausible. However, if each member state were to maintain, to a considerable extent, its autonomy regarding social, health, and education policy, the feasibility prospects of the project would seem much higher. In this sense, the threshold does not require a levelling down of social provision.[9] Hence, the feasibility status of *common* justice in the EU seems to depend critically on its ability *not* to become a *single* justice – that is, to accommodate a variety of welfare models.

Being economically sustainable

Another key aspect of a pervasively feasible political theory is that it should be economically sustainable. For a variety of reasons, one may suspect that this is not the case of the distributive proposals advanced in this study. First, to ensure that every EU citizen attains the threshold may be too costly, particularly if one considers the figures of material deprivation from which this study originally departed. Would an EU threshold imply an unprecedented amount of redistribution? If so, would it be feasible? Secondly, the most likely transferral of resources from the most productive to the least productive economies of the Union could produce huge efficiency costs. Furthermore, extending EU labour law, namely by including provisions for an EU minimum wage and severance payments, could harm the competitiveness of certain member states on global markets. Is my account of distributive justice compatible with the need to modernize labour markets? Thirdly, since social needs tend to increase when the economic performance worsens, it might be hard to sustain the scheme when the latter would be most needed. What sort of fiscal policies are consistent with my proposal? If all member states face times of crisis, how will they be able to allocate further resources to redistribution beyond borders? Finally, allowing for the depreciation of the euro could induce an inflationary crisis, undermining both investment and growth. Would this proposal still be feasible?

There are good reasons to think that the scheme is economically sustainable, at least if certain conditions are met. A preliminary insight on the matter has to do with the potential impact of pre-distribution. In fact, it is plausible to expect that, were reciprocity to be realized in the EU in the terms described in Chapter 3, the number of individuals below the threshold line would be relatively low. Recall that amongst the requirements of reciprocity were (i) a fair EU minimum wage, allowing for a decent life; (ii) the containment of tax competition amongst member states; and (iii) a fair euro exchange rate. A reciprocal economy such as this would promote the achievement of sufficiency through participation in the labour market and alleviate the pressure on the distressed economies of the Eurozone and their social services. Hence, with a fair EU economy, social needs would likely be much lower than they are at present. Under such a scenario, the role of redistribution would be relatively marginal, particularly when compared to that of pre-distribution. As I shall discuss later on, this is promising, since it seems politically easier to change a rule of cooperation than to transfer resources from one group to another. Therefore, if a massive level of redistribution between member states would seem pervasively unfeasible, a limited amount of inter-state transfers is plausible to conceive.[10]

If there may be efficiency costs associated with my proposal, there are also a number of potential economic benefits. Recent empirical studies have demonstrated that certain external shocks – say, a variation in the price of a given commodity – have opposite impacts in different economies in the Union.[11] This suggests that an EU safety net may be regarded as a collective insurance policy against the social risks resulting from poor economic performance.[12] In addition, as I argued in Chapter 3, redistributive transfers would act as an automatic stabilizer in the Eurozone, at least partially compensating for the imbalances of the single currency. This would reduce the gap amongst the different equilibrium exchange rates of the Eurozone members, as well as the need for monetary depreciation. Fair monetary policy is not a comprehensive solution for structural economic imbalances, but it is a necessary condition for any such solution to produce a sizeable effects on the trade accounts of labour-intensive member states.[13] In turn, the inflationary risks could be minimized by moderating the degree of depreciation.[14] Of course, understanding the net impact of my proposals would require the quantification of each of these effects. This task is beyond the scope of this book. Yet if Joseph Stiglitz is right in saying that lower inequality is typically better for economic growth, one may plausibly expect that the benefits of distributive justice will offset its costs.[15]

Furthermore, the economic costs of regulating labour at the EU level should not be overestimated. A first reason is that, if *all* member states were to coordinate their labour codes, the bargaining power of EU workers over multinational companies would be considerably higher. Many firms operating in the common market can easily move to a neighbouring member state where labour market rigidity and salaries are lower. However, mobility of people, goods, and capital is more limited beyond EU borders. Consider, for instance, border controls, tariffs, and restrictions regarding the repatriation of profits. Moving a French factory to China is not as easy as moving it to Poland. In addition, the EU's abundant stocks of technology and high-skilled workers give it sustainable comparative advantages in a variety of niches, which can hardly be delocalized to regions where such resources are less abundant. For example, despite the high labour costs in Denmark, more than 30% of Danish jobs are generated by foreign-owned companies.[16] This reasoning also applies to peripheral member states. First, if the coordination of minimum wages and severance payments is done gradually, and if it is combined with sustained productivity gains linked to the FGC, the net effect of these reforms will be positive in terms of the competitive position of peripheral member states. Second, peripheral economies would still be relatively competitive in terms of labour costs, since the coordinated minimum wage has been defined as a percentage of the median *national* salary. For these reasons, an EU Labour Code is potentially economically sustainable.

In turn, the long-term sustainability of this project seems to be contingent upon the adoption of a particular stand on public finance management. If social needs, indeed, tend to increase when the economic performance worsens, a scenario where the dimension of a crisis is such that it hits all member states, in one way or another, will challenge the sustainability of the scheme. This is notably the case with the financial crisis that started in 2008. A way to achieve the financial capacity to afford the threshold in times of crisis is assuring generous levels of public savings in times of economic growth. In other words, to be feasible, the threshold seems to require the adoption of counter-cyclical macroeconomic policies on the revenue side, namely an increase of taxes in periods of economic expansion. This is politically difficult, but not impossible – in fact, it was a common practice in Western Europe before neoliberal approaches to public finance became dominant. Thus, higher contributions to the EU budget should be used to constitute a provision for times of need. Note that this would be compatible with the general goal of keeping inter-state transfers relatively low. For example, in 2015, raising the level of national transfers to approximately 2% of national GDPs would have generated an additional revenue of 100 billion euro.[17] This is equivalent to the sum of the entire social spending of Greece, Portugal, Romania, and Bulgaria for the same year.[18] Of course, the social needs that EU citizens face *today* could not be addressed by this solution, since such precautionary savings were not made in the past. Yet recall that the present study is forward looking: pervasive feasibility should then be equated with *long-term* resource management. If, as I have suggested, it is possible to effectively anticipate times of economic hardship, the project is sustainable.

However, this point begs the question, is it possible to change the way in which public finances are managed? The same question applies quite stringently to monetary policy, given the recognized preference of Germany for low inflation. It is true that, under the current political conditions, it seems hard to move away from the neoliberal approach to economic and monetary policy. In fact, even the governments belonging to the left spectrum of political ideology have often become scrupulous implementers of austerity politics, thus creating the impression that an alternative approach to governance is simply not available.[19] However, as the EU is getting back to growth, the moods of certain political actors seem to be changing. An illustrative example is the changing position of the IMF, which has recently admitted the disastrous consequences of the Greek bail-outs and called for new policies.[20] In addition, a look back to the history of a previously hegemonic Keynesianism suggests that economic doctrines may dramatically win or lose popularity in the market of ideas.[21] Indeed, as Markus K. Brunnermeier, Harold James, and Jean-Pierre Landau have eloquently put it, the current disputes concerning the Eurozone are mostly a "battle of ideas".[22] Thus a German preference for a low inflation rate may hinder a significant depreciation of the euro in the short run, but there is no reason to think that such a preference cannot change.[23] Therefore, if the frameworks of economic thought are changed – and they *can* be changed – distributive justice will be feasible in the Union.

Being translatable into institutions and policies

Further feasibility challenges arise when one thinks of the type of institutions through which a scheme of distributive justice could be realized in the EU. First, how could such scheme be created in the first place? This is a major question, since social policy does not belong to the list of EU competences under the existing treaties. Secondly, which institution(s) would *coordinate* and *supervise* the implementation of the scheme? Notice that, under this scheme, a number of new tasks would need to be performed, including collecting the EU corporate tax, managing the resources of the FGC, and scrutinizing compliance with the EU threshold by the member states. Thirdly, would this scheme constitute an incentive for free-riding amongst member states? If national governments know that their citizens are ultimately protected by an EU safety net, they may well disinvest in social policy or simply mismanage the resources which are dedicated to it. This would put the sustainability of the scheme at risk. Finally, would the scheme constitute an incentive for welfare tourism? For instance, if certain member states interpret basic goods such as "means of subsistence" and "access to healthcare" in a more generous way, is a mass migration of benefits seekers to be expected?

Let me address these questions in turn. To begin with, implementing a scheme of distributive justice in the EU would, indeed, require either a new treaty or amendments to the existing treaties.[24] Although a few redistributive devices, such as an unemployment insurance scheme, could fit the current legal framework of the common market, a more systematic approach to social justice in the EU would have to be legitimized through the transferral of certain competences on social policy to EU institutions.[25] However, notice that this requirement does not defeat my proposal. First, treaty making is not a rare event in EU history, nor does it happen only in times of prosperity and social peace. In fact, in its history the EU counts eight major treaties of institution building and reform, and some of them constituted a reaction to political crisis in the Union. Second, since, under my proposal, member states would maintain a considerable degree of autonomy concerning social policy, any transferral of competences would be limited. In any case, an EU redistributive scheme would likely require a European agency for social justice, with a mandate to implement and control the scheme. Launching a common agency does not seem to be an impossible challenge for the EU, if one considers the more than 30 agencies currently existing in the Union.[26] Therefore, if the need for a new treaty and institutional reform is a challenge for this project, it does not render it pervasively unfeasible.

The likelihood of large-scale free-riding and welfare tourism would depend on the way in which the scheme was designed. A first barrier against these risks is to establish that the EU would only intervene when the provision of basic goods in a given member state would require a level of expenditure unaffordable for its economy. This could be measured, for instance, through the familiar ratio "social expenditure as % of GDP". Thus, a European agency for social justice would only take action if this ratio went above a certain critical level. At the same time, the scheme would require a firm commitment by member states to make their public services more efficient. This could be assessed periodically by a number of indicators of efficiency of the public services. To prevent welfare tourism, the responsibility to provide income-related benefits could be primarily assigned to the last member state where the worker had been employed for a given period of time. This coverage would be extended to the worker's children and partner. In the case of non-mobile workers, their children, and incapacitated and retired citizens, such primary responsibility could be assigned to the member state where they hold citizenship status. For example, an Italian citizen would qualify to receive social benefits from Finland only if they had been working there recently. Otherwise, they would receive social benefits from Italy.[27] In case Italy lacked the resources to secure a safety net for all its citizens, a European agency for social justice would proceed with budgetary transfers. A scheme thus designed would not offer incentives for welfare tourism. On the contrary, by securing sufficiency at the nation-state level, it would alleviate the pressure on the most prosperous welfare states.

The same agency would be responsible for operationalizing and managing the EU FGC. As mentioned before, the revenues to support this fund would be obtained through a small EU corporate tax, to be collected by national authorities as an additional component of domestic corporate taxes. As an illustrative example, in 2015, a 3% EU corporate tax on the profits of the companies of 21 member states would have generated an approximate revenue of 30 billion euro.[28] This would allow the EU to double its current level of investment in four critical areas: research and innovation, competitiveness of small and medium-size enterprises, vocational training, and sustainable employment.[29] The agency for social justice would then allocate these resources to a portfolio of investments which would target primarily peripheral member states. These investments would follow the logic of subsidiarity which currently applies to structural funds.[30] The two funds would be complementary but distinct: while the existing structural funds would focus on basic socioeconomic infrastructure after accession being, by definition, a temporary instrument, the FGC would work as a permanent adjustment mechanism for external shocks in the global economy. Finally, an EU Labour Code could be produced and executed by the existing institutional framework of the Union. While the Council, the Commission, and the Parliament could work together on the drafting of a proposal, the CJEU would be responsible for its enforcement.

Being consistent with the degree of social solidarity

An issue of major importance is whether the level of social solidarity amongst the peoples of Europe would ever be high enough to implement a scheme of distributive justice. In the absence of bonds of civic friendship, one may reasonably claim, it will be impossible to engage in systematic redistribution. The main reason is that people will not be willing to bear the costs of assisting those who they regard as distant foreigners. As has often been noted, social solidarity at EU level seems much weaker than at the nation-state level. Whether stronger bonds will ever develop remains unclear. If anything, the existing ties may even collapse, as illustrated by Brexit and the emergence of powerful nationalist discourses in a number of member states. In this sense, critics will argue, taxation at the EU level is an utterly utopian project, which would be regarded by many as an inadmissible demand from EU bureaucrats. Hence, instead of holding the pieces of the EU puzzle together, redistribution could become the final act of the EU's history, in a way which reminds us of the tea tax introduced by the British Empire that sparked the independence of their former American colonies. In an EU where inter-state mobility is reduced for large parts of the population, and where a common language and a shared memory are lacking, will EU citizens ever care enough for each other to allow for EU redistribution?

Although these are complicated feasibility issues, a number of points are in order. First, social solidarity does not seem to be completely absent at EU level. Surely, solidarity is much lower than at national level, but this only suggests that a scheme of social justice would be unfeasible if it equated redistribution at EU level with redistribution at national level – a view that this study has entirely rejected. Once we admit that different levels of redistribution may apply to different types of social bonds, the feasibility prospects of my proposal dramatically increase. As I have argued in Chapter 4, it seems more plausible to conceive social solidarity in terms of a matter of degrees on a scale rather than as something that either exists or does not exist. The fact that my proposal relies mainly on pre-distribution, treating redistribution as a residual practice, is consistent with the idea of thicker and thinner degrees of social solidarity. Under this proposal, large-scale redistribution would only take place at the national level, where social bonds are stronger, while residual redistribution would happen at the EU level, where social bonds are weaker. In addition, the insights of social psychology suggest that changing the rules of the common market and the Eurozone requires a lower degree of social solidarity than transferring resources across member states. If, according to a number of studies, the decision on whether to help others is evaluated in cost-benefit terms, it seems plausible to assume that the perceived cost of measures such as an EU Labour Code or a minimum EU corporate tax rate will be much lower than that of transferring resources from one to another member state.[31]

What if, due to the budgetary imbalances of a few member states, EU redistribution turned out to be not merely residual, as this study has assumed, but comprehensive? Admittedly, a higher level of redistribution would only be possible if stronger bonds were to emerge amongst EU citizens. Yet, in the long run, this is not necessarily out of reach for Europe. This is illustrated by three historical examples which demonstrate that social solidarity may increase dramatically under specific circumstances, creating what we might call "redistributive momentums" – that is, opportunities to advance redistributive practices. One example is the New Deal, launched by the US government in the aftermath of the Great Crisis of 1929. The very harsh social conditions faced by the American people generated a widespread awareness that government intervention would be needed to overcome the social consequences of the crisis. Another example is William Beveridge's redistributive plan, launched by the United Kingdom in the aftermath of the Second World War. It has been noted that the implementation of this ambitious plan was only made possible by a strong sense that the social costs of the war should be shared by all British citizens. A third example is the reunification of Germany, which led to one of the most expensive redistributive programmes ever put into practice. Despite having been apart from their eastern counterparts for more than 40 years, western Germans were sensible to their needs, thus they accepted paying the costs of reunification. These examples suggest that social solidarity is not a static but a dynamic variable. For this reason, the lack of social solidarity in the EU should ultimately be treated as a potentially temporary constraint.

III. Timing and agency

In the previous section, I claimed that the proposals presented in this book are within Europe's reach. Yet at least three practical questions will follow: (i) *When* could this framework be implemented? (ii) *Who* could lead and persuade the 27 member states to create a social Europe? (iii) *How* could this agent achieve such goal? Let me begin by addressing the first question. As I have mentioned, the current political conditions of the Union seem to suggest a great deal of prudence in moving forward with integration. Developments such as Brexit, global terrorism, and the refugee crisis have cast doubt on the merits of integration, as well as the future of the EU. In addition, the economic and financial crisis that Europe is just leaving has shaken the foundations of its welfare states. One of the key contentions of this book is that to say that a given policy is feasible is not to say that it could be adopted and implemented as of today. In fact, one thing we learn from the history of European integration is that the EU is resilient to crises, having survived many in the last 60 years. However, there may be a price for waiting too long for appropriate responses. As I have suggested, the lack of a stronger social dimension may constitute a powerful threat against the EU. Thus, the question of *when* poses a difficult dilemma: if we force social reform upon the member states, the EU can disintegrate; if we do not do anything, it may as well break.

The questions of *who* and *how* bring about a number of additional dilemmas. A primary issue is that, even if they have some sympathy for the idea of social reform, the leaders of wealthy member states find it very hard to justify such reforms before electorates which do not seem to be willing to bear the costs of extending justice beyond borders. On the other side of the barricade, even if they understand the need to modernize their economies and public sectors, the leaders of the distressed member states find it increasingly difficult to engage with additional cuts and structural reforms when large segments of their populations are more and more impoverished. At the discursive level, when northern European leaders call for stronger efforts from the south, they may be perceived there as cynical and exploitative; when southern rulers ask for social justice, they may be regarded in the north as complacent and incapable of reforming their countries. In both regions, the pressure from populist political forces only makes political compromise harder. This brings the EU to political deadlock, where each side represents the other as self-interested, undermining the credibility of all partners.

Undoubtedly, this deadlock is bad for everyone. One reason is that such a cleavage has the potential to be politically explosive, as demonstrated by the events in Greece in recent years. We should not lose sight of the magnitude of political instability in this country at the peak of the crisis, as well as of the fact that the Eurozone was very close to a rupture. The EU is by no means safe from a similar set events in the future, yet possibly with more tragic and pervasive consequences. Another reason why this deadlock is so toxic is that it keeps the EU away from a better economic and social equilibrium, which would benefit all member states. As I have suggested, by fostering the exports of southern markets and increasing their incomes, distressed member states would be able to stand on their own feet in the long run. This, in turn, would limit the amount of inter-state transfers required by the conception of distributive justice presented in this book. At the same time, by alleviating the pressure of economic migration to the countries north of the Alps, the populist case would likely be weakened and EU scepticism could more easily be contained. Therefore, distributive justice might leave *all* member states better off, and not only the net recipients of the scheme. Yet the EU needs to take a first step, or we will be trapped in a sort of prisoner's dilemma.

To advance a political strategy to deal with these issues would go beyond the scope of this book. However, a few guidelines may be drawn from what has been proposed in this chapter. One of the first priorities is shifting the political discourse on distributive justice from a *zero-sum* to a *win-win* paradigm. In fact, if winning the public opinions of the wealthiest EU member states is critical for success, this may be achieved by showing that material deprivation in the south has important economic and social costs for the north, and that distributive justice would not become a passport for mismanagement and free-riding. For these reasons, the advocacy of these reform proposals should place great emphasis on the conditionality and subsidiarity of the new model of assistance. In addition, it will be crucial to highlight that the costs of EU social policy would be relatively reduced, addressing the fear that a social Europe may become a gateway for unlimited inter-state transfers. As I have claimed, this is not wishful thinking: it can be achieved, for instance, through a focus on pre-distribution instruments and by setting a cap for redistributive transfers. These guarantees would help building trust amongst member states, facilitating the implementation of the scheme.

Given all that has been said, advocates of social justice should adopt an incremental approach to change that, on the one hand, seizes the existing political opportunities and, on the other hand, attempts to create a 'redistributive momentum' in Europe. On the first account, the EU's return to economic growth and to financial stability has opened a door that had been closed for several years. Social justice can no longer be quickly dismissed on the grounds of being too costly for times of austerity, nor can it be framed as a too-easy way out from the crisis for the "misbehaved" member states. This presents an opportunity to advance the debate. Yet political opportunities should not be taken as given; they need to be seized through effective political agency. For this matter, the advancement of the social Europe programme will certainly require skilful leaders, with the capacity for agenda setting and meaningful dialogue. This willingness to see the world from the perspective of others seems key not only to distributive justice, but also to holding the EU together in the future. In turn, social movements, trade unions, and think tanks can help shaping the ideational context and the political arena in which political authorities operate, creating avenues for a smoother implementation of the reforms.

In 2017, we witnessed an attempt to generate a meaningful discussion on social rights at the EU level: the enactment of the European Pillar of Social Rights. This declaration consists of 20 principles, structured in three chapters: (1) Equal opportunities and access to the labour market; (2) Fair working conditions; and (3) Social protection and inclusion. Its principles cover a wide variety of fields including education, training and lifelong learning, work-life balance, and old-age income and pensions. This statement seems to suffer from the same shortcoming as the Charter of Fundamental Rights of the European Union: it does not generate positive duties for member states, which means that it can be enforced only to a very limited extent. As happened with the charter, EU institutions did not receive additional competences nor resources to fulfil the rights prescribed by the European Pillar of Social Rights. Thus, when drawing the practical implications of the Pillar's principle on "access to basic services", the European Commission makes this point particularly clear: "Member States retain competence in defining, organising, delivering and financing such services at national, regional or local level".[32] Therefore, it is unlikely that this document will lead to tangible changes of the status quo.

However, the European Pillar of Social Rights achieved some progress at the conceptual level: it made the list of (non-enforceable) European social rights not only longer but also more detailed than did any previous statement. For instance, the section on "active support to employment" states that "[t]he long-term unemployed have the right to an in-depth individual assessment at the latest at 18 months of unemployment" – a remarkably concrete target, compared to the relatively broad social goals expressed in the charter and in the treaties.[33] Another illustrative example is the endorsement of adequate minimum wages, "in a way that provide [*sic*] for the satisfaction of the needs of the worker and his/her family in the light of national economic and social conditions".[34] This had been a political taboo for decades, due to the absence of statutory minimum wages in a few member states and to the different collective bargaining models in place. Even if the Pillar does not contain any reference to a coordination mechanism at the EU level, it certainly constituted a step forward. Despite its limited practical implications, the European Pillar of Social Rights sent the signal that social justice is back on the agenda of European institutions. The very fact that this statement could be enacted, with the consent of the European Parliament and the Council of the EU, shows some openness to pursue the debate. This is a signal that advocates of social justice should not miss.

IV. Conclusion

I have argued that the proposals advanced in this book are not only desirable, but also feasible. I claimed that distributive justice fits the political culture of the EU, as long as it respects the current diversity of welfare regimes. I have argued that redistribution at the EU level is economically sustainable if combined with pre-distributive measures and long-term public finance management. I have claimed that a social Europe can better be realized through a change in the treaties and the creation of a European agency for social justice. I have argued that, given that sufficiency – not equality – is the main value behind it, my proposal is consistent with the limited level of social solidarity in the Union. I concluded by arguing that the current economic and political conditions in the EU offer a good opportunity to advance the social agenda.

Notes

1 European Social Survey, *Welfare Attitudes in Europe: Topline Results from Round 4 of the European Social Survey* (November 2012), p. 5.
2 European Social Survey, *Welfare Attitudes* (2008).
3 The concept of overlapping consensus is discussed in John Rawls, "The Idea of an Overlapping Consensus", *Oxford Journal of Legal Studies* 7 (1987), pp. 1–25; and John Rawls, *Political Liberalism* (New York, 2005).
4 It is important to emphasize the point that social safety net policies vary greatly across member states. However, the *conception of justice* underlying such policies – for example, that minimum standards of living should be provided to all citizens – seems to be the same. For a detailed empirical study which stresses the similarities in principle and the differences in scale and scope of minimum social provision policies within the EU, see European Commission, *Minimum Income Schemes in Europe: A Study of National Policies* (2015).
5 Kenneth Nelson has identified a modest yet positive trend of convergence in social safety net policies within the EU. In addition, a recent study by the European Parliament has concluded that "besides the context of an increasing Euroscepticism it is possible to see a progressive evolution towards a few common principles" concerning an EU minimum income. At the more general level of redistributive institutions and practices, Peter Achterberg and Mara Yerkes have claimed that, in Western countries "[m]ore generous, universal welfare states are becoming more liberalized, and liberal welfare states are expanding, which causes convergence in the middle". This is consistent with Fritz Scharpf's finding that "regardless of how much they differ in the patterns of social spending and in their welfare-state institutions, the member states of the European Union are remarkably alike in their revealed preferences for *total social*

spending (measured as a share of GDP)". See, respectively, Kenneth Nelson, "Minimum Income Protection and European Integration: Trends and Levels of Minimum Benefits in Comparative Perspective 1990–2005", *International Journal of Health Services* 31 (2008), pp. 103–124; European Parliament, *Minimum Income Policies in EU Member States* (2017); Peter Achterberg and Mara Yerkes, "One Welfare State Emerging? Convergence versus Divergence in 16 Western Countries", *Journal of Comparative Social Welfare* 25 (2009), pp. 189–201; and Fritz W. Scharpf, *Governing in Europe: Effective and Democratic?* (Oxford, 1999), pp. 177–178 (emphasis in original).

6 An additional point to be made is that most of the basic goods included in the threshold have been given formal legitimacy by the EU Charter on Fundamental Rights, ratified by every member state. The issue, then, is not one of divergent conceptions of justice, but of willingness to take responsibility for their fulfilment.

7 European Commission, "Employment, Social Affairs and Inclusion", http://ec. europa.eu/social/main.jsp?catId=157 (Accessed 16 October 2017) (emphasis in original). In addition, note that EU labour law is a field in clear expansion. Consider, for instance, the recent proposal by the Commission to create an EU regulator with the task of monitoring labour practices at national level. See Jean-Claude Juncker, *The State of the Union Speech* (2017).

8 The exceptions are Austria, Cyprus, Denmark, Finland, Italy, and Sweden. However, note that "[i]n the majority of EU Member States where there is no statutory minimum wage (Austria, Denmark, Finland, Italy and Sweden), the minimum wage level is de facto set in (sectoral) collective agreements". Notice, however, that these amounts are not coordinated, thus incentivizing competition amongst member states. For the quote, see European Foundation for the Improvement of Living and Working Conditions, "Statutory Minimum Wages in the EU 2017".

9 It should be noted that even liberal welfare states tend to provide some sort of social safety net. If there were a particular social service in which levelling up were required, transitional periods could be granted to accommodate social reform. This non-ideal commitment is justifiable in terms of the normative value of self-determination and the practical requisites of temporary feasibility. Yet, as was discussed in Chapter 2, a permanent opt-out from distributive justice at EU level would be incompatible with the idea of common playing field implied by the principle of equality of status.

10 Certain non-ideal commitments could be made to improve the feasibility conditions of EU redistribution in the short run. An illustrative example is a cap on the amount of inter-state transfers, which would address the fear amongst northern electorates that EU redistribution may be a Pandora's box. If such a cap were adopted, two scenarios could happen in the long run: (i) if my argument that EU redistribution would be relatively residual holds, the cap would not have practical significance and could be abandoned; (ii) if the cap proved to be insufficient to cover the needs of EU citizens, a new debate could be launched, with the strategic advantage of EU redistribution constituting already the status quo.

11 See, for instance, Christian Gayer, "A Fresh Look at Business Cycle Synchronization in the Euro Area", *European Economy Economic Papers*

(2007); and Narcissa Balta, "Business Cycle Synchronization in the Euro Area", *Quarterly Report on the Euro Area* 14 (2015), pp. 28–36. Notice that these negative correlations are consistent with the claim presented in Chapter 3 that the positioning of the member states in the international value chain varies significantly.

12 This argument, backed by a sophisticated economic model, is advanced in Árpád Ábrahám, João Brogueira de Sousa, Ramon Marimon, and Lukas Mayr, "On the Design of a European Unemployment Mechanism", *European University Institute Working Paper* (2017).

13 For instance, a structural strategy such as improving the competitive position of a state in the global market by gradually increasing the productivity of factors can be offset by an appreciation of the currency.

14 It is important to stress the point that I regard monetary policy as a complement, not a substitute, to economic policy. Thus, rejecting Milton Friedman's influential claim that economic imbalances should be primarily tackled through monetary policy does not imply subscribing to the argument that monetary policy is entirely irrelevant for successful economic adjustments. Indeed, had depreciation been applied moderately during the peak of the last recession, the social costs of the crisis would have likely been considerably lower. See Milton Friedman and Anna Jacobson Schwartz, *A Monetary History of the United States 1867–1960* (Princeton, 1963).

15 Joseph Stiglitz, *The Price of Inequality* (New York, 2013).

16 Eurofund, *Multinational Companies and Collective Bargaining* (2009), Table 1.

17 This estimate has been calculated based on the transfers to the EU budget reported by the European Commission. For simplicity, I assume *ceteris paribus* conditions in a scenario in which the contributions are raised. However, for a systematic evaluation, a dynamic model would be needed, given that the introduction of a new tax would imply certain distortionary effects, as well as changes in the amount of consumption and saving. The purpose of my (admittedly rough) estimate is to illustrate the point that the level of taxation required at the EU level would likely be very small, particularly when compared to the rates currently applied at the nation-state level. The amount presented already excludes the United Kingdom. For the figures of the EU budget, see European Commission, "EU Expenditure and Revenue 2014–2020", http://ec.europa.eu/budget/figures/interactive/index_en.cfm (Accessed 17 December 2017).

18 Eurostat, "Total General Expenditure on Social Protection" (2015), http://ec.europa.eu/eurostat/statistics-explained/index.php/Government_expenditure_on_social_protection (Accessed 1 December 2017). This indicator includes, for instance, pensions, unemployment benefits, family benefits, and labour market policies.

19 This tendency not to see beyond present-day political and economic arrangements seems to be common in modern societies. On this point, Herbert Marcuse forcefully claimed that, under conditions of cultural and ideological standardization, an external critique to institutions and practices becomes much harder. See Herbert Marcuse, *One-Dimensional Man: Studies in the Ideology of Advanced Capitalist Societies* (New York, 1991).

20 See, for instance, Peter Spiegel, "IMF Criticizes Greece's Bailout Deal with the EU", *Financial Times* (15 July 2015).

21 On this topic, see, for instance, Peter A. Hall (ed.), *The Political Power of Economic Ideas: Keynesianism Across Nations* (Princeton, 1989).

22 Markus K. Brunnermeier, Harold James, and Jean-Pierre Landau, *The Euro and the Battle of Ideas* (Princeton, 2017).

23 It may be argued that, since Germany's preference for a low inflation results from its dramatic inter-war experience, it may be very hard to change. However, it should be noted that, although history is crucial in defining the available courses of action at a given moment of time, its shadow does not last forever. An illustrative example, precisely in Germany, is the changing character of German foreign policy, particularly as far as humanitarian interventions are concerned. Before the Kosovo crisis, the deployment of German troops to a foreign war would have seemed impossible, given the legacy of the Second World War. Yet circumstances changed significantly, and so did the policy outcomes.

24 The issue of how extensive the EU legal reform would have to be to realize my conception of distributive justice depends on which concrete proposal is at stake. For instance, the threshold of basic goods would likely require a new treaty that delegates certain competences of social policy to the EU, whereas an EU Labour Code would be feasible through an amendment to Article 137 that, as proposed by Fritz Scharpf, would add "social inclusion" to the goals of the directives setting minimum labour standards. In turn, an EU minimum corporate tax rate would more easily be put in practice through an intergovernmental agreement. Although more modest changes would be, in principle, easier to implement, all of these proposals are within the reach of the Union, as I shall claim in the next lines. See Fritz W. Scharpf, "The European Social Model: Coping with the Challenge of Diversity", *Journal of Common Market Studies* 40 (2002), p. 663.

25 A number of legal arguments have been made according to which at least certain dimensions of social justice would, in fact, fit the mandate of the treaties, particularly if justified as common market mechanisms. However, as I have argued in Chapter 2, the notion of market citizenship is unsuitable for the EU. In my view, the move towards distributive justice may be gradual and, in some cases, not ideal, but it should be a conscious and publicly debated one.

26 A comprehensive list of EU agencies can be found in European Union, "Agencies and Other EU bodies", https://europa.eu/european-union/about-eu/agencies_ en (Accessed 20 August 2020). Notice that many of these agencies were created to address specific problems, at a moment when they became salient. Consider, for instance, the European Banking Authority (2011), the European Asylum Support Office (2011), and the European Border and Coast Guard Agency (2016).

27 This poses a problem related to different living costs. Indeed, if an Italian citizen were to live in Finland with the Italian minimum income, they might not be able to fulfil their basic needs. This suggests that perfect mobility backed by social benefits can only be achieved if there is sufficient convergence of European economies.

28 Due to limited data availability, this amount refers only to the 21 member states which are also members of the OECD. This figure would then be higher if all

member states were considered. I calculated the amount of wealth of the GDP of each member state which was subjected to corporate taxes. Then I simulated the revenues of additional marginal taxes. Again, distortionary effects were ignored for simplicity. See OECD, "Tax on Corporate Profits (as % of GDP)" (2015), https://data.oecd.org/tax/tax-on-corporate-profits.htm (Accessed 17 December 2017); OECD, "Gross Domestic Product" (2016), https://stats.o ecd.org/index.aspx?queryid=60702 (Accessed 1 December 2017); KPMG, "Corporate Tax Table" (2003–2017), https://home.kpmg.com/xx/en/home/ services/tax/tax-tools-and-resources/tax-rates-online/corporate-tax-rates-tab le.html (Accessed 17 December 2017); and ECB, "Euro Reference Exchange Rate" (averages 2015), https://www.ecb.europa.eu/stats/policy_and_exchang e_rates/euro_reference_exchange_rates/html/index.en.html (Accessed 17 December 2017).

29 European Commission, "European Structural and Investment Funds by Theme" (2014–2020), available at https://cohesiondata.ec.europa.eu/ (Accessed 16 December 2017).

30 Structural funds have been subjected to criticism due to the mismanagement of funds and ad hoc implementation and evaluation frameworks. Yet the point that the efficiency of structural funds management may be increased does not imply that they are an undesirable or an unfeasible policy. On this point see, for instance, John Bradley, Timo Mitze, Edgar Morgenroth, and Gerhard Untiedt, "An Integrated Micro-Macro (IMM) Approach to the Evaluation of Large-scale Public Investment Programmes: The Case of EU Structural Funds", *The Economic and Social Research Institute Working Papers* 167 (2005).

31 For a summary of the different theories which explain why we help others, see Michael A. Hogg, "Social Processes and Human Behaviour: Social Psychology", in Kurt Pawlik and Mark R. Rosenzweig, *The International Handbook of Psychology* (London, 2000), pp. 305–327.

32 European Commission, *Staff Working Document: Monitoring the Implementation of the European Pillar of Social Rights* (2018), p. 87.

33 *European Pillar of Social Rights* (2017), principle 4.

34 Ibid., principle 6.

Conclusion: Towards a just Europe

I should now return to the research questions presented in the Introduction, explaining how I have addressed them. Recall that the research questions were formulated as follows:

> *Does the political and economic configuration of the EU generate distributive duties amongst EU citizens, and/or between member states? If so, what are these duties and under which conditions do they apply?*

I have claimed that the *political* configuration of the EU generates a duty of redistribution amongst EU citizens. The argument proceeded in three steps. First, I established a strong link between coercion and democracy, on the one hand, and distributive justice, on the other hand. I argued that, to have a chance to participate in civic life and to resist arbitrary power, citizens of a democratic polity are entitled to a set of material resources. These means have been described in terms of a threshold of basic goods, which includes subsistence and access to healthcare, to public education, and to the judiciary system. I claimed that, in the absence of any of these goods, citizens may be excluded from civic life, becoming subjects to power. Secondly, I claimed that the conditions which trigger these entitlements – coercion and democracy – fully apply to the European Union. I argued that EU institutions comprise a coercive system which leads member states to comply with its regulations. The primacy of EU law over national law, its direct effect in domestic courts, and the supranational character of the decisions of the CJEU illustrate the coercive nature of the Union. In addition, I argued that the EU is a demoicracy. It combines a set of key democratic institutions, such as free and fair elections for a representative parliament, with a common status of citizenship and multiple *demoi*. Thirdly, I argued that the current political configuration of the EU indicates the way in which responsibilities for redistribution should be allocated across different levels of government. By applying the familiar principle of subsidiarity, I concluded that the EU should act as a safety net for the domestic welfare states, instead of attempting to replace them.

I then argued that the *economic* configuration of the Union generates an inter-state duty to engage with pre-distributive policies. Again, the argument proceeded in three steps. First, I argued that, in any economy with a division of labour, the market should be regarded as a cooperative venture where each job is the precondition for other jobs. For this reason, reciprocity, understood as mutual advantage and mutual respect, is due amongst market participants. In addition, I claimed that reciprocity should apply to what I dubbed the "economic structure" – a set of key features of any given economy, which decisively shape its market outcomes. This structure includes, for instance, conditions of access to capital, endowment with natural resources, terms of trade for goods and services, exchange rates, and border control regimes. Secondly, I argued that the EU has developed a comprehensively shared economic structure, which comprises a common market, a common currency, and freedom of movement. I claimed that the rules embedded in this structure, coupled with globalization, have produced a distributive vicious circle in the EU, which is harmful for certain member states. Thirdly, I claimed that a number of pre-distributive devices should be put in practice to break this vicious circle. Examples of the pre-distributive policies defended in the previous chapters were an EU Labour Code, a minimum EU corporate tax rate, and fair exchange rates. These policies need to be complemented by a redistributive mechanism – an EU Fund for Global Competitiveness funded by a small EU corporate tax. Therefore, economic integration generates a shared responsibility to promote a market where all member states have a fair chance of success.

The duties to redistribute and to pre-distribute are conditional upon normative and feasibility constraints. At the normative level, I have claimed that pre-distribution should be prioritized over redistribution. The reason has been summarized in the following maxim: injustice should be prevented whenever possible and corrected whenever needed. Thus, redistribution should only be applied when pre-distribution is ineffective. I have also emphasized the point that distributive justice should come alongside a commitment by member states to make their domestic welfare systems more efficient. Hence, it will be for the national authorities to demonstrate that they lack the resources to meet the social needs of their citizens, despite their best efforts. In addition, I claimed that the purpose of redistributing across the EU should be to complement the domestic welfare regimes, and neither to substitute for nor to harmonize them. The feasibility prospects of a distributive scheme seem to be dependent on the scale and design of such a scheme. First, to be widely accepted, the amount of inter-state transfers will need to be limited. Note that this is an additional reason why the priority of pre-distribution is auspicious. Secondly, a common scheme will have to consider the diversity of political cultures and historical experiences of the member states. This is why the idea of an EU safety net which leaves much room for domestic social policy is promising. Thirdly, the scheme will require an appropriate institutional setting, which includes a specialized EU agency entrusted with the budgetary and operational coordination of the programme. All things considered, a sufficientarian approach to social justice in the EU seems more desirable and feasible than an egalitarian one.

Let me summarize the main institutional changes that such a scheme would imply. A new treaty would state that competences regarding distributive justice and social policy should be shared by the EU and the member states, according to the principle of subsidiarity. This treaty would create a European agency for social justice, with the purpose of operationalizing the idea of an EU threshold of basic goods. In addition, the new treaty would give the Union limited fiscal capacity to pursue such goals. Accordingly, contributions to the EU budget would be raised to the level of 2% of national GDPs, and a small EU corporate tax would be launched to fund the programmes of the agency. At the level of rule-making, both the Commission and the Parliament would evaluate the design of the common market and the Eurozone in light of the new distributive goals. A minimum EU corporate rate and an EU Labour Code consistent with the different level of prices of member states would be introduced to avoid tax competition and social dumping. The European Central Bank would incorporate distributive concerns when setting targets for the euro exchange rate. In turn, all member states would commit to making their welfare regimes more efficient, being subjected to regular reports on the performance of their social services. These reforms could be introduced gradually, considering the political and economic circumstances of the Union at each moment of time.

These institutional developments would have a major impact on the way we think of the EU. First, they would bring about a paradigm shift in the Union, moving from a logic of *transitional* justice only – that is, economic convergence backed by structural funds – to a logic of *social* justice. Of course, structural funds could still be used as a trigger for the economic development of newly admitted member states. Yet the problem of justice in the EU would no longer be articulated in terms of economic infrastructure, but expressed in terms of social needs. Secondly, under the framework presented here, the rules of the common market and the Eurozone would be assessed not only according to standards of efficiency, but also from the standpoint of social justice. Accordingly, reducing transaction costs would no longer be enough to justify a given policy; one would need to investigate its distributive implications. This alternative framework for EU policy making would render unsustainable the view that the EU is only an economic association. Thirdly, a social Europe of this sort would be incompatible with the conception of an EU at two (or more) speeds. The idea of leaving the distressed member states behind goes against the principles of democratic citizenship and reciprocity advocated in the previous chapters. Crucially, it is inconsistent with the background of shared political and economic institutions of the present-day EU.

Accordingly, participation in a social Europe should become a constitutive part of EU membership. Solidarity would not only be a key European value, but also a consistent set of institutionalized practices backed by adequate EU competences and resources. This would likely make further enlargements costlier and harder, but not impossible, particularly if transitional policies were adopted. For instance, one might establish that redistribution would only apply after a given period of membership, allowing for a degree of economic and social convergence to take place. At the same time, while bringing social justice to the Union's DNA might be a source of contention, refraining from it would not necessarily make further exits from the Union less unlikely. The concession of a seven-year "emergency break" on in-work benefits for EU citizens arriving to the United Kingdom did not prevent Brexit from happening. Perhaps an EU distributive scheme reaching the losers of globalization would have been a more effective remedy. In any case, harsh measures such as those imposed on Greece during the recent financial crisis have the potential to alienate national support for EU membership, thus posing a real threat to the survival of the Union as we know it.

To conclude, it is worth reviewing the three tensions presented in the Introduction of this book, explaining how my proposals would help to address them. Recall that these tensions were (i) a discrepancy between the degrees of political integration and social integration in the Union; (ii) the contrast between the existing legal grounds for an (at least thin) EU social citizenship and the lack of mechanisms to provide and enforce it; and (iii) the paradox raised by the fact that, under the principle of non-discrimination, EU citizens are entitled to the same set of social rights, but only when they live or work in the same member state. My proposals have addressed each of these tensions. First, once a set of pre-distributive and redistributive instruments have been launched, the level of social integration will be consistent with the comprehensive set of shared political and economic institutions. Secondly, if the institutional reforms described here are put into practice, social rights will become enforceable at the EU level, with an unambiguous legal basis in the treaties, and a specialized agency responsible for their fulfilment. Thirdly, insofar as the threshold of basic goods applies to all EU citizens, regardless of their country of origin and residence, it fully realizes the ideal of non-discrimination, applied to social goods. As I have suggested, solving these tensions would not only promote social cohesion but also foster political stability in the Union.

At the opening of this book, I referred to a famous prediction by Robert Schuman dating back to 1950. According to the Schuman Declaration, economic integration would open the way to political and social integration.[1] This became a reality to a remarkable extent: EU member states share not only a prosperous common market, but also representative democratic institutions and a free-movement area. However, as I have claimed, a few crucial dimensions of social integration are yet to be realized. Europeans should not expect that market mechanisms will do the whole job. The purpose of social policy (at whichever level of government) is precisely to address distributive imbalances that the "invisible hand" will not fix. As Schuman perceptively put it, a united Europe can only be built "through concrete achievements which first create a de facto solidarity".[2] It has been a key contention of this book that a social Europe that distributes fairly the benefits and burdens of European integration would be one such achievement. In other words, "a de facto solidarity" is not just a pre-condition of a social Europe – it may also become one of its most significant outcomes. Distributive justice has the potential to strengthen the civic bonds among Europeans and to increase their sense of belonging to a political project that visibly includes them all. Thus the struggle for a social Europe is a quest for a more united Europe. This is, undoubtedly, a cause worth fighting for.

Notes

1 Robert Schuman, *The Schuman Declaration* (9 May 1950).
2 Ibid.

Bibliography

Books and articles

ABIZADEH, Arash, "Cooperation, Pervasive Impact, and Coercion: On the Scope (Not Site) of Distributive Justice", *Philosophy & Public Affairs* 35 (2007), pp. 318–358.

ÁBRÁHAM, Árpád, João Brogueira de Sousa, Ramon Marimon, and Lukas Mayr, "On the Design of an European Unemployment Mechanism", *European University Institute Working Paper* (2017).

ACEMOGLU, Daron, "Good Jobs Versus Bad Jobs", *Journal of Labor Economics* 19 (2001), pp. 1–21.

ACHTERBERG, Peter and Mara Yerkes, "One Welfare State Emerging? Convergence versus Divergence in 16 Western Countries", *Journal of Comparative Social Welfare* 25 (2009), pp. 189–201.

ALBERTUS, Michael, *Autocracy and Redistribution: The Politics of Land Reform* (New York, 2015).

ALESSINA, Alessandro and Nicola Fuchs-Schündeln, "Good-bye Lenin (or Not)? The Effect of Communism on People's Preferences", *American Economic Review* 97 (2007), pp. 1507–1528.

ALEXIADIS, Stilianos, *Convergence Clubs and Spatial Externalities* (New York, 2013).

ALTER, Karen J., "Who are the 'Masters of the Treaty'?: European Governments and the European Court of Justice", *International Organization* 52 (1998), pp. 121–147.

ANARAKI, Nahid Kalbasi, "Effects of Euro Devaluation on Eurozone Exports", *International Journal of Economics and Finance* 6 (2014), pp. 19–24.

ANDERSON, Benedict, *Imagined Communities: Reflections on the Origin and Spread of Nationalism* (London, 2006).

ANDERSON, Elizabeth, "Ethical Assumptions in Economic Theory: Some Lessons from the History of Credit and Bankruptcy", *Ethical Theory and Moral Practice* 7 (2004), pp. 347–360.

———, "What is the Point of Equality?", *Ethics* 109 (1999), pp. 287–337.

ANDERSON, Scott, "The Enforcement Approach to Coercion", *Journal of Ethics and Social Philosophy* 5 (2010), pp. 1–31.

ARENDT, Hannah, *Human Condition* (Chicago, 1998).

ARNESON, Richard, "Distributive Justice and Basic Capability Equality: 'Good Enough' Is Not Good Enough", in A. Kaufman (ed.), *Capabilities Equality: Basic Issues and Problems* (London, 2005).

––––––, "Luck Egalitarianism Interpreted and Defended", *Philosophical Topics* 32 (2004), pp. 1–18.

ATKINSON, A. B. and Joseph Stiglitz, "The Structure of Indirect Taxation and Economic Efficiency", *Social Justice and Public Policy* (Cambridge MA, 1983).

BACON, Francis, "New Atlantis", in *Three Early Modern Utopias* (Oxford, 2008).

BALTA, Narcissa, "Business Cycle Synchronization in the Euro Area", *Quarterly Report on the Euro Area* 14 (2015), pp. 28–36.

BARBER, Benjamin R., "Review: Justifying Justice: Problems of Psychology, Measurement, and Politics in Rawls", *The American Political Science Review* 69 (1975), pp. 663–674.

BAUBÖCK, Rainer, "Recombinant Citizenship", in Martin Kohli and Alison Woodward (eds), *Inclusions and Exclusions in European Societies* (London, 2001).

––––––, "The Three Levels of Citizenship within the European Union", *German Law Journal* 15 (2014), pp. 751–764.

––––––, "Why European Citizenship? Normative Approaches to Supranational Union", *Theoretical Inquiries in Law* 8 (2007), pp. 453–488.

BEDNAR, Jenna, "Authority Migration in Federations: A Framework for Analysis", *PS* 37 (2004), pp. 403–408.

BEITZ, Charles R., "Cosmopolitanism and Global Justice", *The Journal of Ethics* 9 (2005), pp. 11–27.

––––––, *Political Theory and International Relations* (Princeton, 1999).

BELLAMY, Richard, "A Duty-Free Europe? What's Wrong with Kochenov's Account of EU Citizenship Rights", *European Law Journal* 21 (2015), pp. 558–565.

BELLAMY, Richard and Dario Castiglione, "Between Cosmopolis and Community: Three Models of Rights and Democracy within the European Union", in Daniele Archibugi, David Held, and Martin Köhler (eds), *Re-imagining Political Community* (Stanford, 1998).

BENGSON, John, "Experimental Attacks on Intuitions and Answers", *Philosophy and Phenomenological Research* 86 (2013), pp. 495–532.

BENTON, Lauren, *Law and Colonial Cultures: Legal Regimes in World History 1400–1900* (Cambridge, 2002).

BLAKE, Michael, "Distributive Justice, State Coercion, and Autonomy", *Philosophy & Public Affairs* 30 (July, 2001), pp. 257–296.

BLAUBERGER, Michael and Susanne K. Schmidt, "Welfare Migration? Free Movement of EU Citizens and Access to Social Benefits", *Research and Politics* 1 (2014), pp. 1–7.

BLOCH, Marc, *Feudal Society* (New York, 2014).

BODIN, Jean, *On Sovereignty: Four Chapters from the Six Books of the Commonwealth*, ed. Julian H. Franklin (Cambridge, 1992).

BOTHFELD, Silke and Singrid Betzelt (eds), *Activation and Labour Market Reforms in Europe: Challenges to Social Citizenship* (New York, 2011).

BOURDIEU, Pierre, *Distinction: A Social Critique of the Judgment of Taste* (London, 1986).

BRADLEY, John, George Petrakos, and Iulia Traistaru, *Integration, Growth, and Cohesion in the European Union* (New York, 2004).

———, Timo Mitze, Edgar Morgenroth, and Gerhard Untiedt, "An Integrated Micro-Macro (IMM) Approach to the Evaluation of Large-scale Public Investment Programmes: The Case of EU Structural Funds", *The Economic and Social Research Institute Working Papers* 167 (2005).

BREWSTER, Rachel, "Unpacking the State's Reputation", *Harvard International Law Journal* 50 (2009), pp. 231–269.

BRUNNERMEIER, Markus K., Harold James, and Jean-Pierre Landau, *The Euro and the Battle of Ideas* (Princeton, 2017).

BUCHANAN, Allen and Robert O. Keohane, *Justice, Legitimacy, and Self-Determination* (Oxford, 2004).

———, "The Legitimacy of Global Governance Institutions", *Ethics and International Affairs* 20 (2006), pp. 405–437.

———, "Rawls's *Law of Peoples*: Rules for a Vanished Westphalian World", *Ethics* 110 (2000), pp. 697–721.

BÚRCA, Gráinne, "The Future of Social Rights Protection in Europe", in Gráinne De Búrca, Bruno de Witte, and Larissa Ogertschnig (eds), *Social Rights in Europe* (Oxford, 2005).

BYRNE, Ruth M. J., *The Rational Imagination: How People Create Alternatives to Reality* (Cambridge MA, 2005).

CAMPANELLA, Tommaso, *The City of the Sun* (Berkeley, 1981);

CANEY, Simon, "Just Emissions", *Philosophy & Public Affairs* 40 (2012), pp. 255–300.

———, *Justice Beyond Borders: A Global Political Theory* (New York, 2005).

CARENS, Joseph H., *Equality, Moral Incentives, and the Market: An Essay in Utopian Politico-Economic Theory* (Chicago, 1981).

CASAL, Paula, "Why Sufficiency is Not Enough", *Ethics* 117 (2007), pp. 296–326.

CHAKRABARTY, Dipesh, *Provincializing Europe: Postcolonial Thought and Historical Difference* (Princeton, 2000).

CHEN, Ruo, Gian Maria Milesi-Ferretti, and Thierry Tressel, "External Imbalances in the Eurozone", *Economic Policy* 73 (2013), pp. 101–142.

CHENEVAL, F. and F. Schimmelfennig, "The Case for Demoicracy in the European Union", *Journal of Common Market Studies* 51 (2013), pp. 334–350.

CHORAFAS, Dimitris N., *Sovereign Debt Crisis: The New Normal and the Newly Poor* (New York, 2011).

CHORLEY, Matt, Claire Ellicott, and David Wilkes, "Thatcher's Chancellor Nigel Lawson Warned Tory PM Her Poll Tax Was 'Completely Unworkable and Politically Catastrophic'", *Daily Mail Online* (30 December 2014).

CHRISTIANO, Thomas, "Is Democratic Legitimacy Possible for International Institutions?", in Daniele Archibugi, Mathias Koenig-Archibugi, and Raffaele Marchetti (eds), *Global Democracy: Normative and Empirical Perspectives* (Cambridge, 2011).

CLOSA, Carlos, "Citizenship of the Union and Nationality of Member States", *Common Market Law Review* 32 (1995), 487–518.

COHEN, G. A., "Expensive Tastes Rides Again", in Justine Burley (ed.), *Dworkin and His Critics* (Malde, 2004), pp. 3–29.

_____, "Facts and Principles", *Philosophy & Public Affairs* 31 (2003), pp. 211–245.

_____, "On the Currency of Egalitarian Justice", *Ethics* 99 (1989), pp. 906–944.

_____, "The Pareto Argument for Inequality", *Social Philosophy and Policy* 12 (1995), pp. 160–185.

COHEN, Joshua and Charles F. Sabel, "Extra Rempublicam Nulla Justitia?", *Philosophy & Public Affairs* 34 (2006), pp. 147–175.

_____, "Global Democracy?", *New York University Journal of International Law and Politics* 37 (2006), pp. 763–797.

COURT OF JUSTICE OF THE EUROPEAN UNION, Press Release 146/14 by the Court of Justice of the European Union, 11 November 2014.

CRISP, Roger, "Equality, Priority, and Compassion", *Ethics* 113 (2003), pp. 745–763.

DAHL, Robert, "Can International Organizations Be Democratic? A Skeptic's View", in Ian Shapiro and Casiano Hacker-Cordon (eds), *Democracy's Edges* (Cambridge, 1999).

_____, *Democracy and its Critics* (New Haven, 1989).

DALLMAYR, Fred, "Cosmopolitanism: Moral and Political", *Political Theory* 31 (2003), pp. 421–442.

DANIELS, Norman, "Reflective Equilibrium", in Edward N. Zalta (ed.), *The Stanford Encyclopedia of Philosophy* (2013), http://plato.stanford.edu/arch ives/win2013/entries/reflective-equilibrium/, (Accessed 1 June 2016).

DE GRAUWE, Paul, "Design Failures in the Eurozone: Can They Be Fixed?", *LSE Europe in Question Discussion Paper Series* 57 (2013).

_____, "The Governance of a Fragile Eurozone", *CEPS Working Document* 346 (2011), pp. 1–25.

DE ROOVER, Raymond, "The Concept of the Just Price: Theory and Economic Policy", *The Journal of Economic History* 18 (1958), pp. 418–434.

DEARDORFF, Alan V., "General Validity of the Law of Comparative Advantage", *Journal of Political Economy* 88 (1980), pp. 941–957.

DESCARTES, René, *A Discourse on the Method* (Oxford, 2008).

DOBSON, Lynn, *Supranational Citizenship* (Manchester, 2006).

DOWNS, George and Michael A. Jones, "Reputation, Compliance, and International Law", *Journal of Legal Studies* 31 (2002), pp. S95–S114.

DUTTON, Paul V., *Origins of the French Welfare State: The Struggle for Social Reform in France 1914–1947* (Cambridge, 2002).

DWORKIN, Ronald, *Sovereign Virtue: The Theory and Practice of Equality* (Harvard, 2002).

EASTLUND, David, "Utopophobia", *Philosophy & Public Affairs* 42 (2014), pp. 113–134.

ELEFTHERIADIS, Pavlos, "Why Germany is the Eurozone's Biggest Free-Rider", *Fortune* (22 October 2014).

ESPING-ANDERSON, Gøsta, *The Three Worlds of Welfare Capitalism* (Cambridge, 2004).

EUROFUND, *Multinational Companies and Collective Bargaining* (2009).

EUROPEAN CENTRAL BANK, "Public Investment in Europe", *ECB Economic Bulletin* 2 (2016).

EUROPEAN COMMISSION, *Annual Report on Intra-EU Labour Mobility 2016: Second Edition* (2017).

———, *Minimum Income Policies in EU Member States* (2017).

———, *Minimum Income Schemes in Europe: A Study of National Policies* (2015).

———, *Staff Working Document: Monitoring the Implementation of the European Pillar of Social Rights* (2018).

EUROPEAN UNION, "Agencies and Other EU bodies", https://europa.eu/european-union/about-eu/agencies_en (Accessed 20 August 2020).

FABO, Brian and Sharon Sarah Belli, "(Un)believable Wages? An Analysis of Minimum Wage Policies in Europe from a Living Wage Perspective", *IZA Journal of Labour Policy* 6 (2017), pp. 1–11.

FERNÁNDEZ-MACIAS, Enrique and Carlos Vacas-Soriano, "A Coordinated European Union Minimum Wage Policy?", *European Journal of Industrial Relations* 22 (2016), pp. 97–113.

FERRARO, Fabrizio, Jeffrey Pfeffer, and Robert I. Sutton, "Economics Language and Assumptions: How Theories Can Become Self-fulfilling", *Academy of Management Review* 30 (2005), pp. 8–24.

FERRERA, Maurizio, "The Contentious Politics of Hospitality: Intra-EU Mobility and Social Rights", *European Law Journal* 22 (2016), pp. 791–805.

FLANAGAN, Owen, *The Varieties of Moral Personality: Ethics and Psychological Realism* (Cambridge MA, 1991).

FLEISCHACKER, Samuel, *A Short History of Distributive Justice* (Harvard, 2004).

FØLLESDAL, Andreas, "Citizenship: European and Global", in Nigel Dower and John Williams (eds), *Global Citizenship: A Critical Introduction* (Edinburgh, 2002), pp. 71–83.

———, "Federal Inequality Amongst Equals: A Contractualist Defence", *Metaphilosophy* 32 (2001), pp. 236–255.

FORST, Rainer, "Towards a Critical Theory of Transnational Justice", *Metaphilosophy* 32 (2001) .

FRANKFURT, Harry, "Equality as a Moral Ideal", *Ethics* 98 (1987), pp. 21–43.

FRASER, Nancy, *Social Justice in the Age of Identity Politics: Redistribution, Recognition, Participation* (Berlin, 1998).

FRIEDMAN, Milton, and Anna Jacobson Schwartz, *A Monetary History of the United States 1867–1960* (Princeton, 1963).

FRIESE, Heidrun and Peter Wagner, "Survey Article: The Nascent Political Philosophy of the European Polity", *Journal of Political Philosophy* 10 (2002), pp. 342–364.

GAYER, Christian, "A Fresh Look at Business Cycle Synchronization in the Euro Area", *European Economy Economic Papers* (2007).

GENDLER, Tamar Szabo, *Thought Experiment: On the Powers and Limits of Imaginary Cases* (New York, 2013).

GILABERT, Pablo, "The Feasibility of Basic Socioeconomic Human Rights: A Conceptual Exploration", *The Philosophical Quarterly* 59 (2009), pp. 659–681.

GOODIN, Robert E., "Political Ideals and Political Practice", *British Journal of Political Science* 25 (1995), pp. 37–56.

GRIMM, Dieter, "Does Europe Need a Constitution?", *European Law Journal* 1 (1995), pp. 282–302.

GUTZMAN, Andrew, *How International Law Works: A Rational Choice Theory* (Oxford, 2008).

HAAGH, Louise, *The Case for Universal Basic Income* (Cambridge, 2019).

HAAS, Ernst B., "Turbulent Fields and the Theory of Regional Integration", *International Organization* 30 (1976), pp. 173–212.

HABERMAS, Jürgen, "The Constitutionalization of International Law and the Legitimation Problems of a Constitution for World Society", *Constellations* 15 (2008), pp. 444–455.

_____, *The Crisis of the European Union: A Response* (Cambridge, 2012).

_____, "The Postnational Constellation and the Future of Democracy", *The Postnational Constellation: Political Essays* (Cambridge, 2001).

HACKER, Jacob S., "The Institutional Foundations of Middle Class Democracy", in *Priorities for a New Political Economy: Memos to the Left* (London, 2011), pp. 33–38.

HALL, Peter A. (ed.), *The Political Power of Economic Ideas: Keynesianism Across Nations* (Princeton, 1989).

_____, "Varieties of Capitalism in Light of the Eurocrisis", *Journal of European Public Policy* 25 (2017), pp. 7–30.

HARDT, Michael and Antonio Negri, *Empire* (Cambridge MA, 2001).

HARE, R. M., *Freedom and Reason* (Oxford, 1963).

HARRIS, Bernard, *The Origins of the British Welfare State: Society, State and Social Welfare in England and Wales* (Basingstoke, 2004).

HARRIS, Jose, *William Beveridge: A Biography* (Oxford, 1997).

HARRIS, Nigel, "The Economics and Politics of the Free Movement of People", in Antoine Pécoud and Paul de Guchteneire (eds), *Migration Without Borders: Essays on the Free Movement of People* (New York, 2007).

HAUSMAN, Daniel M. and Michael S. McPherson, "Economics, Rationality, and Ethics", in Daniel M. Hausman (ed.), *The Philosophy of Economics: An Anthology* (Cambridge, 1994).

HAWTHORN, Geoffrey, *Plausible Worlds: Possibility and Understanding in History and the Social Sciences* (Cambridge, 1991).

HAYEK, F. A., *The Constitution of Liberty* (Abingdon, 2006).

_____, *Law, Legislation and Liberty* (London, 1998).

HECHTER, Michael and Christine Horne, "The Problem of Social Order", in Michael Hechter and Christine Horne (eds), *Theories of Social Order* (Stanford, 2003).

HELD, David, *Models of Democracy* (Cambridge, 2006).

HEMERIJCK, Anton, "The Quiet Paradigm Revolution of Social Investment", *Social Politics* 22 (2015), pp. 242–256.

HOBBES, Thomas, *Leviathan*, ed. Noel Malcolm (Oxford, 2014).

HOFFMANN, Stanley, "Obstinate or Obsolete? The Fate of the Nation-State and the Case of Western Europe", *Daedalus* 95 (1966), pp. 862–915.

HOGG, Michael A., "Social Processes and Human Behaviour: Social Psychology", in Kurt Pawlik and Mark R. Rosenzweig, *The International Handbook of Psychology* (London, 2000), pp. 305–327.

HUEMER, Michael, *Ethical Intuitionism* (New York, 2005).

HUFFSCHMID, Jörg (ed.), *Economic Policy for a Social Europe: A Critique of Neo-liberalism and Proposals for Alternatives* (New York, 2005).

HULLER, Thorsten, "Out of Time? The Democratic Limits of EU Demoicracy", *Journal of European Public Policy* 23 (2016), pp. 1407–1424.

HUME, David, *A Treatise of Human Nature* (Oxford, 1896).

HUNGER, Peter, *Living High and Letting Die: Our Illusion of Innocence* (New York, 1996).

INOTAI, András, "The Czech Republic, Hungary, Poland, Slovak Republic, and Slovenia", *Winners and Losers of EU Integration: Policy Issues for Central and Eastern Europe* (Washington, 2000).

INSTITUTO NACIONAL DE ESTATÍSTICA, *Estatísticas do Comércio Internacional* (2014).

INTERNATIONAL LABOUR OFFICE and the Secretariat of the World Trade Organization, *Trade and Employment: Challenges for Policy and Research* (2007).

JANSEN, Marion, "International Trade and the Position of European Low-Skilled Labour", *World Trade Organization Staff Working Paper* (2000).

JENSEN, Mark, "The Limits of Practical Possibility", *The Journal of Political Philosophy* 17 (2009), pp. 168–184.

JOHNSON, Miles, "FTSE Chiefs Earn 183 Times Average Salary of UK Workers", *Financial Times*, 17 August 2015, https://www.ft.com/content/b3d0225e-4416-11e5-af2f-4d6e0e5eda22 (Accessed 20 August 2020).

JULIUS, A. J., "Nagel's Atlas", *Philosophy & Public Affairs* 34 (2006), pp. 176–192.

JUNCKER, Jean-Claude, *State of Union Address 2017*, https://ec.europa.eu/comm ission/presscorner/detail/en/SPEECH_17_3165 (Accessed 27 February 2020).

KANT, Immanuel, "On the Common Saying: This May Be True in Theory But It Does Not Apply in Practice", in Hans Reiss (ed.), *Kant's Political Writings* (Cambridge, 1991).

KEANE, John, *Global Civil Society?* (Cambridge, 2003).

KEATING, Michael, "Social Citizenship, Solidarity and Welfare in Regionalized and Plurinational States", *Citizenship Studies* 13 (2009), pp. 501–513.

KELLY, Paul, "How Political is Political Liberalism?", *Liberalism* (Cambridge, 2005).

KENNER, Jeff, "Economic and Social Rights in the EU Legal Order: The Mirage of Indivisibility", in Tamara K. Harvey and Jeff Kenner, *Economic and Social Rights under the EU Charter of Fundamental Rights: A Legal Perspective* (Oxford, 2003).

KEYNES, John Maynard, "Economic Possibilities for Our Grandchildren", in Lorenzo Pecchi and Gustavo Piga (eds), *Keynes Revisited: Economic Possibilities for Our Grandchildren* (Cambridge MA, 2008).

KOCHENOV, Dimitry, "EU Citizenship without Duties", *European Law Journal* 20 (2014), pp. 482–498.

KRUGMAN, Paul, "Increasing Returns in a Comparative Advantage World", in *Comparative Advantage, Growth, and the Gains from Trade and Globalization: Festschrift Papers in Honor of Alan V. Deardorf* (Ann Arbor, 2010).

————, "Revenge of the Optimum Currency Area", *NBER Macroeconomics Annual 2012* 27 (2012), pp. 439–448.

KRUGMAN, Paul, Maurice Obstfeld, and Marc J. Melitz, *International Economics: Theory and Policy* (Harlow, 2015).

KUHN, Thomas S., *The Structure of Scientific Revolutions* (Chicago, 2012).

KUMM, Matias, "Beyond Golf Clubs and the Judicialization of Politics: Why Europe Has a Constitution Properly So Called", *The American Journal of Comparative Law* 54 (2006), pp. 505–530.

LABORDE, Cécile, "Republicanism and Global Justice: A Sketch", *European Journal of Political Theory* 9 (2010), pp. 48–69.

LÆGAARD, Sune, "Feasibility and Stability in Normative Political Philosophy: The Case of Liberal Nationalism", *Ethical Theory and Practice* 9 (2009), pp. 399–416.

LAMBACH, Daniel, "Oligopolies of Violence in Post-Conflict Societies", *German Institute of Global and Area Studies Working Papers* 62 (2007).

LAMOND, Grant, "The Coerciveness of Law", *Oxford Journal of Legal Studies* 20 (2000), pp. 39–62.

LAWFORD-SMITH, Holly, "Understanding Political Feasibility", *The Journal of Political Philosophy* 21 (2003), pp. 243–259.

LEAMER, Edward E., "The Heckscher-Ohlin Model in Theory and Practice", *Princeton Studies in International Finance* 75 (1995).

LIJPHART, Arend, *Patterns of Democracy: Government Forms and Performance in Twenty-Six Countries* (Yale, 1999).

LIPSEY, R. G. and Kelvin Lancaster, "The General Theory of the Second Best", *The Review of Economic Studies* 24 (1956/57), pp. 11–32.

LOCKE, John, *Two Treatises of Government*, ed. Peter Laslett (Cambridge, 1988).

MAAS, Willem, "Varieties of Multilevel Citizenship", in William Maas (ed.), *Multilevel Citizenship* (Philadelphia, 2013).

MACDONALD, Terry and Miriam Ronzoni, "Introduction: The Idea of Global Political Justice," *Critical Review of International Social and Political Philosophy* 15 (2008), pp. 521–533.

MACKINNON, Catherine A., *Toward a Feminist Theory of the State* (Cambridge MA, 1998).

MADURO, Miguel Poiares, "A New Governance for the European Union and the Euro: Democracy and Justice", *RCSAS Policy Papers* (2012).

———, "Europe's Social Self: The Sickness Unto Death", in Jon Shaw (ed.), *Social Law and Policy in an Evolving European Union* (Oxford, 2000).

———, "O Superavit Democrático Europeu", *Análise Social* 35 (2001), pp. 119–152.

MAJONE, Giandomenico, "The European Community Between Social Policy and Social Regulation", *Journal of Common Market Studies* 31 (1993), pp. 153–170.

MANKIW, N. Gregory, "The Growth of Nations", *Brookings Papers on Economic Activity* 1 (1995), pp. 275–326.

MARCUSE, Herbert, *One-Dimensional Man: Studies in the Ideology of Advanced Capitalist Societies* (New York, 1991).

MCINTYRE, Alisdair, *After Virtue* (London, 2013).

MEEHAN, Elizabeth, *Citizenship and the European Union* (Bonn, 2000).

MELITZ, Marc J., "When and How Should Infant Industries Be Protected?", *Journal of International Economics* 66 (2005), pp. 177–196.

MEYERS, Chris, "Wrongful Beneficence: Exploitation and Third World Sweatshops", *Journal of Social Philosophy* 35 (2004), pp. 319–333.

MILLER, David, *Justice for Earthlings: Essays in Political Philosophy* (Cambridge, 2013).

———, *National Responsibility and Global Justice* (Oxford, 2007).

———, *On Nationality* (Oxford, 1997).

MÖLLER, Kai, *The Global Model of Constitutional Rights* (Oxford, 2012).

MORAVCSIK, Andrew and F. Schimmelfennig, "In Defence of the 'Democratic Deficit': Reassessing Legitimacy in the European Union", *Journal of Common Market Studies* 40 (2002), pp. 603–624.

———, "Liberal Intergovernmentalism", in A. Wiener and T. Diez (eds), *European Integration Theory* (Oxford, 2009), pp. 67–87.

MORE, Thomas, *Utopia* (Cambridge, 1989).

MUNDELL, Robert A., "A Theory of Optimum Currency Areas", *The American Economic Review* 51 (1961), pp. 656–665.

NAGEL, Thomas, "Moral Luck", *Mortal Questions* (Cambridge, 1979).

———, "The Problem of Global Justice", *Philosophy & Public Affairs* 33 (2005), pp. 113–147.

NELSON, Kenneth, "Minimum Income Protection and European Integration: Trends and Levels of Minimum Benefits in Comparative Perspective 1990–2005", *International Journal of Health Services* 31 (2008), pp. 103–124.

NICOLAIDIS, Kalypso, "The Idea of European Demoicracy", in Julie Dickson and Pavlos Eleftheriadis, *Philosophical Foundations of European Law* (Oxford, 2012).

NÖLKE, Andreas and Arkan Vliegenthart, "Enlarging the Varieties of Capitalism: The Emergence of Dependent Market Economies in East Central Europe", *World Politics* 61 (2009), pp. 670–702.

NOZICK, Robert, *Anarchy, State and Utopia* (Malden, 1974).

———, "Coercion", in Sidney Morgenbesser, Patrick Suppes, and Morton White (eds), *Philosophy, Science, and Method: Essays in Honor of Ernest Nagel* (New York, 1969), pp. 440–472.

NUSSBAUM, Martha C., *Creating Capabilities* (Cambridge MA, 2011).

OECD, *Focus on Inequality and Growth*, December 2014.

OFFE, Claus, *Europe Entrapped* (Cambridge, 2015).

———, "Social Protection in a Supranational Context: European Integration and the Faces of the 'European Social Model'", in Pranab Bardhan, Samuel Bowles, and Michael Wallerstein (eds), *Globalization and Egalitarian Redistribution* (Princeton, 2006).

OKIN, Susan Moller, *Justice, Gender, and the Family* (New York, 1989).

OLSEN, Espen D. H., "European Citizenship: Mixing Nation State and Federal Features with a Cosmopolitan Twist", *Perspectives on European Politics and Society* 14 (2013), pp. 505–519.

O'NEILL, Onora, *Justice Across Boundaries: Whose Obligations?* (Cambridge, 2016).

ONGLEY, Sophia F., Marta Nola, and Tina Malti, "Children's Giving: Moral Reasoning and Moral Emotions in the Development of Donation Behaviors", *Frontiers in Psychology* 23 (2014), pp. 1–8.

OTTAVIANO, Gianmarco, "European Integration and the Gains from Trade", in Harald Badinger and Volker Nitsch (eds), *The Routledge Handbook of European Integration* (New York, 2016).

PAGER, Devah and Hana Shepherd, "The Sociology of Discrimination: Discrimination in Employment, Housing, Credit, and Consumer Markets", *Annual Review of Sociology* 34 (2008), pp. 181–204.

PETERSON, Matt and Christian Barry, "Who Must Pay for the Damage of the Gobal Financial Crisis", in Ned Dobos, Christian Barry, and Thomas W. Pogge (eds), *Global Financial Crisis: The Ethical Issues* (New York, 2011).

PETTIT, Philip, "Freedom in the Market", *Politics, Philosophy and Economics* 5 (2006), pp. 131–149.

_____, "The Globalized Republican Ideal", *Global Justice: Theory, Practice, Rhetoric* 9 (2016), pp. 47–68.

PHILLIPS, Michael, "Reflections on the Transition from Ideal to Non-ideal Theory", *Noûs* 19 (1985), pp. 561–562.

PIERSON, Paul, "The Path to European Integration: A Historical-Institutionalist Analysis", in Wayne Sandholtz and Alec Stone Sweet (eds), *European Integration and Supranational Governance* (Oxford, 1998), pp. 28–59.

PIKETTY, Thomas, *Capital in the Twenty-First Century* (Cambridge MA, 2014).

PLATO, *The Republic* (Oxford, 2008).

POGGE, Thomas W., *Realizing Rawls* (Ithaca, 1989).

POPPER, Karl, "Science: Conjectures and Refutations", in *Conjectures and Refutations: The Growth of Scientific Knowledge* (London, 1963).

_____, "Utopia and Violence", in *Conjectures and Refutations: The Growth of Scientific Knowledge* (New York, 1989).

PORTER, Michael E., *The Competitive Advantage of Nations* (New York, 1998).

PRITCHARD, Michael S., "Rawls's Moral Psychology", *The Southwestern Journal of Philosophy* 8 (1977), pp. 59–72.

QUESNAY, François, *Tableau Économique des Physiocrates* (Paris, 1969).

RÄIKKÄ, Juha, "The Feasibility Condition in Political Theory", *The Journal of Political Philosophy* 6 (1998), pp. 27–40.

RAWLS, John, "Deuxième Lettre", in John Rawls and Philippe Van Parijs, *Three Letters on* The Law of Peoples *and the European Union* (2003), https://cdn.ucl ouvain.be/public/Exports%20reddot/etes/documents/RawlsVanParijs1.Rev.p hil.Econ.pdf (Accessed 16 December 2017).

_____, "The Idea of an Overlapping Consensus", *Oxford Journal of Legal Studies* 7 (1987), pp. 1–25.

_____, "The Idea of Public Reason Revisited", *The University of Chicago Law Review* 64 (1997), pp. 765–807.

_____, *The Law of Peoples* (Cambridge MA, 2001).

_____, *Political Liberalism* (New York, 2005).

_____, "The Sense of Justice", *The Philosophical Review* 72 (1963), pp. 281–305.

_____, *A Theory of Justice: Revised Edition* (Cambridge MA, 1999).

RICARDO, David, *On the Principles of Political Economy and Taxation* (Indianapolis, 2004).

RICHARDSON, Henry S., "Moral Reasoning", in Edward N. Zalta (ed.), *Stanford Encyclopedia of Philosophy* (Fall 2018), https://plato.stanford.edu/archives/fall 2018/entries/reasoning-moral/ (Accessed 3 October 2019).

RONZONI, Miriam, "The European Union as a Demoicracy: Really a Third Way?", *European Journal of Political Theory* 16 (2017), pp. 210–234.

———, "The Global Order: A Case of Background Injustice? A Practice-Dependence Account", *Philosophy & Public Affairs* 37 (2009), pp. 229–256.

ROOS, Christof, "Freedom of Movement in the EU and Welfare State Closure: Welfare Regime Type, Benefit Restrictions, and Their Implications for Social Mobility", in Melike Wulfgramm, Tonia Bieber, and Stephan Leibfried (eds), *Welfare State Transformations and Inequality in OECD Countries* (2016).

ROSSET, Jan, Nathalie Giger, and Julian Bernauer, "More Money, Fewer Problems? Cross-Level Effects of Economic Deprivation on Political Representation", *West European Politics* 36 (2013), pp. 817–835.

ROUSSEAU, Jean-Jacques, *The Social Contract* (Oxford, 1998).

SANGIOVANNI, Andrea, "Global Justice, Reciprocity, and the State", *Philosophy & Public Affairs* 35 (2007), pp. 3–39.

———, "Non-Discrimination, In-Work Benefits, and Free Movement in the EU", *European Journal of Political Theory* 16 (2017), pp. 143–163.

———, "Solidarity in the European Union: Problems and Prospects", in Julie Dickson and Pavlos Eleftheriadis (eds), *Philosophical Foundations of European Union Law* (Oxford, 2012).

SAPONTZIS, Steve F., "'Ought' Does Imply 'Can'", *The Southern Journal of Philosophy* 29 (1991), pp. 382–393.

SARTORI, Giovanni, "Concept Misformation in Comparative Politics", *American Political Science Review* 64 (1970), pp. 1033–1053.

SCANLON, Thomas, *What We Owe to Each Other* (Cambridge MA, 1998).

SCHARPF, Fritz W., "The European Social Model: Coping with the Challenge of Diversity", *Journal of Common Market Studies* 40 (2002), pp. 645–670.

———, *Governing in Europe: Effective and Democratic?* (Oxford, 1999).

SCHEURMAN, William E., "Cosmopolitanism and the World State", *Review of International Studies* 40 (2014), pp. 419–441.

SCHMITTER, Philippe C. and Michael W. Bower, "A (Modest) Proposal for Expanding Social Citizenship in the European Union", *Journal of European Social Policy* 11 (2001), pp. 55–65.

SCHUMAN, Robert, *The Schuman Declaration* (9 May 1950), https://europa. eu/european-union/about-eu/symbols/europe-day/schuman-declaration_en (Accessed 16 December 2017).

SCHUMPETER, Joseph A., *Capitalism, Socialism and Democracy* (New York, 2008).

SEN, Amartya, *Development as Freedom* (New York, 1999).

———, *The Idea of Justice* (London, 2010).

———, "What Do We Want from a Theory of Justice", *The Journal of Philosophy* 103 (2006), pp. 251–238.

SEWELL JR, William H., "The Concept(s) of Culture", in Victoria E. Bonnell and Lynn Hunt (eds), *Beyond the Cultural Turn: New Directions in the in the Study of Society and Culture* (Berkeley, 1999).

SHAW, Jon, "Citizenship of the Union: Towards Post-National Membership?", in *Collected Courses of the Academy of European Law* (The Hague, 1998).

SHER, George, "Ancient Wrongs and Modern Rights", *Philosophy & Public Affairs* 10 (1981), pp. 3–17.

SHIELDS, Liam, *Just Enough: Sufficiency as a Demand of Justice* (Edinburgh, 2016).

SHKLAR, Judith N., "Putting Cruelty First", *Daedalus* 111 (1982), pp. 17–28.

SIDGWICK, Henry, *The Methods of Ethics* (Cambridge, 2012).

SIL, Rudra and Peter J. Katzenstein, "Analytical Eclecticism in the Study of World Politics: Reconfiguring Problems and Mechanisms across Research Traditions", *Perspectives on Politics* 8 (2010), pp. 411–431.

SIMMONS, John A., "Ideal and Nonideal Theory", *Philosophy & Public Affairs* 38 (2010), pp. 5–36.

SINGER, Peter, "Famine, Affluence and Morality", *Philosophy & Public Affairs* 1 (1972), pp. 229–243.

SLEAT, Matt, "Realism, Liberalism and Non-ideal Theory or, Are There Two Ways to do Realistic Political Theory?", *Political Studies* 64 (2016), pp. 27–41.

SMITH, Adam, *An Inquiry Into the Nature and Causes of the Wealth of Nations* (Indianapolis, 1993).

SMITH, Melanie, "The Evolution of Infringement and Sanction Procedures: Of Pilots, Diversion, Collisions, and Circling", in *The Oxford Handbook of European Union Law* (Oxford, 2015).

SNORRASON, Snorri Thomas, *Asymmetric Economic Integration: Size Characteristics of Economies, Trade Costs, and Welfare* (New York, 2012).

SOLT, Frederick, "Economic Inequality and Democratic Political Engagement", *American Journal of Political Science* 52 (2008), pp. 48–60.

SPIEGEL, Peter, "IMF criticizes Greece's Bailout Deal with the EU", *Financial Times* (15 July 2015).

STEARNS, Peter N., "Forecasting the Future: Historical Analogies and Technological Determinism", *The Public Historian* 5 (1983), pp. 30–54.

STEARS, Marc, "The Vocation of Political Theory: Principles, Empirical Enquiry and the Politics of Opportunity", *European Journal of Political Theory* 4 (2005), pp. 325–350.

STIGLITZ, Joseph, *The Price of Inequality* (New York, 2013).

STILZ, Anna, "Is There an Unqualified Right to Leave", in Sarah Fine and Lea Ypi (eds), *Migration in Political Theory: The Ethics of Movement and Membership* (Oxford, 2016).

STRANGE, Susan, *Mad Money* (Manchester, 1998).

STRAWSON, Galen, "The Impossibility of Moral Responsibility", *Philosophical Studies* 75 (1994), pp. 5–24.

SUZUKI, Kazuto, "The EU as a Regulatory Empire", *Hokkaido Journal of New Global Law and Policy* 2 (2009), pp. 141–159.

SWIFT, Adam, "Public Opinion and Political Philosophy: The Relation between Social-Scientific and Philosophical Analyses of Distributive Justice", *Ethical Theory and Moral Practice* 2 (1999), pp. 337–363.

TESSMAN, Lisa, *Moral Failure: On the Impossible Demands of Morality* (Oxford, 2015).

THOMPSON, Janna, "Historical Injustice and Reparation: Justifying Claims of Descendants", *Ethics* 112 (2001), pp. 114–135.

TIMMONS, Mark, *Moral Theory: An Introduction* (Lanham, 2001).

TOMZ, Michael, "The Effect of International Law on Preferences and Beliefs", Working Paper (Stanford, 2008).

TRANSPARENCY INTERNATIONAL, *Poverty, Aid and Corruption* (2007).

TRATTNER, Walter I., *From Poor Law to Welfare State: A History of Social Welfare in America* (New York, 1999).

TUORI, Klaus, "Has Euro Area Monetary Policy Become Redistribution By Monetary Means? 'Unconventional' Monetary Policy as a Hidden Redistributive Mechanism", *European Law Journal* 22 (2016), pp. 838–868.

UNICEF, "Skills Development", https://www.unicef.org/education/skills-devel opment (Accessed 27 February 2020).

VALENTINI, Laura, "Coercion and (Global) Justice", *The American Political Science Review* 105 (2011), pp. 205–220.

————, "Ideal vs Non-Ideal Theory: A Conceptual Map", *Philosophy Compass* 7/9 (2012), pp. 654–664.

————, "Justice, Charity, and Disaster Relief: What, if Anything, is Owed to Haiti, Japan, and New Zealand?", *American Journal of Political Science* 57 (2013), pp. 491–503.

————, *Justice in a Globalized World: A Normative Framework* (Oxford, 2011).

VAN PARIJS, Philippe, "Must Europe Be Belgian?", in *Just Democracy: The Rawls-Machiavelli Programme* (Colchester, 2011).

————, "Première Lettre", in John Rawls and Philippe Van Parijs, *Three Letters on* The Law of Peoples *and the European Union* (2003), https://cdn.uclouvai n.be/public/Exports%20reddot/etes/documents/RawlsVanParijs1.Rev.phil. Econ.pdf (Accessed 16 December 2017).

————, "Why Surfers Should be Fed: The Liberal Case for an Unconditional Basic Income", *Philosophy & Public Affairs* 20 (1991), pp. 101–131.

VAN PARIJS, Philippe and Yannick Vanderborght, *Basic Income: A Radical Proposal for a Free Society and a Sane Economy* (Cambridge MA, 2017).

————, "From Euro-Stipendium to Euro-Dividend", *Journal of European Social Policy* 11 (2001), pp. 342–346.

VANDENBROUCKE, Frank, Anton Hemerijck, and Bruno Palier, "The EU needs a Social Investment Pack", *OSE Opinion Paper 5* (2011).

WALDRON, Jeremy, "Superseding Historical Injustice", *Ethics* 103 (1992), pp. 4–28.

WALZER, Michael, "Achieving Global and Local Justice", *Dissent* 58 (2011), pp. 42–48.

————, *Spheres of Justice: A Defence of Pluralism and Equality* (New York, 1983).

WEBER, Max, "Politics as a Vocation", in David Owen and Tracy B. Strong (eds), *The Vocation Lectures* (Indianapolis, 2004).

WEILER, J. H. H., "The Transformation of Europe", *The Yale Law Journal* 100 (1991), pp. 2403–2483.

————, "To be a European Citizen – Eros and Civilization", *Journal of European Public Policy* 4 (1997), pp. 495–519.

WEIMER, David L. and Aidan R. Vining, *Policy Analysis: Concepts and Practice* (New York, 2011).

WENAR, Leif, "Reparations for the Future", *Journal of Social Philosophy* 37 (2006), pp. 396–405.

WEST, Darell M., "The Costs and Benefits of Immigration", *Political Science Quarterly* 126 (2011), pp. 427–443.

WIENER, Antje, "Assessing the Constructive Potential of Union Citizenship – A Socio-Historical Perspective", *European Integration Online Papers* 1 (1997), file:///C:/Users/jtl/AppData/Local/Packages/Microsoft.MicrosoftEdge_8w ekyb3d8bbwe/TempState/Downloads/SSRN-id302708%20(1).pdf (Accessed 16 December 2017).

WILLIAMS, Eric, *Capitalism and Slavery* (Chapel Hill, 1994).

WORLD BANK, *Migration and Remittances Factbook: Third Edition* (2016).

WORLD HEALTH ORGANIZATION, "Universal Health Coverage", https://www.who.int/health-topics/universal-health-coverage#tab=tab_1 (Accessed 27 February 2020).

YOUNG, Iris Marion, *Responsibility for Justice* (New York, 2011).

_____, "Taking the Basic Structure Seriously", *Perspectives on Politics* 4 (2006), pp. 91–97.

YPI, Lea, *Global Justice and Avant-Garde Political Agency* (Oxford, 2011).

_____, "Statist Cosmopolitanism", *Journal of Political Philosophy* 16 (2008), pp. 48–71.

YPI, Lea, Robert E. Goodin and Christian Barry, "Associative Duties, Global Justice, and the Colonies", *Philosophy & Public Affairs* 37 (2009), pp. 103–135.

Legal documents, indicators, and databases

Aicep, "Fluxos de Investimento Directo de Portugal com o Exterior (1996–2014)", http://www.portugalglobal.pt/PT/Biblioteca/Paginas/FluxosInvestimentoDi rectoPortugalExterior2009_JanJunho.asp (Accessed 20 December 2017).

Charter of Fundamental Rights of the European Union (2000).

Communication from the Commission – Implementation of Article 260(3) of the Treaty (2011).

Community Charter of the Fundamental Social Rights of Workers (1989).

Convention Limiting the Hours of Work in Industrial Undertakings to Eight in the Day and Forty-eight in the Week (1991).

Elisabeta Dano and Florin Dano v. Jobcenter Leipzig.

EUR-Lex, "The Direct Effect of European law", https://eur-lex.europa.eu/legal-con tent/EN/TXT/HTML/?uri=LEGISSUM:l14547 (Accessed 6 December 2018).

EUR-Lex, "Precedence of European Law", http://eur-lex.europa.eu/legal-content/ EN/TXT/?uri= URISERV%3Al14548 (Accessed 6 December 2018).

European Central Bank, "Euro Reference Exchange Rate" (averages 2015), https://www.ecb.europa.eu/stats/policy_and_exchange_rates/euro_reference_exchang e_rates/html/index.en.html (Accessed 17 December 2017).

European Commission, "Employment, Social Affairs and Inclusion", http://ec.europa.eu/social/ main.jsp?catId=157 (Accessed 16 October 2017).

_____, "EU Expenditure and Revenue 2014–2020", http://ec.europa.eu/budget/ figures/interactive/index_en.cfm (Accessed 17 December 2017).

————, "European Structural and Investment Funds by Theme" (2014–2020), https://cohesiondata.ec.europa.eu/ (Accessed 16 December 2017).

————, *White Paper on Social Policy* (1994).

European Court of Human Rights, *Guide of Article 6 of the Convention on Human Rights: Right to a Fair Trial* (2019).

European Foundation for the Improvement of Living and Working Conditions, "Statutory Minimum Wages in the EU 2017", https://www.eurofound.europa.eu/observatories/eurwork/articles/statutory-minimum-wages-in-the-eu-2017 (Accessed 16 October 2017).

European Pillar of Social Rights (2017).

European Social Charter (1961, revised in 1996).

European Social Survey, *Welfare Attitudes* (2008).

European Social Survey, *Welfare Attitudes in Europe: Topline Results of Round 4 of the European Social Survey* (November 2012).

Eurostat, "GDP per Capita in PPS" (2016), http://ec.europa.eu/eurostat/tgm/table.do?tab =table&init=1&language=en&pcode=tec00114&plugin=1 (Accessed 1 December 2017).

————, "Hourly Labour Costs" (2004–2016), http://ec.europa.eu/eurostat/statistics-explained/index.php/Hourly_labour_costs (Accessed 1 December 2017).

————, "Proportion of Employees Earning Less than 105% of the Minimum Wage" (2014), http://ec.europa.eu/eurostat/statistics-explained/index.php/Minimum_wage_statistics (Accessed 1 December 2017).

————, "Severely Materially Deprived People" (2017), https://ec.europa.eu/eurostat/statistics-explained/index.php/Material_deprivation_statistics_-_early_results (Accessed 1 September 2018).

————, "Total General Expenditure on Social Protection" (2015), http://ec.europa.eu/eurostat/statistics-explained/index.php/Government_expenditure_on_social_protection (Accessed 1 December 2017).

————, "Unemployment Rate" (2017), https://ec.europa.eu/eurostat/statistics-explained/index.php?title=Unemployment_statistics (Accessed 1 September 2018).

Judgment of the Court of 15 July 1964, *Flaminio Costa v. ENEL*.

KPMG, "Corporate Tax Table" (2003–2017), https://home.kpmg.com/xx/en/home/services/tax/tax-tools-and-resources/tax-rates-online/corporate-tax-rates-table.html (Accessed 17 December 2017).

OECD, "Gross Domestic Product" (2016), https://stats.oecd.org/index.aspx?queryid=60702 (Accessed 1 December 2017).

————, "Structural Unemployment" (2002–2015), http://stats.oecd.org/Index.aspx?QueryId =613 65 (Accessed 1 December 2017).

————, "Tax on Corporate Profits (as % of the GDP)" (2015), https://data.oecd.org/tax/tax-on-corporate-profits.htm (Accessed 17 December 2017).

Treaty on European Union (1993).

Treaty on the Functioning of the European Union (2007).

World Inequality Database (2015), https://wid.world/ (Accessed 17 December 2017).

World Values Survey, "Government Responsibility", Wave 6 (2010–2014).

Index

arbitrary rule 3, 35, 61

basic structure 43–44, 52, 57,
   88–89, 109
Bauböck, Rainer 11, 23, 53, 71, 84
border control regimes 89, 91,
   109, 164
Brexit 6, 153, 155, 166
burdens
   of integration 1, 97, 167
   of social citizenship 75, 80

capability approach 25
capital-intensive 47, 111
capitalism 35, 41, 58, 114, 116, 123,
   140, 142
centralization 75, 80
Charter of Fundamental Rights of the
   European Union 2–3, 21, 157
circumstances of justice 12, 57,
   109, 121
citizenship
   democratic 11, 34–35, 61, 68, 165
   dominant conception of 11
   EU 11, 19, 21, 70–74, 84
   levels of 11–12, 23, 69, 71, 73,
      75, 84
   multilevel 8, 11, 12, 23, 61, 67–68,
      72, 83
   national 10, 72, 73, 74
   social 12, 19, 22–23, 60, 74–75, 77,
      80–81, 110, 112–113, 166
   status 3, 7, 10, 19, 39, 41, 55, 72,
      76, 80, 152
   studies 1, 8, 11, 23, 61
coercive practices 28, 34, 40, 65
collective action 33, 94, 96
colonialism 28, 29, 33, 100–101

common market 19–23, 83–84, 86–89,
   91, 93, 95–97, 101, 106, 108–109,
   111, 113, 149, 152, 154, 161,
   164–166
comparative advantage 91, 92, 95
compensation 6, 32–33, 45, 91, 111,
   113
competitiveness 87, 93, 94, 96, 97, 101,
   112–113, 148, 153
   see also EU Fund for Global
      Competitiveness (FGC)
"constrained" feasibility tests 20, 112,
   123–124, 125
context-dependency 37
convergence thesis 1
cooperation
   benefits of 48
   fair terms of 43
   need for 42
   rules of 20, 43, 89, 91, 104, 107
   scheme of 42, 46, 49, 50, 87
   system of 2, 28, 49, 89, 140
cosmopolitanism 8, 10, 22, 81, 136,
   142
Court of Justice of the European Union
   (CJEU) 3, 7, 21, 65, 66–67, 70,
   85, 105, 153, 163
criteria of validity 14

Dahl, Robert 25, 40, 53, 67–69, 71, 82
democratic deficit 5, 21, 61, 83
democratic duty to redistribute 18, 19,
   27, 31, 33–34, 36, 39, 40–41, 49,
   51, 60–62, 67, 71–72, 76, 80–81,
   114
democratic institutions 3, 19, 38,
   40–41, 45, 68–69, 71–72, 78, 80,
   83, 164, 166

democratic legitimacy 7, 19, 56, 76, 104
demoi 3, 11, 19, 41, 60, 69, 72, 80, 84, 163
demoicracy 19, 23, 60–61, 67, 68–72, 76–77, 80, 83–85, 163
demos 5, 11–12, 68–69, 71, 80, 83–84
distributional pattern 32
distributive vicious circle 19, 86, 93–97, 106, 109, 164
domination 28, 40

economic growth 48–49, 82, 115, 122, 126, 130, 147, 149, 150, 156
economic policy 56, 90, 97, 112, 115, 160
economic reciprocity 18–19, 27, 31, 38, 39–42, 44–45, 47–48, 51, 57, 86–87, 89, 100, 109
economic structure 15, 43–44, 47, 57–58, 86–91, 110, 164
economic sustainability 77, 134
efficiency 5, 20, 36, 42, 47, 49, 92, 98, 103, 125, 133–134, 142–143, 148–149, 152, 162, 165
equality
    ideal of 39
    of opportunity 28, 47, 89, 106–107, 109, 117, 159
    socioeconomic 11
    of status 10, 19, 73, 75, 77–80
EU budget 77, 97, 144, 150, 160, 165
EU corporate tax 20, 86, 96–97, 109, 151, 153–154, 165
EU Fund for Global Competitiveness (FGC) 20, 87, 97, 99, 109, 145, 150, 151–153, 164
EU income tax 77
EU labour code 86, 96–97, 109, 113, 145, 150, 153–154, 161, 164–165
EU minimum wage 20, 99, 147–149
Eurogroup 88, 103
European agency for social justice 152, 158
European Central Bank 103
European Commission 21, 66, 117, 147, 157, 158–160, 162
European Community 67, 69, 87
European Community of Coal and Steel 67
European Court of Human Rights 37, 54

European Globalization Adjustment Fund 97, 114
European Parliament 22, 66, 69–70, 116, 158–159
European Pillar of Social Rights 157, 162
European social model 21, 95, 113, 114, 161
Eurozone crisis 6, 101–102
exploitation 28, 30, 40, 43, 45–46, 50, 57, 101
external shocks 44, 95, 149, 153
externalities 91, 104

fair euro exchange rate 86, 145, 149
feasibility
    pervasive 119, 126–127, 131, 134, 137, 150
    temporary 20, 125–126, 147, 159
federation 7, 13, 94, 120
free trade 19, 27, 50, 59, 95
freedom of movement 4, 19, 22, 71, 86–87, 89, 91, 104, 106–107, 117, 164
free-riding 5, 7, 77, 94, 108, 112, 151, 152, 156

generalized compliance 19, 41, 60, 62, 67, 72
global minimum of reciprocity 50, 87
globalization 19, 41, 62, 93, 110–111, 113, 130, 164, 166
    see also European Globalization Adjustment Fund

Habermas, Jürgen 13, 24, 41, 56, 110
high-skilled workers 105, 150
human agency 20, 199, 125, 137
human needs 36–37
humanitarian duties 8

ideal theory 119–120, 138
identity
    collective 68
    common 11, 71
    European 69
individual choice 44, 46, 56, 58
individual liberty 17, 74
inequality 23, 29, 39–40, 46, 48, 58, 98, 114, 117, 122, 132, 139, 149, 160

integration
  benefits of 4
  burdens of 97
  economic 1, 7, 9, 19, 27, 29, 50,
    51, 62, 87, 90, 93, 95, 97–98,
    113–114, 166
  European 1, 23, 78, 83–84, 89, 111,
    113, 155, 159, 164, 167
  EU 19, 89, 103, 113, 175
  gains of 89
  level of 99
  political 2, 166
  process of 95
  regional 62, 83
  social 1–2, 6, 166
interdependence 10, 13, 26, 33, 43,
  48–50, 87
international community 31, 87
international competition 57, 92, 96
International Criminal Court (ICC)
  28, 40, 64–65, 82
International Labour Organization
  (ILO) 51, 59
International Monetary Fund (IMF)
  40, 48, 151, 161
international trade 28, 40, 50–51, 59,
  92, 111–112
international value chain 92, 101, 112,
  160
intuition 16–17, 25, 31

labour
  division of 42, 43, 57, 87, 89, 101,
    164
  -intensive 47, 95–96, 98, 111
  law 44–45, 90, 147–148, 159
  markets 46, 94–95, 97, 148–149
  regulation 19, 30, 35, 44–51, 98
  relations 44, 47, 87, 91, 114
  standards 59, 94, 161
  see also EU labour code;
    International Labour
    Organization (ILO)
levelling down 5, 7, 49, 79, 146–148
levelling the playing field 32, 53, 96
liberalization 92–93, 97, 111
low-skilled workers 47, 105, 107, 111
luck 9, 39, 44, 56

Maastricht Treaty 11
macroeconomic stabilizers 102
means of subsistence 19, 36–38, 61,
  106, 145, 151

minimum EU corporate tax rate 20,
  86, 96, 109, 154, 164
monetary policy 22, 44–45, 47–48,
  90, 115, 149, 151, 160
monopoly of force 19, 29, 60, 62–64,
  66
moral arbitrariness of birth 9
moral hazard 79
multinational firms 28, 40
mutual advantage 41–42, 49, 57,
  87–88, 108, 114, 164
mutual respect 42, 44, 47, 58, 87,
  107–108, 114, 164

Nagel, Thomas 9, 22, 27, 28–29,
  33–34, 50–52, 58
national responsibility 98–100, 109,
  114
non-ideal theory 119–120, 137–138
Nozick, Robert 15, 25, 43–44, 57, 81,
  129, 142

Offe, Claus 13, 24, 113
opportunity gap 5
Organisation for Economic
  Cooperation and Development
  (OECD) 48, 58, 110, 117,
  161–162
overlapping consensus 20, 146–147,
  158

patterns of specialization 86, 93
political culture 20, 36–37, 46, 119,
  126–127, 130–133, 135, 137,
  145–148, 158
political theory 14–16, 22, 24, 26,
  41, 52, 59, 83, 99, 117–121, 126,
  137–138, 141–142, 148
poor policy choices 1, 19, 86, 99–100,
  102
poverty gap 5
power
  arbitrary 15, 36, 46–47, 74, 76, 97,
    104, 107, 163
  coercive 9, 28, 33–34, 72
  distribution of 7, 80
  economic 45, 47
  political 62, 73, 161
  resistance to 18, 34, 41, 51, 61
  subjects to 35, 61, 163
pre-distribution 20, 27, 32, 53, 89,
  95–96, 103, 107, 144, 149, 154,
  156, 164

price stability 102
principle
  of conferral 76
  of justice 134
  of non-discrimination 2, 4, 20, 107
  of proportionality 76, 85
  of subsidiarity 76, 85, 163, 165
prioritization 78
production possibility frontiers 92

Rawls, John 8, 12–13, 15, 22–23,
  25–26, 52, 54–57, 59, 89, 109–
  110, 117, 121–122, 133, 137–139,
  142–143, 158
reflective equilibrium 16–18, 25
refugee crisis 6, 17, 155
Ricardo, David 91–92, 110

safety net 19, 54, 60, 75, 77, 81, 147,
  149, 151–152, 158–159, 163–164
Sangiovanni, Andrea 13, 24, 59, 108,
  110, 118
Schuman, Robert 1, 21, 166–167
second-class citizens 107
self-determination 73, 108–109, 138,
  159
self-fulfilling liquidity crisis 102
self-government 10, 19, 37, 45, 74–75,
  79–80, 108
sense of justice 7, 38, 46, 55, 129, 131,
  142
single currency 19, 50, 86–89, 91,
  101–104, 106, 115–116, 149
social dumping 19, 97, 113, 165
social engineering 38, 74, 124, 132
social Europe 112, 155–158, 165–167
social solidarity 5, 10, 12, 20, 29, 73,
  80, 89, 98–99, 119, 127, 135–137,
  145, 153–154, 155, 158
sovereign debt crisis 99, 101, 114
sovereignty 13, 28–29, 71, 81, 98
specialized system of coercion 60, 62,
  66, 67, 80
Stability and Growth Plan 94–95
standardization of social policy 6, 62,
  78–79

state intervention 44
statism 8, 10
structural funds 6, 87, 97, 102, 111,
  114, 153, 162, 165
structural reforms 97, 102–104, 155
subject of justice 31, 52
sufficiency 13, 20, 38, 39, 53–54,
  56, 74, 77–78, 107, 144, 149,
  152, 158
supremacy of EU law 66, 71

tax competition 10, 94, 149, 165
technology-intensive 97
terms of trade 43, 48, 89, 92, 101, 164
threshold of basic goods
transaction costs 5, 102, 165
transfer union 89, 116
Treaty of Lisbon 70, 84, 103
Treaty on the Functioning of the
  European Union (TFEU) 3, 21,
  67, 82, 84

unanimity 6, 71
UNICEF 37, 54
United Nations (UN) 28, 65

Van Parijs, Philippe 12, 23, 55, 109,
  110, 116, 138

Weber, Max 60, 62, 81
welfare
  models 73, 75, 81, 148
  states 77, 152, 155, 158–159, 163
  systems 5, 19, 60, 75, 77, 81, 94,
  106, 146, 164
  tourism 108, 151
willingness to work 38, 55
world government 28
World Health Organization (WHO)
  37, 54
World Trade Organization (WTO) 28,
  40, 44, 64–65, 90–91, 110–111
worse-performing member states 19,
  97

Young, Iris Marion 43, 57, 95

EU authorised representative for GPSR:
Easy Access System Europe, Mustamäe tee 50,
10621 Tallinn, Estonia
gpsr.requests@easproject.com